Chapters of the Sages

A Psychological Commentary on Pirkey Avoth

Reuven P. Bulka

JASON ARONSON INC.
Northvale, New Jersey
London

Library of Congress Cataloging-in-Publication Data

Bulka, Reuven P.
    Chapters of the sages : a psychological commentary on Pirkey Avoth / by Reuven Bulka.
        p. cm.
    Text of Avot in Hebrew and English.
    Rev ed. of: As a tree by the waters.
    ISBN 0-56821-133-3
    1. Mishnah. Avot –Commentaries. 2. Mishnah. Avot –Psychology.
1994. III. Mishnah. Avot. English. 1994. IV. Title.
BM506.A23B78 1994
296.1'23 – dc20   93-34041

Manufactured in the United States of America. Jason Aronson Inc. offers books and cassettes. For information and catalog write to Jason Aronson Inc., 230 Livingston Street, Northvale, New Jersey 07647.

In loving memory of

EFRAYIM YECHEZKEL BULKA

16 Elul 5736 — 18 Cheshvan 5737

In his short life,
he was the inspiration
for so much

Contents

Acknowledgments

This psychological commentary on Pirkey Avoth was originally published under the title, *As a Tree by the Waters*.

It was published first as a hardcover volume and later as a paperback. It went through a number of print runs and was used by many study groups as a text for exploring this most seminal source of Jewish ethics applied to life.

The volume had gone out of print and would probably have remained so had it not been for Arthur Kurzweil at Jason Aronson, Inc., Publishers. Arthur literally rescued this work from potential oblivion by making it part of a Jewish classics series.

I thank Arthur for his making sure that this volume would continue to be available to the general public. Thanks also are extended to Yaakov Feldheim, the original publisher, for his help in facilitating the republication of *As a Tree by the Waters*, now under new title.

It is quite heartening to know that this, my first book, has been designated a classic. It means so much, especially since it was written as a memorial to our son, who died so suddenly after a short sojourn in this world.

Certainly Arthur Kurzweil and his staff are a classy group, so the volume by definition has class.

Special thanks to Muriel Jorgensen of Jason Aronson, Inc., for all her efforts to assure the high quality of the republication.

It is my fervent hope that this volume will continue to be studied by all those who desire to learn more about the surpassing excellence of Jewish ethical tradition.

Introduction

Pirkey Avoth, which is normally referred to as "Ethics of the Fathers," should be more precisely translated as "Chapters of the Sages." In the spirit of mediating between these two alternatives, it may be said that Pirkey Avoth are chapters of ethics. They are chapters containing guiding principles for a Jewish way of life. To be exact, they are more than merely ethics, they are what may be termed "ultimate ethics," or the way the human being should behave consistent with God's plan. This relates to the social dimension but, at the same time, transcends it.

The principles enunciated in Pirkey Avoth are written as Mishna. The first five chapters form what may be termed a Talmudic tractate. Each *mishna*, or short paragraph, is a terse, succinct, and pointed statement relating to one or another aspect of life. Sometimes a *mishna* will contain only one basic idea, at other times, two or more ideas. Together the ideas expressed in Pirkey Avoth add up to a profound expression of the human situation in a Torah context.

Traditionally Pirkey Avoth occupies a very special place in the Jewish home. Even those who may not have studied other Talmudic tractates have had some exposure to Pirkey Avoth. There are some who may not learn Pirkey Avoth, but would, in fact, recite it as part of prayer; for it has become part of the warp and woof of Sabbath afternoon activity in the summer months between Pesach and Rosh Hashana. Individuals and groups meditate over the statements in Pirkey Avoth and try to elicit from it renewed meaning from week to week, from month to month, and from year to year.

Pirkey Avoth, then, is not a remote and abstract text. It is rather one which is part of the Sabbath Siddur. Though custom has established a set pattern for the study of Pirkey Avoth in the summer, it should not be restricted to the summer. It is, in reality, a year-round pursuit.

Because Pirkey Avoth is so essential to understanding the Jewish way of life, there has been literally a proliferation of commentary on it. The great sages from every generation, using differing methodologies, have continually probed the deeper meanings of Pirkey Avoth.

With the ready availability of an abundance of commentaries on Pirkey Avoth, one is likely to question the necessity of yet another such commentary. Of course, any justification for another commentary involves, in one way or another, the claim that "this book is different." This author is no different in claiming that this book is indeed different. It is quite likely that some of the commentary may have already been suggested by others, but the underlying purpose of this work is different.

The primary concern of this book is to attempt gaining an understanding of the connections and linkages — connections within each *mishna* and linkages between one *mishna* and another. Obviously, Rabbi Yehuda haNasi, when he compiled this tractate, did not do so haphazardly. There was a reason why he chose the specific statements and a reason why he chose to order them the way he did. If a number of statements are quoted in the name of a Tanna, they obviously are not only significant but also interrelated. This work, then, is an attempt to uncover the connection between diverse statements within each *mishna* and the underlying themes which link one *mishna* to the next. The commentary does not resort to explication through outside sources, even other Talmudic passages; it rather attempts to understand each *mishna* on its own. The internal connections and *mishna*-to-*mishna* linkages often open new and illuminating insights into human behavior patterns.

Pirkey Avoth is divided into six chapters. Each of them may be seen as addressing different dimensions of existence. I have suggested titles for each of the chapters. Understandably, the titles are not exhaustive and perfectly descriptive, but they give the general thrust of what the chapters attempt to achieve.

Chapter One is titled "The Fundamentals—An Exercise in Tradition." In this chapter, the transmissional flow of Jewish values is vividly established. Starting from Sinai and continuing through with the great sages to Rabban Shimon the son of Gamliel, this chapter introduces via these learned sages many of the fundamental principles involved in Jewish life, such as Torah, prayer, charity, responsibility to the self, and responsibility to the community.

Chapter Two, titled "The Path for Life," concerns itself with the proper path upon which an individual should embark. It includes integration of the social and religious dimensions and contains various insights concerning one's relationship to the community and one's relationship to one's material being. It contains statements by various disciples on the right path for life and subsequent statements by these disciples which relate back to their views concerning the essential ingredients in one's life-path.

Chapter Three, titled "The Sanctification of Life," concerns itself with the various means by which an individual can avoid life's pitfalls and sanctify one's sojourn on earth. It addresses such matters as one's eating, one's conversation, the sacredness and seriousness of life, and the ways of measuring whether one is indeed expressing life the way it should be expressed.

Chapter Four, titled "The Integration of Values," is concerned with the values which become part of the human personality, the ingredients and the attitude which make for a true human being. This chapter speaks about such elements as might, wealth, wisdom, dignity, sincerity, the need to continually improve, the importance of having a good reputation, and generally seeing this world as a preparatory for the world to come.

Chapter Five, titled "Torah, History, and Nature," is a partial culmination of the previous four chapters. It indicates how the foundations for the proper expression of Torah were established by God in the process of creation and carried through via God's role in history. It speaks of the various natural aberrations which occur through the abuse of Torah. These serve to show how the design of the world was intended to reinforce Torah orientation. Chapter Five also addresses itself to the various attitudes and personality types, the variations of human nature, and concludes with recommendations on how best to naturally develop a Torah personality through a chronological, educational progression.

Chapter Six, which is technically not Mishna as the previous five chapters are, but is, in fact, *baraitha,* has been called *kinyan torah,* or "The Acquisition of Torah." This chapter expresses many of the ideas that were projected in the previous five chapters. It focuses in sharply on what is meant by a Torah-true personality. It establishes that such an appellation is not easily gained, but that once gained, it encompasses all that is good in life.

By chapter design, Pirkey Avoth begins with the *fundamentals,* then moves on to speak about the recommended *path* for life. In this path, one must confront life in its *sanctity.* By so doing, one integrates into the self the *values* which relate to life's sanctity. The weaving of Torah ideas into the fabric of *history* and the essence of human *nature* is the final Mishnaic chapter, ending with the climactic statements that everything is in Torah and that with proper exertion, one will be rewarded with the benefits of a Torah-life. The final chapter rounds out the work by spelling out how one acquires a Torah personality and the natural outgrowths of this acquisition.

This, then, is a general overview of *Chapters of the Sages.* It is, of course, a conjecture on my part, as indeed is the entire thrust of the commentary. Together with a new translation of the basic text, it is hoped that this approach does not trespass the boundaries of logic and legitimate interpretation. In actuality, the commentary is not expansive, but terse. It relates to the basic questions implicitly, through short connective threadings and development of the unifying theme in each *mishna* itself. The commentary does not indulge in too much elaboration — this is left to the reader. I do not assume that this commentary will answer all questions. I will be content if it serves as a catalyst towards opening up new vistas for further insight into this most significant work.

כָּל יִשְׂרָאֵל יֵשׁ לָהֶם חֵלֶק לְעוֹלָם הַבָּא, שֶׁנֶּאֱמַר
וְעַמֵּךְ כֻּלָּם צַדִּיקִים לְעוֹלָם יִירְשׁוּ אָרֶץ נֵצֶר מַטָּעַי
מַעֲשֵׂה יָדַי לְהִתְפָּאֵר:

All Israelites have a portion in the world-to-come,
as it is said: "And your people, all righteous,
shall inherit the land forever, the branch of My
plantings, the work of My hands, to glorify Me"
(Yeshayahu 60:21).

This statement is an introductory note which is recited
weekly during the period between Pesach and Rosh
Hashana before studying the appropriate chapter of the
week. Like its counterpart at the close of each chapter, it is
a constant, and appears to be a tone-setter for the study of
Jewish ethics. In effect, it establishes the framework within
which Jewish ethics operate.

All Israelites have a portion in the world-to-come
posits, in a terse but powerful manner, the notion that all
people have the capacity to actualize the good. They are
not doomed by any predestination to evil, nor are they
dependent on a vicarious atoning and redeeming process.
They begin life not from square one, nor from a negative
starting point. They begin life with an assumed righteousness, with a share in the real estate of eternal life. If the true
human nature is allowed to express itself, the natural
status quo prevails, that of guaranteed eternality. Ethics
are hereby projected as the human way to behave, as the
normative and natural way to be.

The proof text for this statement seems to pick up this
theme of naturalness. The human being is called *the
branch of My plantings*, the human being's ethical devel-

15

opment is as natural as the branch's development from the tree. The tree has many branches, but one trunk. The picture painted is of diverse individuals, all unique in their capacities, and all branching out in their unique searches for meaning, but all connected to the source, to the trunk. Pirkey Avoth is the trunk, all of us the branches.

Ultimately, this branching out through connectedness to the lifeline of the trunk serves *to glorify Me.* God made his creatures with the propensity for good, but ethical action is not programmed, it is a matter of choice. God is not glorified by puppets who react in cause-and-effect manner to God's string pulling. God is glorified by the human choice to be Godly.

Eternal life is projected as the land which shall be inherited forever. It is the soil which feeds the trunk which branches out into life.

The reader begins the journey through Jewish ethics with a share of the world-to-come. The reader is told that the ethics to be presented are not beyond human expression. From the distance, they may seem difficult, even unreachable, but, in essence, they are geared to bringing forth the natural human propensity for goodness. It is with this positive attitude that the study and practice of Jewish ethics is approached.

CHAPTER **1**❀ פרקי אבות

The fundamentals

an exercise in tradition

אָ מֹשֶׁה קִבֵּל תּוֹרָה מִסִּינַי וּמְסָרָהּ לִיהוֹשֻׁעַ
וִיהוֹשֻׁעַ לִזְקֵנִים וּזְקֵנִים לִנְבִיאִים
וּנְבִיאִים מְסָרוּהָ לְאַנְשֵׁי כְנֶסֶת הַגְּדוֹלָה: הֵם אָמְרוּ
שְׁלֹשָׁה דְבָרִים, הֱווּ מְתוּנִים בַּדִּין וְהַעֲמִידוּ
תַלְמִידִים הַרְבֵּה וַעֲשׂוּ סְיָג לַתּוֹרָה:

1 Moshe received the Torah from Sinai
and transmitted it to Yehoshua, and
Yehoshua to the Elders, the Elders to the
Prophets, and the Prophets transmitted it to the
Men of the Great Assembly. They [the Men of the
Great Assembly] emphasized three things: Be
cautious in judgment, raise up many disciples,
and make a fence around the Torah.

The first *mishna* expounds on the most basic of questions:
What is the source of the ethics which are about to be
proposed? Are the values contained in Pirkey Avoth the
subjective self-expression of the sages, or are they objective
values which transcend time and space?

The ethical norms of Avoth begin with statements by
members of the Great Assembly, and continue with expressions by their students and the students of their
students. The members of the Great Assembly, however,
were working within a tradition, the tradition received from
the Prophets, who in turn received it from the Elders, and
the Elders from Yehoshua, and Yehoshua from Moshe, and
Moshe, of course, from God (Sinai). The values of the
members of the Great Assembly emanate directly from
God's Torah. Torah is seen as the Jewish lifestyle, and the

ethics of Avoth relate the objective values of Sinai to the subjective individual situation. Jewish ethics derive from God but reside in the individual.

This opening tracing of the route of tradition establishes a vital principle in Jewish ethics. There is room for each person to branch out in a unique fashion, but it must be within the framework of the revealed objective values. They are the parameters within which the expression of values must take place. The general direction and goal of the ethical system is concretized, but there are various routes to the goal. Self-transcendence toward the goal is the essential dynamic, but how each individual will specialize and in what sphere of endeavor are left to choice.

BE CAUTIOUS IN JUDGMENT: Tradition must take seriously each person's individuality. Each person is unique, each situation equally unique. Though at all times the Law (Torah) is the guiding factor, it is wrong to fit all people into a set equation, with the resolution of a court case or personal situation programmed according to a specific set and demanding only a mental push of the right button. The Law must not depersonalize; it must respond to each unique circumstance uniquely. The judge or counselor dare not say that this case is familiar, something like one that came before me last week, and can therefore be dispensed with easily.

RAISE UP MANY DISCIPLES: If caution in judgment concerns itself with the otherness of each individual and the judge's sacred responsibility to respect this otherness, *raise up many disciples* is concerned with the hierarchy in society, and the possible development of the class of the intelligent and the class of the ignorant. Normally, those in positions of power and influence desire to protect such position, by denying others the means for encroaching. In Jewish life, no one occupies a more esteemed and respected position than the scholar. The acknowledged scholar is looked to for leadership, and is followed when rendering a decision. Protectionism, however, has no place in the hierarchy of wisdom. The scholar who has acquired knowledge is obliged to share that knowledge, to raise up many disciples, to try as hard as possible to make dependency on the one scholar unnecessary. The scholar attained this rank because others shared their wisdom. The scholar is thus obliged to extend that very process. Law and its wisdom do not belong to the privileged few, they are the inheritance of the entire community.

MAKE A FENCE AROUND THE TORAH: If *Be cautious in judgment* protects the humaneness of the law, and *raise up many disciples* ensures that the law is shared and taught, *make a fence around the Torah* guards against the Torah (law) becoming an end in itself. The law is sacred, but making it an end in itself would distort this sanctity and turn it into a form of idolatry. Sensitivity and balance are achieved through hedging around the law, making trespass less likely by placing a fence within the fence. The law is structured somewhat like a circle, with the human being inside the circle and being urged inward toward the core. A fence around the law tightens the circle, hones more sharply the boundaries, and thus moves the person ever more forcefully into the core. If Sabbath is a core experience made possible by the host of Biblical restrictions which channel human expression, Rabbinic additions extend these restrictions even further, and prohibit any action which, however slightly, approximates the Torah prohibition. This eliminates almost totally possible diversions, and thus serves to focus on the real intent of the law, to drive the individual toward the true fulfillment to be found in the human dimension. The law is not an end in it-

שִׁמְעוֹן הַצַּדִּיק הָיָה מִשְּׁיָרֵי כְּנֶסֶת
הַגְּדוֹלָה. הוּא הָיָה אוֹמֵר, עַל־שְׁלשָׁה
דְבָרִים הָעוֹלָם עוֹמֵד, עַל הַתּוֹרָה וְעַל הָעֲבוֹדָה וְעַל
גְּמִילוּת חֲסָדִים:

2 Shimon the righteous was one of the
last survivors of the Great Assembly.
He used to say: The world stands on three
things — on the Torah, on the Sacred Service,
and on the practice of loving-kindness.

---

self, it is rather a means. It is not the end point of Judaism,
instead merely its beginning.

The underlying theme in the three comments by the
Men of the Great Assembly would thus be "Do not get
carried away with the law." Do not let adherence to the law
make you insensitive to the individual; do not let love of the
law and the power it brings you make you neglect the
obligation to share its wisdom; do not let dedication to
the law become a dogmatic observance which is an end in
itself rather than just the beginning of your contribution.
In a word, view the law with balance, sensitivity, and
humaneness.

MISHNA 2

Not only the law, Torah, but also two other ingredients are
vital to the world. These three ingredients and their se-
quence are crucial to fully understanding this *mishna.*
Torah refers to what God has given to the people, *Sacred
Service* to what the people have given to God, and *loving-*

kindness refers to that which the people give to other people.

TORAH is the lifestyle of the Jew, that which fills life with meaning and directs the individual to the ultimate goals of life. Through the experience of living a Torah-oriented life in its full authenticity, one senses that the fulfillments it brings are a gift from God. It is immediately recognized that God gave the Torah not for God's sake, but for the people's sake. God is glorified through observance, but it is the people who gain.

SACRED SERVICE, or true worship, is the natural spontaneous gratitude that is expressed by the beneficiaries of this great gift toward the Bestower. It is based on a profound understanding of the concern of God for the people. God's loving concern causes a sincere loving appreciation by the people. Prayer, of course, is a value in and of itself, but it is greatly enhanced through the links forged by the Torah.

THE PRACTICE OF LOVING-KINDNESS should be the natural climax of one's true relationship with God. Once it is recognized that Torah is an ultimate form of sharing, in which the person has been given the means by which to be Godly (by emulating His kindness — *imitatio Dei*), the desire to share with other human beings in loving-kindness should automatically ensue. If God, in sharing, has given everyone the ability to be Godly, then every individual is constrained to see the Divine element in the other, and share the self with the other. From authentic religiousness necessarily flows true human concern.

On these three pillars, signifying God's relationship with the people, the people's relationship with God, and the people's relationship with one another, does the world stand. The hope that these relationships will fuse together

ג אַנְטִיגְנוֹס אִישׁ סוֹכוֹ קִבֵּל מִשִּׁמְעוֹן
הַצַּדִּיק. הוּא הָיָה אוֹמֵר, אַל־תִּהְיוּ
כַּעֲבָדִים הַמְשַׁמְּשִׁין אֶת־הָרַב עַל־מְנָת לְקַבֵּל פְּרָס,
אֶלָּא הֱווּ כַּעֲבָדִים הַמְשַׁמְּשִׁין אֶת־הָרַב שֶׁלֹּא עַל־
מְנָת לְקַבֵּל פְּרָס וִיהִי מוֹרָא שָׁמַיִם עֲלֵיכֶם:

3 Antigonus of Socho received the tradition from Shimon the righteous. He
used to say: Be not like servants who serve their
master for the sake of receiving a reward; rather
be like servants who serve their master not for the
sake of receiving a reward, and let the awe of
Heaven be upon you.

---

into their ultimate expression is what keeps the world
going. The primary responsibility of humankind is to
perfect these relationships. This is the target of the human
endeavor.

MISHNA 3

This *mishna* further elaborates on aspects of service and
prayer. There are many dimensions to prayer. Prayer
establishes a link between God and the individual. Prayer,
in a group setting, forges community. Prayer keeps the
individual and community attuned and responsive. In
praying for what is lacking, one constantly remembers the
vacuum.

Prayer is also seen as a cause-and-effect process. One
asks God for something, be it good health, family joy,
communal redemption, or even wealth. When one's rela-

tionship with God resides in the cause-and-effect dimension, and the approach to faith and its values is based on anticipated gain, such faith is on shaky ground and open to disappointment, disenchantment, and the inability to face life realistically. Prayer should not be an act of investment in some eventual advantage; prayer should be of value for its own sake. The relationship it forges with God is reason enough to pray. Values should not be lived for the sake of any future aggrandizement, for the sake of receiving a reward. The living of the value is its own reward.

The prospect of meeting the leader of a country surely excites the person involved. Such a meeting is a thrill of its own. It would be absurd for one who is visiting a leader to expect some tangible reward for the experience. The visit is its own reward; the relationship, if it develops, ample recompense. Gratitude for having a minute with the leader is the normal reaction.

LET THE AWE OF HEAVEN BE UPON YOU, so that the thrill of having a relationship with God, and the prospect of a dialogue with Transcendence, is independent of any material wish. Once the cause-and-effect dimension of material gain is eliminated, the room that is needed for an authentic service of God, in awe, is created. *Letting* that awe be *upon* the person indicates that once the material obstacles are removed, the authentic relationship will ensue on its own, the awe will let itself be upon the person.

ד יוֹסֵי בֶּן־יוֹעֶזֶר אִישׁ צְרֵדָה וְיוֹסֵי בֶּן־יוֹחָנָן
אִישׁ יְרוּשָׁלַיִם קִבְּלוּ מֵהֶם. יוֹסֵי בֶּן־יוֹעֶזֶר
אִישׁ צְרֵדָה אוֹמֵר, יְהִי בֵיתְךָ בֵּית וַעַד לַחֲכָמִים
וֶהֱוֵה מִתְאַבֵּק בַּעֲפַר רַגְלֵיהֶם וֶהֱוֵה שׁוֹתֶה בַצָּמָא
אֶת־דִּבְרֵיהֶם:

4 Yose the son of Yoezer, of Tsereda, and Yose the son of Yochanan, of Jerusalem, received the tradition from them [Shimon, Antigonus, and the teachers who followed them]. Yose the son of Yoezer, of Tsereda, says: Let your house be a meeting place for the wise, cover yourself with the dust of their feet, and drink their words thirstily.

One of the three main foundations of the world, the learning and living of Torah, is here more fully explored in its educational aspect. Education is usually seen as an institutionalized aspect of life. Schools and other public-oriented facilities provide a variety of programs to satisfy all ages.

Essentially, however, education is not an institution as much as a way of life. The learning process cannot be localized in time and space. Instead, the life of each family should be an education. The doors of knowledge should never be closed, and every house should inspire the ambience of wisdom by being *a meeting place for the wise.*

A step beyond making one's home a meeting place for the wise is the covering of oneself *with the dust of their feet.* The desire to learn should not be relegated to places which

26

are comfortable or pleasant. Even when dust will cover the learner the educational process should not cease.

If *Let your house be a meeting place for the wise* speaks of education as beyond institutions and permeating all of life, and *cover yourself with the dust of their feet* urges the educational process even in discomfort, *drink their words thirstily* speaks of the knowledge-seeker. Just as water is a basic need for sustaining life, so is proper knowledge the water of human existence. Water is not an option, nor is education. The seeker of knowledge should approach learning with the seriousness of the desert-hiker in search of water. It is not a nice title before the name or a few letters after it, it is existence itself.

The emphasis on drinking thirstily suggests that in education, the acquisition of knowledge is not even the prime value. Instead, it is the subjective condition of seeking, desiring, wanting to learn, which is fundamental. From the right desire and orientation knowledge will come, but the key is the desire itself. The right desire guarantees the continuousness of education. Studies can never be completed, as the need for water is never completely suspended.

ה יוֹסֵי בֶּן־יוֹחָנָן אִישׁ יְרוּשָׁלַיִם אוֹמֵר, יְהִי
בֵיתְךָ פָּתוּחַ לָרְוָחָה וְיִהְיוּ עֲנִיִּים בְּנֵי
בֵיתֶךָ וְאַל־תַּרְבֶּה שִׂיחָה עִם הָאִשָּׁה, בְּאִשְׁתּוֹ אָמְרוּ
קַל וָחֹמֶר בְּאֵשֶׁת חֲבֵרוֹ. מִכָּאן אָמְרוּ חֲכָמִים כָּל־
הַמַּרְבֶּה שִׂיחָה עִם הָאִשָּׁה גּוֹרֵם רָעָה לְעַצְמוֹ
וּבוֹטֵל מִדִּבְרֵי תוֹרָה וְסוֹפוֹ יוֹרֵשׁ גֵּיהִנֹּם:

5 Yose the son of Yochanan, of Jerusalem, says: Let your house be opened wide, let the poor be members of your household, and do not engage in excessive idle chatter with women. This was said with regard to one's wife; how much more does it apply to a friend's wife. From this the sages derived that one who engages in excessive idle chatter with women causes harm to himself and desists from Torah study, and his end is that he will inherit Gehinnom.

The third foundation, the practice of loving-kindness, is the subject of this *mishna*. There is a need to be concerned with the world, and there is a need to be aware of one's immediate environment. Too often the dedication and commitment of people in the work or volunteer situation is not found at home. Outsiders' problems are taken earnestly, but the home is taken for granted. A balance between inside and outside is vital, lest the inside be deprived and the outside merely used for opportunistic reasons.

Firstly, *Let your house be opened wide,* so that social concern is authentic, and not relegated to office hours. Second, *let the poor be members of your household,* so that those who come to you for material or spiritual help do not feel like strangers in an alien environment, but like members of the house. In fact, a society which is structured along the lines of helpers and seekers of help tends to create the classes of the manipulators and the manipulated. Thus, even in being helped the individual's sense of confidence is shattered, and a feeling of dependency, even inadequacy, confirmed. True help comes in the form of friendship, and friendship is less likely to project from behind a desk, and more likely from a living room sofa.

True concern for the plight of others, even showing that concern in the home, should not be at the expense of one's wife. If one has a home which is receptive to the outside, it is not just the open door, but also the internal warmth, which makes it possible. Furthermore, if one has the time and patience to show serious empathy for the problems of outsiders, there must be ample room for empathizing with one's wife. A wife is not just there for small talk, nor is she to be seen as the household servant who must do the bidding of the boss. If one takes that attitude to his wife, it is likely to spill over in the attitude to women in general.

In this distorted perception of women, the ultimate loser is man. It is he who *causes harm to himself,* in that by disparaging his partner he thereby disparages himself, and begins a dangerous dehumanizing process. The partner is seen as a thing rather than a being, the depersonalization of the partner eventually depersonalizes the husband, who, in this distorted world-view, will become alienated from all meaningful endeavor, will *desist from Torah study,* and shrink away spiritually.

יְהוֹשֻׁעַ בֶּן־פְּרַחְיָה וְנִתַּאי הָאַרְבֵּלִי קִבְּלוּ
מֵהֶם. יְהוֹשֻׁעַ בֶּן־פְּרַחְיָה אוֹמֵר, עֲשֵׂה לְךָ
רַב וּקְנֵה לְךָ חָבֵר וֶהֱוֵה דָן אֶת־כָּל־הָאָדָם לְכַף
זְכוּת:

6 Yehoshua the son of Perachya and Nittai of Arbel received the tradition from them [Yose the son of Yoezer and Yose the son of Yochanan]. Yehoshua the son of Perachya says: Make a teacher for yourself, acquire a companion for yourself, and judge all individuals charitably.

Rather than desist from Torah study, one should realize that education is a continual process. If the essence of the individual involves a constant transcending of the self, then education is the means through which awareness of self and responsibility is heightened. The human being is in a continual striving process, and the value education of Torah is that which makes the transcending possible. As such, it is vital that every individual take pains to ensure the perpetuity of the educational process. This is best achieved by *making a teacher for yourself,* one who surpasses you in knowledge and will bridge the gaps in your own education.

The values taught by the appointed teacher are not merely to be digested, they must be lived. But values cannot be lived in isolation, they demand sharing. Thus, *acquire a companion for yourself,* so that what is learned can be immediately taught and lived with another. This

ז נִתַּאי הָאַרְבֵּלִי אוֹמֵר, הַרְחֵק מִשָּׁכֵן רָע
וְאַל־תִּתְחַבֵּר לְרָשָׁע וְאַל־תִּתְיָאֵשׁ מִן־
הַפּוּרְעָנוּת:

7 Nittai of Arbel says: Keep far away
from a bad neighbor, do not consort
with a wicked person, and do not despair of
retribution.

---

translates theory into reality and abstract knowledge into
human wisdom.

There is a natural tendency to think of knowledge
acquired as a superior state of being. This may be so, but it
is equally dangerous to view others, less knowledgeable, as
inferior. Knowledge used to put down others is knowledge
abused.

Thus, *judge all individuals charitably*. The other
person may not have been blessed with the same opportunities as you, or even with the same native intelligence.
The fact that you seem to know more only places upon you
a greater responsibility to understand others and judge
them favorably. Assume that had the same opportunities
been open to them, they would be where you are now.

Ultimately, then, true wisdom must bring with it a
well-honed sensitivity to humankind that makes room for
the less knowledgeable. It is a necessary balance to ensure
that the wise retain a measure of humility and refrain from
propelling themselves above society.

MISHNA 7

Learning is a continual process, and the proper atmosphere
for learning needs to be maintained. Human beings are

finite. They are prone to error and subject to influence. To keep the flow of the educational process of life in a positive direction, it is important to choose the right social conditions. Therefore, *Keep far away from a bad neighbor,* for the subtle influences of the immediate surroundings can creep into one's lifestyle very slowly and imperceptibly.

However, a society in which those who exhibit upright behavior are radically separated from those who are destructive or inhumane dooms the inhumane to the status quo. With no positive example to follow, there is little possibility for climbing out of the rut. Moreover, this very isolationism breeds an insensitivity among the upright and even a dangerous self-righteousness and sense of superiority. Therefore, *do not consort with a wicked person,* do not form an association with the wicked, but do not detach yourself from the wicked entirely. Maintain a contact, keep the lines of communication open, in full awareness of the wicked reality and positive potentiality.

Those who take this balanced approach, committed to a lifestyle of goodness but equally cognizant of the bad around them which should be redirected, are likely to become frustrated by the sense of futility in trying to make inroads in a cruel, almost impenetrable world. If indeed cruelty proliferates, one is likely to one day ask who is right, and to question one's own commitment. In a world ruled by the majority, it is natural to doubt whether a minority of humane individuals are in the right. Therefore, *do not despair of retribution,* do not associate the majority with the truth, and do not let the apparent happiness and prosperity of the cruel people detract from your own dedication to righteous behavior. For, in fact, there are two types of values, the values of the moment and ultimate values. The values of the moment relate to immediate gain, and are opportunistic, often insensitive and too often cruel. Ultimate values relate to ultimate truths, truths which are

ח יְהוּדָה בֶּן טַבַּאי וְשִׁמְעוֹן בֶּן שָׁטַח קִבְּלוּ
מֵהֶם. יְהוּדָה בֶּן־טַבַּאי אוֹמֵר, אַל־תַּעַשׂ
עַצְמְךָ כְּעוֹרְכֵי הַדַּיָּנִין וּכְשֶׁיִּהְיוּ בַּעֲלֵי הַדִּין עוֹמְדִים
לְפָנֶיךָ יִהְיוּ בְעֵינֶיךָ כִּרְשָׁעִים וּכְשֶׁנִּפְטָרִים מִלְּפָנֶיךָ
יִהְיוּ בְעֵינֶיךָ כְּזַכָּאִין כְּשֶׁקִּבְּלוּ עֲלֵיהֶם אֶת־הַדִּין:

8 Yehuda the son of Tabbai and Shimon the son of Shetach received the tradition from them [Yehoshua the son of Perachya and Nittai of Arbel]. Yehuda the son of Tabbai says: In the office of judge do not act as counsel, and when the litigants stand before you consider them as guilty, but when they depart from you having accepted the judgment, consider them as innocent.

---

eternal in time and space, and whose eternality will vindicate the trials of the moment. Such futuristic orientation will help to counter the despair of the present.

MISHNA 8

A combination of the right environment and proper education is likely to bring an individual into prominence, even into positions where knowledge is a requisite, such as becoming a judge. From the perspective of intellect, judging others is not so difficult. The human aspect, dealing with the judge's relationship with the litigants, poses more problems. The judge must at one and the same time be concerned and detached. Insensitivity to people hardens the judge, making such an arbiter clearly unfit to understand really human problems. On the other hand, a judge who is too involved is likely to judge by compassion rather than justice, and, in this manner, compromises the law and is party to the breakdown of societal equilibrium.

The judge must retain sensitivity, but as a judge dare not *act as counsel.* One or both of the litigants should not be helped by the judge. There is room for concern, but it is extra-legal. In fact, even though in everyday life one is obliged to judge each person charitably, in the administration of justice each litigant is to be viewed as *potentially guilty,* and likely to be pronounced guilty by the judge.

This attitude pertains only in the court of law and during the case itself. Once the case is concluded and the litigants depart *having accepted the judgment, consider them as innocent.* Sitting in judgment of others is an enterprise which should be relegated to the courts. Even the judge who sits and critically analyzes a case should not thereby pronounce a judgment on the character of the litigants. Once judged in the specific case, they become people, as pure and innocent as they were before potentially guilty. Immediately after the close of the case, the judge should come down from the pedestal and relate on a one-to-one, equal basis with those whom he has judged. In the final analysis, the position of judge should not be viewed as a status, but as a task.

מ שִׁמְעוֹן בֶּן־שֶׁטַח אוֹמֵר, הֱוֵה מַרְבֶּה
לַחֲקוֹר אֶת־הָעֵדִים וֶהֱוֵה זָהִיר בִּדְבָרֶיךָ
שֶׁמָּא מִתּוֹכָם יִלְמְדוּ לְשַׁקֵּר:

9 Shimon the son of Shetach says: Examine the witnesses thoroughly; and be careful with your words, lest through them they learn to lie.

If previously the judge is cautioned to view as potentially guilty the litigants in the case, now the judge is urged to view with equal suspicion the witnesses in the case. A judge must have an affirmative attitude to humankind in everyday life, but in court, righteousness must not be assumed. In litigation, caution and suspicion are the rule.

The *witnesses must be examined thoroughly,* with no assumptions based on reputation or position. And, in the process of interrogation, the judge must exercise great care not to lead the witnesses in any direction. The witness must not be led by the judge to believe that the judge desires a specific statement or assertion to be made. In such an instance, even if the judge's intentions are pure, the witness, ostensibly coaxed to lie, will be able to pin the blame on the judge and also look cynically on the judicial process.

Admittedly, this is an unnatural way of relating to people, but this very unnaturalness serves to reinforce the idea that judging people, even for a judge, is not natural. It is the exception rather than the norm.

שְׁמַעְיָה וְאַבְטַלְיוֹן קִבְּלוּ מֵהֶם. שְׁמַעְיָה
אוֹמֵר, אֱהַב אֶת־הַמְּלָאכָה וּשְׂנָא אֶת־
הָרַבָּנוּת וְאַל־תִּתְוַדַּע לָרָשׁוּת:

10 Shemaya and Avtalyon received the tradition from them [Yehuda the son of Tabbai and Shimon the son of Shetach]. Shemaya says: Love work, hate positions of lordship, and do not seek to become intimate with the ruling authorities.

Though judging is a vital aspect of the social order, still one must not seek positions of power; rather, one should apply oneself to life in an unassuming manner. Work is that which gives the individual the means to meet the needs of everyday physical existence. Through earning one's sustenance, one is able to maintain the state of health which is vital to any meaningful endeavor.

Thus, *Love work,* as it is so closely tied to life's purpose. Work, however, should not be seen as an end in itself, as if one's entire life gains meaning through work and one's entire energy supply is spent on work.

Thus, *hate positions of lordship,* in which you are the boss and therefore responsible for the work of others and the fate of a company. As a boss, or lord, one is likely to develop a boss mentality, ordering people around and manipulating them for greater gain. The boss is so caught up in the work cycle and the need to succeed that life itself passes by without even a wink.

Lordship poses a greater danger, in that it addicts the lord to a superior status and urges the lord to seek out

יא אַבְטַלְיוֹן אוֹמֵר, חֲכָמִים הִזָּהֲרוּ
בְּדִבְרֵיכֶם שֶׁמָּא תָחוּבוּ חוֹבַת גָּלוּת
וְתִגְלוּ לִמְקוֹם מַיִם הָרָעִים וְיִשְׁתּוּ הַתַּלְמִידִים
הַבָּאִים אַחֲרֵיכֶם וְיָמוּתוּ וְנִמְצָא שֵׁם שָׁמַיִם
מִתְחַלֵּל:

11 Avtalyon says: Scholars — be careful with your words lest you incur the penalty of exile, and will be exiled to a place of evil waters, and the disciples who follow you will drink from them and die, and thus the Name of Heaven will be profaned.

---

others in more privileged positions. Once the status-seeker starts climbing the ladder, only the ultimate gives real satisfaction. But do not fall into that trap and *seek to become intimate with the ruling authorities*. It will become immediately obvious to you that the status of rulership is hardly deserved, and the mode of expression in this high society blatantly artificial. In high society the main staple is party rather than study.

One maintains a true perspective on life by associating with those who do not wear masks or hide behind status. Work and workers are where human expression is likely to be found.

MISHNA 11

Although one should not seek to join the high society of rulership, this does not mean that one should publicly denigrate the ruling authorities or even be insensitive to their potential reactions.

Precisely because the rulers are likely to legislate laws which are unfair and even cruel, as they are removed from the grass roots, precisely for this reason is the scholar who is committed to communal concern likely to rebel or protest.

Scholars, however, carry on their shoulders a heavy responsibility. They have a community which follows them, the community of people thirsting for knowledge. The scholar must therefore weigh very carefully any remark of protest before making it. If there is a chance the protest will awaken the slumbering authorities to what is just, the protest should be made. But if the protest is likely to be met by a violent reaction, the exile of the scholar from the community to an isolated area removed from the immediate pale, then second thought must be given. It is good to be a hero, but irresponsible to be a hero when other people are likely to suffer. The students of the scholar, dutifully following even to *a place of evil waters,* a place divorced from communal roots and lacking in spiritual vibrancy, are still in a developmental phase. The disparity between what they are taught and their new environment may create conflict in them, and lead them away from their tradition. Though they will be thought of as students of the scholar, they will go a different way, even possibly *profaning the Name of Heaven* through their misrepresentation.

This scenario may seem a bit far-fetched, but it is not outside the realm of possibility. The ethics of protest demand that the scholar-protester be concerned with more than getting an opinion expressed to rid the self of guilt. The scholar must weigh with meticulous care the full implications and possible ramifications of the outburst.

הָלֵּל וְשַׁמַּאי קִבְּלוּ מֵהֶם. הָלֵּל אוֹמֵר, **יב**
הֶוֵה מִתַּלְמִידָיו שֶׁל־אַהֲרֹן אוֹהֵב שָׁלוֹם
וְרוֹדֵף שָׁלוֹם אוֹהֵב אֶת־הַבְּרִיּוֹת וּמְקָרְבָן לַתּוֹרָה:

12 Hillel and Shammai received the tradition from them [Shemaya and Avtalyon]. Hillel says: Be of the disciples of Aharon, loving peace and pursuing peace, loving humankind and bringing them near to the Torah.

In exhibiting meticulous care and concern for others, Aharon is an outstanding model. Even today it is possible to *be a disciple of Aharon.* Being a disciple does not mean merely to listen to the lectures of a teacher, in which case presence would be mandatory. Being a disciple means to follow the teachings of the sage or saint. This following transcends time and spans the generations.

The difference between *loving peace* and *pursuing peace* is the difference between passivity and activity. More precisely, pursuing peace is the natural tendency of one who truly loves peace. It is a necessity to fully appreciate the need for peace as a societal norm and love peace before one can authentically venture out to pursue peace. But, once having been convinced of the need for peace and therefore loving it, one cannot help but pursue it.

Still, even peace is not the ultimate goal. Peace is a stable equilibrium, a form of social homeostasis. It is too static to be viable, and is likely, lacking directedness, to give birth to irritation, frustration, and eventual disintegration of the peace.

Peace must be based on a love of humankind and a concern for its development. Once peace is achieved, the

יג הוּא הָיָה אוֹמֵר, נְגִיד שְׁמָא אֲבַד שְׁמֵה וּדְלָא מוֹסִיף יָסֵף וּדְלָא יַלִיף קְטָלָא חַיָב וְדְאִשְׁתַּמַּשׁ בְּתָגָא חֲלָף:

13 He [Hillel] used to say: One who seeks a name loses one's name, one who does not increase knowledge decreases it, one who does not study deserves to die, and one who makes use of the crown will die.

---

immediate task is to give life direction and purpose. *Loving humankind and bringing them near to the Torah* gives peace the directedness and value orientation which at once ensures the peace and brings personal and communal harmony.

MISHNA 13

Though the goal, in peace, is to bring individuals close to the Torah, there are many wrong ways to approach Torah study.

ONE WHO SEEKS A NAME LOSES ONE'S NAME. If the person approaches the educational process with the view to gaining status or power, such lust is likely to be obvious to students and teachers, and will stand in the way of gaining recognition. The knowledge might be there, but its integration into the person is missing, so that true human knowledge is replaced by an individual who has knowledge but is not knowledgeable.

ONE WHO DOES NOT INCREASE KNOWLEDGE DECREASES IT. The human being is involved in a never-ending becoming process. The fulfillment of today is no excuse to relax; it is an inspiration to greater fulfillment tomorrow. The missed opportunity to improve can never be retrieved, for the time which passes is not open to recall. Standing still, not increasing knowledge, is thus a regression, for it kills the present potential. In human striving, there is no neutral gear. It is either forward or reverse.

ONE WHO DOES NOT STUDY DESERVES TO DIE. Of course, one who consciously turns the back on learning cuts the self off from meaningful living. Viable life is thus reduced to mere existence and value realization radically rejected. Such rejection of the educational process maintains life as a quantity but kills its quality. Such a blatant suicide of quality deserves quantitative death.

ONE WHO MAKES USE OF THE CROWN WILL DIE. Even though education is pursued for its own sake, once knowledge is acquired it can easily be used to gain unfair advantage. Once the person realizes that one possesses what others lack but desire to have, a trend toward selling knowledge may develop. This means that those who cannot pay will not be taught. Such arrogant allocating of wisdom to one's self as a private possession is likely to stultify the know-it-all owner and breed intellectual and moral stagnation. In the end, such use of the crown of knowledge may bring about the erosion of knowledge and an intellectual perdition worse than death itself.

This *mishna* is written in Aramaic. Perhaps the reason for this is that Hillel addresses himself to the assimilated, who have joined the quest for social prominence and have rejected Torah values. Hillel speaks to them, cautions them about the importance of Torah and the futility of social climbing.

יַד הוּא הָיָה אוֹמֵר, אִם אֵין אֲנִי לִי מִי לִי
וּכְשֶׁאֲנִי לְעַצְמִי מָה אָנִי וְאִם לֹא עַכְשָׁו
אֵימָתָי:

14 He [Hillel] used to say: If I am not for myself, who is for me? When I am for myself only, what am I? And if not now, when?

There are many wrong ways to approach acquisition of wisdom, and many wrong ways to approach life. The proper approach to life is a delicate balance between responsibility for oneself and concern for the other.

IF I AM NOT FOR MYSELF, WHO IS FOR ME? No individual can step out into the world with a poor self-image and expect to make important contributions to human betterment. The neglect of self makes the neglectful person a poor choice for helping others. The beginning of all responsibility, and indeed the end of all responsibility, is to and for the self. The ignoramus cannot teach, the uninformed cannot enlighten, the shaky self cannot counsel. Any individual who is not for one's self, who asks *who is for me?*, must be told the blunt answer — *nobody*. Such a person will be for nobody and nobody will be for that person.

Self-worth based on concern for one's development dare not become self-centeredness. The individual must always ask this question: *When I am for myself only, what am I?* In blunt terms, the answer is *a deficient human being*. A true human being gravitates toward the other, and recognizes that existence in isolation impedes the human process, both for the self and for others.

Some individuals may recognize the natural human

שַׁמַּאי אוֹמֵר, עֲשֵׂה תוֹרָתְךָ קֶבַע אֱמוֹר **טז**
מְעַט וַעֲשֵׂה הַרְבֵּה וֶהֱוֵה מְקַבֵּל אֶת־כָּל־
הָאָדָם בְּסֵבֶר פָּנִים יָפוֹת:

15 Shammai says: Make your Torah study
a fixed duty, say little and do much,
and greet all people with a cheerful countenance.

---

condition of concern for the other quite early in life. Others
may be given a rude awakening at a later stage. It will dawn
on these late-bloomers that they are deficient, and they
may seek to defer confrontation with responsibility. But, *if
not now, when?* No matter whether the awakening occurs
at an early or later stage, the demands of the hour preclude
procrastination. In fact, the best way to climb out of the rut
of self-centeredness is not in stages of disengagement from
the self. Such deferral merely delays the inevitable and
wastes precious moments of goodness. Instead, the best
way out of self-centeredness is now, immediately and with
finality. There is no sense punishing the self with guilt for
past failings when present fulfillments are beckoning.
Present achievements atone for the past and restore the
balance between responsibility for the self and concern for
the other.

IF NOT NOW, WHEN? Possibly never. Therefore, now!

MISHNA 15

In the delicate balance which must be struck between self-
improvement and social obligation, it is necessary to
establish guidelines which guarantee the development of
self and community.

It is important never to get so lost in helping others that the self is forgotten. *Make your Torah study a fixed duty,* so that the time needed to develop your own self is sacred and inviolable, to be compromised only in emergency.

If indeed the purpose of study is to translate acquired wisdom into practice, it is wise to *say little and do much,* so that little energy is wasted on talking about what has been or will be achieved, and all energies and time dedicated to real achievement. This saves time for more achievement or greater periods of study.

The bent towards helping, laudable though it is, may eventuate into a welfare-giving personality so intent on giving that it ignores the recipient. Though it is prudent to *say little and do much,* it is absurd to extend this principle to one's approach to people. To be abrupt in the interests of time, or impatient in the interests of pressing commitments is to depersonalize the process of sharing. Therefore, *greet all people with a pleasant countenance.* You are helping people with faces and personalities, people who are sensitive and need warmth as much as they may need help. Do not cut off your nose to spite their face. Insensitivity to the individual hardens the personality and may neutralize the innate desire to help. Always be aware and attentive to the people you relate with, and ensure that sharing itself is not dehumanized.

רַבָּן גַּמְלִיאֵל אוֹמֵר, עֲשֵׂה לְךָ רַב
וְהִסְתַּלֵּק מִן הַסָּפֵק וְאַל־תַּרְבֶּה לְעַשֵּׂר
אֲמָדוֹת:

16 Rabban Gamliel says: Provide yourself with a teacher and remove yourself from doubt, and do not give excessive tithe through guesswork.

The areas of self-improvement and social obligation are complex and intricate, and demand the guidance of a reliable authority to make the right decision. The need to *make a teacher for yourself* as expressed in *mishna 6* is complemented with the need to *Provide yourself with a teacher.* There is need for a teacher to educate, and need for a teacher to *remove yourself from doubt.* The former teaches the student who desires to learn, the latter guides the student who needs a decision. Some teachers can educate well, but have difficulty reaching definitive conclusions in concrete matters of law. Others are expert at rendering decisions even though not the best educators. Each possesses a much needed strength. Oftentimes, the two strengths are fused, in which case choice of teacher is a choice for learning and decision making. When the strengths are best found in different individuals, proper provision should be made accordingly.

A teacher to guide and decide is needed even if one takes the more stringent side in matters of doubt. The fear is not that one may underestimate responsibility, at least at first, but that responsibility may be overstated. Thus, *do not give excessive tithe through guesswork.* An inexact approach to clearly delineated responsibility, such as the

45

רן שִׁמְעוֹן בְּנוֹ אוֹמֵר, כָּל־יָמַי גָּדַלְתִּי בֵּין
הַחֲכָמִים וְלֹא מָצָאתִי לַגּוּף טוֹב
מִשְּׁתִיקָה וְלֹא הַמִּדְרָשׁ עִקָּר אֶלָּא הַמַּעֲשֶׂה, וְכָל־
הַמַּרְבֶּה דְּבָרִים מֵבִיא חֵטְא:

17 Shimon his [Gamliel's] son says: All
my days I have grown among the Sages,
and have found nothing better for the body than
silence; study is not most important, rather
doing, and one who proliferates words brings sin.

---

obligation to give away a tenth of produce, allows haphazardness to creep into the dynamics of observance. This
haphazardness eventually leads to understating responsibility, even though it started with well-intentioned over-
statement. One must be meticulous toward one's duties,
lest their sacred nature be compromised and the observance itself improperly actualized. Even though you are educated, do not be above having a teacher to guide you in
matters of doubt.

MISHNA 17

The proper guide, the recognized authority, leads not only
through words, but even through silence, an activistic
silence. One who is busy talking has no time for doing, and
one who is busy doing has no time or need for talking.

It is obvious that the silence which makes meaningful
action more likely is good for the soul. It makes fulfillment
and the satisfaction it brings a source of spiritual nourish-
ment. What is less obvious is that silence is good for the
body. If experience in living with sages shows that there is

יח רַבָּן שִׁמְעוֹן בֶּן־גַּמְלִיאֵל אוֹמֵר, עַל־
שְׁלֹשָׁה דְבָרִים הָעוֹלָם קַיָּם עַל הָאֱמֶת
וְעַל הַדִּין וְעַל־הַשָּׁלוֹם שֶׁנֶּאֱמַר אֱמֶת וּמִשְׁפַּט שָׁלוֹם
שִׁפְטוּ בְּשַׁעֲרֵיכֶם:

18 Rabban Shimon the son of Gamliel says: The world is preserved through three things: truth, justice, and peace, as it is said: "Administer truth and the justice of peace in your gates" (Zechariah 8:16).

---

nothing better for the body than silence, it speaks of the importance of the body as well as the importance of silence. The body is vital for it supplies the raw energy which makes effective human action possible. Silence is vital because it makes human action more likely to be elicited.

Since *study is not most important, rather doing,* the virtues of silence are readily apparent.

The talker locks the self up in a world of words, and denies the body muscles the exercise that comes with good deeds. Eventually, the body is so enervated from inaction that a spiritual laziness overtakes the talker, who may even reject responsibilities which are pressing and demand action. Thus, *one who proliferates words brings sin.*

One can never know the consequences of bad habits. It is therefore best to avoid cultivating them.

MISHNA 18

Silence is basic for the body. There are similarly basics for the corporate body of humankind, for the world. If *mishna* 2 deals with the three pillars on which the world stands, namely, *Torah, Sacred Service,* and the *practice of loving-kindness,* this culminating *mishna* of the first chapter deals with the three things which preserve the world. The pillars of *mishna* 2 are the utopian goals, the ultimate which humankind should strive for and which are the basis for even starting the human condition. All of Avoth may be seen as the attempt to clearly define these three pillars and how they are best made a reality. The three pillars are the summit.

The summit, however much it must remain the focus of our strivings, is preceded by a long climb. In the meantime, there are certain requisites which must be fulfilled if the world is to preserve itself and avoid destruction. These requisites are *truth, justice, and peace.*

Truth is the basis of all social contact. If what one says is not what one means, suspicion and alienation will reign instead of trust and acceptance.

Justice is the basic staple for social responsibility. Humans must respect the rights, property, and dignity of others, and legislate the protection of these ingredients. In truth, we say what we mean. In justice, we mean what we say. Together, truth and justice merge to make *peace* possible. Peace without truth is a fraud; peace without justice the harbinger of chaos. The peace which is founded in truth and justice can at least *preserve the world,* and ensure its availability so that those who desire to reach the summit of *Torah, Sacred Service, and the practice of loving-kindness* can attempt the climb.

רַבִּי חֲנַנְיָא בֶּן־עֲקַשְׁיָא אוֹמֵר, רָצָה הַקָּדוֹשׁ בָּרוּךְ
הוּא לְזַכּוֹת אֶת־יִשְׂרָאֵל לְפִיכָךְ הִרְבָּה לָהֶם תּוֹרָה
וּמִצְוֹת. שֶׁנֶּאֱמַר יְיָ חָפֵץ לְמַעַן צִדְקוֹ יַגְדִּיל תּוֹרָה
וְיַאְדִּיר:

Rabbi Chananya the son of Akashya says: The
Holy One, blessed be He, desired to make Israel
worthy, therefore He gave them Torah and commandments in abundance, as it is said: "God
was pleased for the sake of His righteousness to
magnify and glorify the Torah" (Yeshayahu 42:21).

This concluding statement is, like the introduction, a
constant. It is recited after the completion of the pertinent
chapter during the period between Pesach and Rosh
Hashana, when Pirkey Avoth is studied every Sabbath.

If the introduction is the tone-setter, inculcating the
conviction that human beings have the potential for good
and begin with eternality, the conclusion links the ideas
projected in the Mishna with everyday life.

The meticulous detail of Jewish ethics, apart from the
detail in commandments, is potentially mind-boggling.
The student of Jewish ethics as well as the student of the
entire Talmud deserves to be told why all the commandments and their infinite detail are necessary.

God *desired to make Israel worthy, therefore He gave*
them Torah and commandments in abundance. If the
individual is expected to attain ethical excellence and
continually strive for self-betterment, then life itself must
contain the ingredients to ensure that process. Learning

can never legitimately cease, nor can the fulfillment of commandments. These literally fill each minute of each hour of each day. There is no room for the existential vacuum, no room for the emptiness which comes from having nothing to do or to strive towards. One who is committed to the Torah track cannot afford to be derailed. The fact that each fulfillment brings in its train the seeds of another fulfillment guards quite adequately against diversion. Total immersion in the world of Torah values is a cleansing experience, bringing individual humanness into sharp focus, making the individual meritorious and worthy.

The proof text refers to God's being pleased, *for the sake of His righteousness, to magnify and glorify the Torah.* The magnification and glorification of the Torah is achieved in practice because in theory it was so intended to envelop all of life. In God's justice, this is a source of pleasure. Nothing pleases God more than to see His creations at their best. Nothing brings out the best as well as the totality of Torah. And only because Torah is a totality is this possible.

With such inspiration one may venture to translate the vastness of Jewish ethics into everyday life. It is a herculean task, but a necessary and rewarding one.

CHAPTER **2** ✤

The path

for life

28

אַ רַבִּי אוֹמֵר, אֵיזוֹ הִיא דֶּרֶךְ יְשָׁרָה שֶׁיָּבוֹר
לוֹ הָאָדָם כָּל־שֶׁהִיא תִּפְאֶרֶת לְעוֹשֶׂהָ
וְתִפְאֶרֶת לוֹ מִן הָאָדָם, וֶהֱוֵה זָהִיר בְּמִצְוָה קַלָּה
כְּבַחֲמוּרָה שֶׁאֵין אַתָּה יוֹדֵעַ מַתַּן שְׂכָרָן שֶׁל־מִצְווֹת,
וֶהֱוֵה מְחַשֵּׁב הֶפְסֵד מִצְוָה כְּנֶגֶד שְׂכָרָהּ וּשְׂכַר
עֲבֵרָה כְּנֶגֶד הֶפְסֵדָהּ. הִסְתַּכֵּל בִּשְׁלשָׁה דְבָרִים וְאֵין
אַתָּה בָא לִידֵי עֲבֵרָה, דַּע מַה־לְמַעְלָה מִמְּךָ עַיִן
רוֹאָה וְאֹזֶן שׁוֹמַעַת וְכָל־מַעֲשֶׂיךָ בַּסֵּפֶר נִכְתָּבִים:

1 Rabbi [Yehuda haNasi] says: Which is
the right path that a person should
choose? That which is an honor to the one who
does it and which also brings honor from humankind; be scrupulous with a light precept as with a
weighty one, for you do not know the reward
given for each precept; reckon the loss incurred in
the performance of a commandment against its
reward and the gain obtained through committing a transgression against its loss. Concentrate on three things and you will not fall into the
grip of sin: know what is above you — a seeing
eye, a hearing ear, and all your deeds being recorded in the book.

Every individual lives in two dimensions, the dimensions of
personal and social responsibility. Personal responsibility is
the responsibility for the self, the obligation to live up to
the ideal as envisaged by God and transmitted through

commandment. This area of life expression is one which should not be lived at the expense of society. True religiousness involves an integration of personal responsibility with social awareness, a life style which is *an honor to the one who does it and brings honor from humankind.*

Concerning the life of personal responsibility and the living of authentic Torah truth, it is important not to compromise by setting up priorities in the form of indispensable and dispensable commandments. What may seem trivial may have great meaning and impact on the individual. Every commandment was given because it has purpose in the development of human potential and is part of a whole. To achieve *honor to the one who does it* one must be *scrupulous with a light precept as with a weighty one.*

With regard to social awareness, a distinction must be made between being popular and being respected. There is a momentary thrill connected with belonging to the crowd, but ultimately it is an empty feeling, disconnected as it is from any real and lasting value. There may be some momentary *gain obtained through committing a transgression* or a sense of momentary loss of an experience or thrill *incurred in the performance of a commandment,* but these should be weighed against the more profound feeling of achievement for doing something positive and the likely feelings of remorse for doing something negative. That which *brings honor from humankind,* as opposed to passing popularity, is that which is by definition honorable and laudable.

It is understandably difficult for the average person to adhere to the demands of inner responsibility and social awareness. One is easily sidetracked or enticed by the prospect of instant pleasure. To stay on the *right path, concentrate on three things,* on the fact that all actions are seen, all utterances heard, and all deeds recorded in the book. The person who sees the self as constantly confronted

רַבָּן גַּמְלִיאֵל בְּנוֹ שֶׁל־רַבִּי יְהוּדָה הַנָּשִׂיא
אוֹמֵר, יָפֶה תַלְמוּד תּוֹרָה עִם דֶּרֶךְ אֶרֶץ
שֶׁיְּגִיעַת שְׁנֵיהֶם מַשְׁכַּחַת עָוֹן וְכָל־תּוֹרָה שֶׁאֵין עִמָּהּ
מְלָאכָה סוֹפָהּ בְּטֵלָה וְגוֹרֶרֶת עָוֹן וְכָל־הָעוֹסְקִים
עִם־הַצִּבּוּר יִהְיוּ עוֹסְקִים עִמָּהֶם לְשֵׁם שָׁמַיִם שֶׁזְּכוּת
אֲבוֹתָם מְסַיַּעְתָּם וְצִדְקָתָם עוֹמֶדֶת לָעַד וְאַתֶּם
מַעֲלֶה אֲנִי עֲלֵיכֶם שָׂכָר הַרְבֵּה כְּאִלּוּ עֲשִׂיתֶם:

2 Rabban Gamliel, the son of Rabbi Yehuda haNasi, says: The study of Torah combined with an occupation is an excellent thing, for the exertion demanded by both together causes sin to be forgotten, while any Torah study without work ultimately fails and causes sin. Let all who occupy themselves with the community do so for the sake of Heaven, for the merit of their fathers sustains them and their righteousness endures forever. And as for you [says God], I consider you worthy of great reward as if you had accomplished it.

---

by God, whether alone or in the alluring atmosphere of peers, will make decisions and embark on a lifestyle that is ultimately honorable, even if presently unpopular.

MISHNA 2

This *mishna* extends further the themes of personal responsibility and social awareness.

In the sphere of personal responsibility, a delicate

balance is suggested. The importance of Torah in life could possibly lead the individual to neglect the pressing needs of everyday. Such an extreme commitment is self-defeating, for *Torah study without work ultimately fails and causes sin.* Torah study needs the sustaining power of an income from a purely practical view. In addition, one who is locked up in Torah study and oblivious to immediate needs will soon be rudely awakened to the reality that though Torah nourishes the soul, the body cannot survive without food. One who places all the eggs in the Torah basket and is then disappointed is likely to turn away totally from Torah. A balanced approach of *Torah combined with an occupation is an excellent thing,* as it fills the day with proper concern for things physical and spiritual, and thus *causes sin to be forgotten.*

In the sphere of social awareness, one who decides to spend time and effort for the sake of the community should do so not in the expectation of recognition or reward, but *for the sake of Heaven.* Where the motivation for communal involvement is personal glory, it is likely that important decisions will be made on a personality rather than issue basis. The lure of immediate power may blind the communal worker to the real but presently unpopular truth, and real dedication in a selfless way will be missing. If actions and decisions are based on God's will and design, they are likely to be in the true interests of the community.

The individual who is involved with the community for the right reason is not alone. Such present commitment is linked to the past and the future. It is enhanced by the past dedication of previous communal workers who were equally devoted. At the same time, since the dedicated worker is a link in the chain, all achievements will be passed on to the benefit of posterity, so that *the merit of their fathers sustains them and their righteousness endures forever.*

The idealist who links the self with the community will

גֵ הֱווּ זְהִירִין בָּרָשׁוּת שֶׁאֵין מְקָרְבִין לוֹ
לְאָדָם אֶלָּא לְצֹרֶךְ עַצְמָן נִרְאִין כְּאוֹהֲבִין
בִּשְׁעַת הֲנָאָתָן וְאֵין עוֹמְדִין לוֹ לְאָדָם בִּשְׁעַת דָּחֳקוֹ:

3 Be cautious with the ruling authorities, for they befriend a person only for their own needs. They appear as friends when it is to their advantage, but they do not stand by the individual at the time of that person's distress.

---

undoubtedly find some measure of frustration in attempting to improve the community. Sometimes the community is not ready for new ideas and not receptive to plans that respond to challenge. It takes the tireless efforts of the committed few to make the necessary impact. On occasion, one person's great idea might not be accepted during that person's lifetime, but the seed has been sown for a successor to develop. Even if the idea does not meet with immediate success, or even fails, it has paved the way. In communal endeavor, nothing goes to waste. Today's failure may become tomorrow's success. Surely one should not desist from trying for fear of failure. God says, *I consider you worthy of great reward as if you had accomplished it.* The dedication to a necessary goal is a value in and of itself, even though the goal is not realized. It is as if the goal has been accomplished, even though the actual accomplishment might come in the next generation, or even perhaps never.

MISHNA 3

The communal worker, in representing the community, is likely to become involved with the ruling authorities. The

57

normal person usually enjoys meeting with higher-ups, even more being friends with them. It is even possible that a communal representative become so enamored of this friendship that, in order to maintain it, communal needs are sacrificed.

Thus, the admonition to *Be cautious with the ruling authorities.* If they befriend, it is *only for their own needs.* Their relationship is a superficial one, in which a person is used to advantage, *their advantage,* but they are not there to help when they are needed, *at the time of that person's distress.*

As a general rule, authority figures *appear* as friends. Appearance hides the true feeling in most instances. There are times when the friendship may be genuine, but it is hard to tell. Caution seems to be in the best interests of the person involved and the community. To rely on the flimsy hopes of a dubious friend is to invite possible disaster; to subordinate communal needs to the development of a superficial friendship is to betray the community. The ruling authority is primarily interested in self, while the communal servant should at all times be interested in the welfare of the community.

ך הוּא הָיָה אוֹמֵר, עֲשֵׂה רְצוֹנוֹ כִּרְצוֹנֶךָ
כְּדֵי שֶׁיַּעֲשֶׂה רְצוֹנְךָ כִּרְצוֹנוֹ. בַּטֵּל רְצוֹנְךָ
מִפְּנֵי רְצוֹנוֹ כְּדֵי שֶׁיְּבַטֵּל רְצוֹן אֲחֵרִים מִפְּנֵי רְצוֹנֶךָ:

4 He [Rabban Gamliel] used to say: Do His will as if it were your own will, so that He may do your will as if it were His will. Nullify your will before His will, so that He may nullify the will of others before your will.

If the public servant is not to rely on the friendship of the ruling authority, shaky as such reliance is, reliance on God is another matter. Reliance on God is the foundation of the community, but God relates to the community and to the individual as a mirror reflection. One who incorporates the will of God into the self, such that all actions are consistent with and express the perceived will of God, is likely to find that God relates in the same way, actualizing the will of the devoted servant as if it were God's will.

The amalgamation of God's will unto the self comes in two stages. The first stage is *Do His will as if it were your own will.* This stage is one of consistent expression, where the person's desires and God's wishes are in harmony. What the person does is what God wants for the person, and also what the person wants, so that God's will is easily absorbed into the self.

The second stage is *Nullify your will before His will.* This is the more difficult stage, as it involves a clash of desires; God's desire on one side, and the individual's desire on the other. Here what the individual wants is not what God wants, and the individual is called upon to acknowledge that what God wants is better for the person. Nullifi-

הֵלֵּל אוֹמֵר, אַל־תִּפְרוֹשׁ מִן־הַצִּבּוּר וְאַל־
תַּאֲמִין בְּעַצְמְךָ עַד יוֹם מוֹתְךָ וְאַל־תָּדִין
אֶת־חֲבֵרְךָ עַד שֶׁתַּגִּיעַ לִמְקוֹמוֹ וְאַל־תֹּאמַר דָּבָר
שֶׁאִי אֶפְשָׁר לִשְׁמוֹעַ שֶׁסּוֹפוֹ לְהִשָּׁמֵעַ וְאַל־תֹּאמַר
לִכְשֶׁאֶפָּנֶה אֶשְׁנֶה שֶׁמָּא לֹא תִפָּנֶה:

5 Hillel says: Do not separate yourself from the community; do not be sure of yourself until the day of your death; do not judge your fellow until you have been in that person's position; do not say of a thing that it cannot possibly be understood, for ultimately it will be understood; and do not say "When I have leisure I will study," for you may never have leisure.

---

cation of the person's will is not a sacrifice, but a positive decision based on faith in God's omniscience. The result of this act of the will is that God *may do your will as if it were His will* and also *may nullify the will of others before your will.*

Herein is expressed the idea that to the extent to which the individual resides in the Divine dimension, to that extent God resides in the human dimension.

MISHNA 5

Herein is expressed in clear terms the need each individual has for community. No one should feel so self-assured and ego-centric that it is possible to live alone, apart from society. *Do not separate yourself from the community,* in the assumption you are above the mediocre crowd.

The person who separates from the community feels superior, and perhaps even immune from the elements which would compromise moral development. Such a person feels secure and sure of the self, but is admonished *do not be sure of yourself until the day of your death.* Do not assume that you are able to reach your potential alone, without the help and assurance of those with more wisdom and experience than you. And certainly do not assume you have reached the limits of your potential, else the rest of your life be spent in stagnation. Only when you die can your contribution to life be assessed.

The feeling of superiority that causes an individual to separate from the community may be caused by a negative view of the general public, who seem so inferior. *Do not judge your fellow until you have been in that person's position.* Other people's achievements may be less than your own, but if you were in their position it is likely that you would not have done better. Since you can never really place yourself in the biological-sociological-psychological position of others, it is impossible for you to judge and condemn them. Your task is not to judge, but to graciously accept others and willingly interact with them.

One who feels intellectually superior to others is likely to not only separate from them, but to underestimate their capacities. But *do not say of a thing that it cannot possibly be understood, for ultimately it will be understood.* Do not think your views are beyond the intellectual reach of the general community, such that you recoil from even proposing them, and thereby doom the community to stagnation. Rather, you should assume a positive stance toward the community, and see them as being capable of understanding and commitment.

Finally, a person with a superiority complex is prone to think that study has been completed, that there is not much left to learn, and what is left can be deferred to the

הוּא הָיָה אוֹמֵר, אֵין בּוּר יְרֵא חֵטְא וְלֹא
עַם הָאָרֶץ חָסִיד וְלֹא הַבַּיְשָׁן לָמֵד וְלֹא
הַקַּפְּדָן מְלַמֵּד וְלֹא כָּל־הַמַּרְבֶּה בִסְחוֹרָה מַחְכִּים
וּבְמָקוֹם שֶׁאֵין אֲנָשִׁים הִשְׁתַּדֵּל לִהְיוֹת אִישׁ:

6 He [Hillel] used to say: The empty
person cannot be sin-fearing, the ig--
norant person cannot be pious, the diffident
person cannot learn, the temperamental person
cannot teach, and not everyone who is deeply
involved in business becomes wise. And in a place
where there are no people, strive to be a person.

---

onset of leisure. But *do not say "When I have leisure I will
study," for you may never have leisure.* Do not assume you
know it all and that all future study is optional. With such
an attitude you are likely to perpetually postpone future
study, study which is obviously so necessary precisely
because you think it is not.

This *mishna* recommends that the approach to
community and self be done with true humility. Such an
approach will ensure good relations with the community
and maintain the process of communal and personal
betterment.

MISHNA 6

The moral character of the individual should not be
divorced from intellectual pursuit. Only one who is well
educated in all the aspects of human endeavor can be fully
aware of one's responsibilities to God and people.

THE EMPTY PERSON CANNOT BE SIN-FEARING. The empty person is not even aware of what is wrong and why it is wrong, and so can hardly be expected, in daily life, to behave in a sin-fearing manner. *The ignorant person cannot be pious.* Ignorance is a notch above emptiness. The ignorant person is not empty, but also far from full. Such a person might be aware of the norms and prohibitions which are to be exercised and avoided, respectively, but cannot really exhibit the true commitment which emanates from positive affirmation. Just knowing what to do without understanding why makes real piety a difficult proposition.

Piety is achieved through becoming fully aware of the ways and the whys of Torah. It is an educational process. That process must of necessity begin from zero, from the point of emptiness toward reaching fullness. *The diffident person cannot learn.* One who is ashamed because of ignorance will remain mired in that position. The very process of education is an escape from ignorance, but in this escape present ignorance is already assumed, so that there is really nothing to be ashamed of.

The teacher is also obliged to take this into account for the teaching process. *The temperamental person cannot teach.* The teacher who explodes at the student because the student does not know is unfair to the student and to the educational process. The teacher must always be aware that it is precisely because the student does not know that teaching is needed. The temperamental person, like the shy student, is not profoundly aware of why education is needed, and therefore cannot be part of the process.

There are some people who, though ostensibly deeply involved in business, still are able to develop themselves and to increase their learning. But *not everyone who is deeply involved in business becomes wise.* The fact that others may become wise even though heavily involved in business does not imply that everyone can do so. Education

ז אַף הוּא רָאָה גֻלְגֹּלֶת אַחַת שֶׁצָּפָה עַל־
פְּנֵי הַמָּיִם. אָמַר לָהּ, עַל דְּאַטֵּיפְתְּ
אַטְיפוּךְ וְסוֹף מְטַיְפָיִךְ יְטוּפוּן:

7 Moreover, he [Hillel] saw a skull
floating on the surface of the water.
He said to it: Because you drowned others, they
drowned you, and ultimately, those who drowned
you will themselves be drowned.

---

must be seen as the most important striving, and each
individual must measure how much time can be spent on
business without compromising intellectual and moral
development.

One who has, through these notions, reached a state of
piety based on the firm footing of a solid education, should
not then plaster that status over the community. The state
of piety is also a state of humility. But modesty in this
sense should not be taken to extremes. *In a place where
there are no people, strive to be a person.* Where there are
leaders, there is no need to push for the top, but where
leadership is missing, one should not hide one's acquired
wisdom. Instead it must be shared for the benefit of the
community.

MISHNA 7

This statement seems to be connected with the last
statement of the previous *mishna,* about the striving to be a
person where there are no people.

The importance of not becoming embroiled in power
struggles is illustrated quite drastically through Hillel's
experience of finding a floating skull in the water. Quite

likely it was the end result of a person striving to be a person where others were already entrenched. It was obviously a murder with vengeance, as the floating skull would indicate.

The skull is told — *Because you drowned others, they drowned you.* You tried to push yourself to the top, and in the process probably pushed aside those who stood in your way. This no doubt caused bitter hatred and led to their killing you.

Ultimately, those who drowned you will themselves be drowned. They are caught up in the same power game as you were, and even though, through killing you, they may have reached the top, others will eventually envy that position and will be forced to kill the present incumbents just as they killed you.

The message is clear — Do not push for power; do not thrust yourself into the public arena. Only when a glaring vacuum appears should one strive to become the leader, and, even then, not for the sake of power, but only to serve, willingly but with humility.

As in Chapter 1, *mishna* 13, Hillel here speaks in Aramaic. Perhaps he is addressing one who presumably assimilated, and became involved in ego concerns instead of Torah pursuits. The implications of social climbing are enunciated by Hillel in the aforementioned *mishna*. Here Hillel bemoans the fate of political name-seekers.

ח הוּא הָיָה אוֹמֵר, מַרְבֶּה בָשָׂר מַרְבֶּה
רִמָּה, מַרְבֶּה נְכָסִים מַרְבֶּה דְאָגָה, מַרְבֶּה
נָשִׁים מַרְבֶּה כְשָׁפִים, מַרְבֶּה שְׁפָחוֹת מַרְבֶּה זִמָּה,
מַרְבֶּה עֲבָדִים מַרְבֶּה גָזֵל, מַרְבֶּה תוֹרָה מַרְבֶּה
חַיִּים, מַרְבֶּה יְשִׁיבָה מַרְבֶּה חָכְמָה, מַרְבֶּה עֵצָה
מַרְבֶּה תְבוּנָה, מַרְבֶּה צְדָקָה מַרְבֶּה שָׁלוֹם. קָנָה שֵׁם
טוֹב קָנָה לְעַצְמוֹ, קָנָה לוֹ דִבְרֵי תוֹרָה קָנָה לוֹ חַיֵּי
הָעוֹלָם הַבָּא:

8 He [Hillel] used to say: The more flesh, the more worms; the more possessions, the more worry; the more women, the more witchcraft; the more maidservants, the more lewdness; the more men-servants, the more robbery. The more Torah, the more life; the more schooling, the more wisdom; the more counsel, the more understanding; the more charity, the more peace. One who has acquired a good name has made an acquisition for the self; one who has acquired the words of Torah has acquired life in the world to come.

The person can be caught up either in the materialistic, self-serving syndrome, or the spiritual syndrome. One is enticing but self-defeating, the other less auspicious but more meaningful. The ultimate results in the political arena are related in the previous *mishna*. Here, the difference between an ego-centered, materialistic lifestyle and a truly spiritual one are projected.

SYNDROME 1 — *the materialistic*

THE MORE FLESH, THE MORE WORMS. The desire to have, to consume, to gluttonously devour is usually the first bad habit in the materialistic syndrome. But overeating does nothing for the body, and the only real impact of corpulence is that after death, there will be more flesh to rot, which will attract more worms. One who overeats is likely to think twice if made aware that all the eating is only to feed the worms.

THE MORE POSSESSIONS, THE MORE WORRY. The glutton who grows up will not only desire wealth to feed the appetite for food, but also to feel totally satisfied. However, increasing possessions does not bring increasing satisfaction as much as it brings increasing worry. Happiness is a state of mind, not a state of wealth.

THE MORE WOMEN, THE MORE WITCHCRAFT. The glutton who seeks pleasure thinks in terms of quantity rather than quality. Ten wives are by definition better than one in this view. But more wives only increases the internecine strife amongst them in vying for attention. This increases bickering and brings unhappiness instead of pleasure. The quality of one true love relationship is more meaningful and lasting than ten superficial relationships.

THE MORE MAIDSERVANTS, THE MORE LEWDNESS; THE MORE MEN-SERVANTS, THE MORE ROBBERY. The empire builder will try to impress others with the amount of wealth attained. One way to do this is to increase the staff which maintains the empire. But bringing maidservants and men-servants into a home which hardly needs them invites in them the emptiness that comes from having little to do. This will drive the maidservants into lewdness and the

men-servants into robbery. Everybody loses in this wayward lifestyle.

As far as the materialistic syndrome is concerned,
more is less.

SYNDROME 2 — *the spiritual*

THE MORE TORAH, THE MORE LIFE. Instead of feeding the
body, with Torah one feeds the soul. The Torah elicits from
life its virtues and qualities, such that it increases life and
enhances its quality. Torah is less flesh, less sensual
pleasure, but more lasting meaning.

THE MORE SCHOOLING, THE MORE WISDOM. Instead of
spending time accumulating wealth, which only increases
worry, it is better to sit and study. The rewards of study are
increased wisdom, which is, again, a more lasting virtue
and an integral part of the person.

THE MORE COUNSEL, THE MORE UNDERSTANDING. To have
many wives is, in fact, to have less. A deep relationship of
true immersion with one another is the ideal. But insofar as
the spiritual values of life are concerned, one's perspective
and insights are greatly improved through learning from
the wisdom and counsel of others, who offer varied experience and differing perspectives.

THE MORE CHARITY, THE MORE PEACE. Bringing into one's
employ people who are not needed and who, in their
frustration, will seek deviant forms of expression, is the
wrong way to spend money. True charity, which protects
the dignity of the recipients, also erases the tension
between the haves and the have-nots. The poor will see the
rich as true friends interested in their welfare, thereby
bringing peace and har-money.

מַ רַבָּן יוֹחָנָן בֶּן־זַכַּאי קִבֵּל מֵהַלֵּל וּמִשַּׁמַּאי.
הוּא הָיָה אוֹמֵר, אִם לָמַדְתָּ תּוֹרָה הַרְבֵּה
אַל־תַּחֲזִיק טוֹבָה לְעַצְמְךָ כִּי לְכָךְ נוֹצָרְתָּ:

9 Rabban Yochanan the son of Zakkai received [the tradition] from Hillel and Shammai. He used to say: If you have learned much Torah do not ascribe any merit to yourself, because this is the purpose for which you were formed.

One who resorts to true charity will undoubtedly gain a good name. This is a true acquisition. *One who has acquired a good name has made an acquisition for the self.* Wealth is what one has, a good person is what one is. This is an acquisition which is for the self, which reflects on the nature of the person and symbolizes that person's character.

The seeker of fame, fortune, and pleasure lives the present as if it were endless, as if it were the sum total of life. When that ends, nothing remains. But *one who has acquired the words of Torah has acquired life in the world to come.* One who has integrated Torah into one's lifestyle gains not only in present quality, but in future eternality. Eternal values bring eternal life.

MISHNA 9

Those who have acquired Torah will, quite naturally, feel good about it. The feeling which Torah learning and living brings is hard to anticipate, as any emotion is hard to anticipate. But the impact of the Torah experience is one which fills the person with awe and uplifts spiritually.

י חֲמִשָּׁה תַלְמִידִים הָיוּ לוֹ לְרַבָּן יוֹחָנָן בֶּן־
זַכַּאי. וְאֵלּוּ הֵן: (רבי) אֱלִיעֶזֶר בֶּן־
הוֹרְקְנוֹס (רַבִּי) יְהוֹשֻׁעַ בֶּן־חֲנַנְיָא (רַבִּי) יוֹסֵי הַכֹּהֵן
(רַבִּי) שִׁמְעוֹן בֶּן־נְתַנְאֵל וְ(רַבִּי) אֶלְעָזָר בֶּן־עֲרָךְ:

10 Rabban Yochanan the son of Zakkai had five disciples. They are: R. Eliezer the son of Horkenos, R. Yehoshua the son of Chananya, R. Yose the priest, R. Shimon the son of Nethanel, and R. Elazar the son of Arach.

The good feeling from Torah should not, however, become an ego trip. *Do not ascribe any merit to yourself, because this is the purpose for which you were formed.* Anything less than a Torah life would negate the very purpose of creation. Torah life is laudable, but it should not be seen as something extraordinary, relegated to the few who are thereby privileged people. Instead, Torah should be seen as the basic norm, that which is basic and essential, that which legitimizes the fact of creation. It is existence itself, nothing special or superimposed on existence. In this perspective, one who has learned much Torah will not become ego-inflated but will instead realize, in humility, that this is what life is all about.

MISHNA 10

Rabban Yochanan definitely had more than five disciples. The five mentioned here each manifested unique traits which related to their study and their relationship with their teacher.

Each was a unique person, who specialized in different

יא הוּא הָיָה מוֹנֶה שִׁבְחָם. (רַבִּי) אֱלִיעֶזֶר בֶּן־הוֹרְקְנוֹס בּוֹר סוּד שֶׁאֵינוֹ מְאַבֵּד טִפָּה (רַבִּי) יְהוֹשֻׁעַ בֶּן־חֲנַנְיָא אַשְׁרֵי יוֹלַדְתּוֹ (רַבִּי) יוֹסֵי הַכֹּהֵן חָסִיד (רַבִּי) שִׁמְעוֹן בֶּן־נְתַנְאֵל יְרֵא חֵטְא וְ(רַבִּי) אֶלְעָזָר בֶּן־עֲרָךְ כְּמַעְיָן הַמִּתְגַּבֵּר:

11 He [Rabban Yochanan] used to enumerate their merits. R. Eliezer the son of Horkenos is a plastered cistern which does not lose a drop; R. Yehoshua the son of Chananya, happy is she who bore him; R. Yose the priest is a pious man; R. Shimon the son of Nethanel is a sin-fearing man; and R. Elazar the son of Arach is like a spring which continually increases its flow.

---

areas of Torah endeavor. They symbolize the different types of students. Their traits are the basic traits of students. Some emulate one or the other, others combine two or more of the characteristics. But the five students of Rabban Yochanan illustrate, with their lifestyles and abilities, the basic patterns of teacher-student relations, and the basic patterns of learning itself.

MISHNA 11

The teacher expounds on the attributes of his disciples. Rabbi Eliezer the son of Horkenos is a *plastered cistern which does not lose a drop.* He retains with precise exactness every word that has been transmitted to him by his teacher. He obviously values the teaching and considers any word lost as a missing treasure.

71

Rabbi Yehoshua the son of Chananya is of such noble character that *happy is she who bore him*. He has obviously been nursed from the earliest stages on the highest principles of the Torah, such that they are well ingrained and integrated into his personality. Everything that he is taught is thus incorporated into an already solid foundation. Everything that he is taught is readily absorbed and becomes part of him, alive and real.

Rabbi Yose the priest is a *pious man*. He has learned much and sees his role as giving over what he has learned to others in a self-effacing way. He is not interested in the honor and glory that are associated with learning, but, in his piety, with selflessly transmitting Torah to all who would desire to learn.

Rabbi Shimon ben Nethanel is a *sin-fearing man*. He is acutely aware of the importance of Torah in life, and therefore extra cautious about what he says and how he says it. He is careful not to mislead or give false impressions that may lead to sin. He thinks things through very carefully and meticulously before speaking about them.

Rabbi Elazar the son of Arach is like a *spring which continually increases its flow*. He has a keen mind which is able to see the underlying principles at work in Torah, is further able to abstract these principles and apply them to the problems that arise. He sees the natural conclusions which Torah principles extend toward, and is thus able to broaden the scope of what he has been taught.

Undoubtedly each of the students possessed, in some measure, the attributes of the others. They all retained at least some of what they were taught, integrated the teachings and were devoted to transmitting them, were cautious in what they said and able, on occasion, to suggest brilliant solutions to difficult problems. But each also excelled in the attribute by which he was described and for which he was most appreciated. To retain what is taught, to make it

יב הוּא הָיָה אוֹמֵר, אִם יִהְיוּ כָל־חַכְמֵי
יִשְׂרָאֵל בְּכַף מֹאזְנַיִם וֶאֱלִיעֶזֶר בֶּן־
הוֹרְקְנוֹס בְּכַף שְׁנִיָּה מַכְרִיעַ אֶת־כֻּלָּם: אַבָּא שָׁאוּל
אוֹמֵר מִשְּׁמוֹ, אִם יִהְיוּ כָל־חַכְמֵי יִשְׂרָאֵל בְּכַף
מֹאזְנַיִם וֶאֱלִיעֶזֶר בֶּן־הוֹרְקְנוֹס אַף עִמָּהֶם וְאֶלְעָזָר
בֶּן־עֲרָךְ בְּכַף שְׁנִיָּה מַכְרִיעַ אֶת־כֻּלָּם:

12 He [Rabban Yochanan] used to say: If all the sages of Israel were in one pan of the balance scale and Eliezer the son of Horkenos in the other, he would outweigh them all. Abba Shaul said in his [Rabban Yochanan's] name: If all the sages of Israel were in one pan of the balance scale, and even Eliezer the son of Horkenos with them, and Elazar the son of Arach in the other, he would outweigh them all.

---

part of the personality, to be devoted to sharing it with others, to be cautious about what one says, to be able to extend the learning to new situations, all these are the vital ingredients of Torah learning.

MISHNA 12

There are two views attributed to the teacher, Rabban Yochanan, on the relative importance of the attributes of his students. The analogy to the balance scale is noteworthy, as it illustrates the point that all attributes are vital, all carry some weight, with the only matter for debate being which is the most weighty, the most vital.

One view is that Rabbi Eliezer the son of Horkenos, the

73

plastered cistern who retains all, outweighs the others and possesses the most vital trait of the students. By not forgetting the smallest detail of his Rabbi's teaching, he illustrates the importance of maintaining tradition in its entirety; that nothing should be lost from generation to generation. The further one is from the revelation on Sinai, the further one is from the source of Jewish life, and the more it is necessary to retain in total the wisdom of Sinai.

The second view sees Rabbi Elazar the son of Arach, the *spring which continually increases its flow,* as the most vital. His ability to perceive the thrust of Torah and apply it to the new problems of the day is most crucial for the flourishing of Jewishness. This assures that the Torah is a living system which is responsive to the needs of the hour, and able to extend into every aspect of existence.

The other ingredients are vital, but the ability to retain and to apply are most vital for the community.

יג אָמַר לָהֶם, צְאוּ וּרְאוּ אֵיזוֹ הִיא דֶרֶךְ טוֹבָה
שֶׁיִּדְבַּק בָּהּ הָאָדָם. רַבִּי אֱלִיעֶזֶר אוֹמֵר
עַיִן טוֹבָה. רַבִּי יְהוֹשֻׁעַ אוֹמֵר חָבֵר טוֹב. רַבִּי יוֹסֵי
אוֹמֵר שָׁכֵן טוֹב. רַבִּי שִׁמְעוֹן אוֹמֵר הָרוֹאֶה אֶת־
הַנּוֹלָד. רַבִּי אֶלְעָזָר אוֹמֵר לֵב טוֹב: אָמַר לָהֶם,
רוֹאֶה אֲנִי אֶת־דִּבְרֵי אֶלְעָזָר בֶּן־עֲרָךְ מִדִּבְרֵיכֶם
שֶׁבִּכְלַל דְּבָרָיו דִּבְרֵיכֶם:

13 He [Rabban Yochanan] said to them
[his disciples]: Go forth and see which
is the good way to which a person should cleave.
R. Eliezer says — A good eye; R. Yehoshua
says — A good friend; R. Yose says — A good
neighbor; R. Shimon says — One who foresees
that which will be; R. Elazar says — A good
heart. He [Rabban Yochanan] said to them: I
prefer the words of Elazar the son of Arach to
yours, for your words are included in his words.

The answers the students give to Rabban Yochanan reflect
the essence of their respective personalities.

Rabbi Eliezer, the *plastered cistern,* who sees the
beauty in every word uttered by his teacher, suggests the
importance of a good eye; of seeing the good in everything.
If such an attitude is adopted to people, one will behave
positively toward them and bring out their best, thus
uplifting society.

Rabbi Yehoshua, the naturally good person who
projects the feeling that *happy is she who bore him,* says

that being a *good friend* is the best way. To make others happy when they are down, to help them when they need help, to be sensitive to others, these are the hallmarks of a good friend and the best way for a person to be.

Rabbi Yose, the *pious man,* recommends being a *good neighbor.* The good neighbor respects the property, privacy, and dignity of others, gives them a sense of security, and thus creates an atmosphere of mutual respect. It is a mark of piety to be careful of what belongs to others and a crucial element in a viable society.

Rabbi Shimon, the *sin-fearing man,* proposes that the best way is to be *one who foresees that which will be.* The sin-fearing man is very wary of consequences, and makes doubly sure of himself before doing anything. Making sure means to foresee what will be, what are the consequences of a specific action. With such care, it will be difficult to do wrong and easier to do good and kind deeds.

Rabbi Elazar, the *spring which continually increases its flow,* advocates having a *good heart.* The good heart is attentive to the concerns of others and responds to these concerns. Like the spring which intellectually perceives the principles of Torah and extends these principles to communal and individual concerns, the good heart perceives a need and reacts to it.

The students seem to extend the main attributes of their approach to scholarship into life itself.

The teacher, Rabban Yochanan, sees the worth of each student's view, and surely sees how these views emanate from their personalities. But he leans to Rabbi Elazar's feeling that a good heart is *the good way,* for it includes the rest. A person with a good heart has a good eye, is a good friend and neighbor, and sees the consequences of actions. A good heart feeds sustenance to an entire body; a good heart feeds feeling to an entire community.

יד אָמַר לָהֶם, צְאוּ וּרְאוּ אֵיזוֹ הִיא דֶרֶךְ
רָעָה שֶׁיִתְרַחֵק מִמֶּנָה הָאָדָם, רַבִּי
אֱלִיעֶזֶר אוֹמֵר עַיִן רָעָה. רַבִּי יְהוֹשֻׁעַ אוֹמֵר חָבֵר
רָע. רַבִּי יוֹסֵי אוֹמֵר שָׁכֵן רָע, רַבִּי שִׁמְעוֹן אוֹמֵר
הַלֹוֶה וְאֵינוֹ מְשַׁלֵם, אֶחָד הַלֹוֶה מִן־הָאָדָם כְּלֹוֶה
מִן־הַמָּקוֹם, שֶׁנֶּאֱמַר לֹוֶה רָשָׁע וְלֹא יְשַׁלֵם וְצַדִּיק
חוֹנֵן וְנוֹתֵן. רַבִּי אֶלְעָזָר אוֹמֵר לֵב רָע. אָמַר לָהֶם,
רוֹאֶה אֲנִי אֶת־דִּבְרֵי אֶלְעָזָר בֶּן־עֲרָךְ מִדִּבְרֵיכֶם
שֶׁבִּכְלַל דְּבָרָיו דִּבְרֵיכֶם:

14 He [Rabban Yochanan] said to them
[his disciples]: Go forth and see which
is the evil way from which a person should keep
away. R. Eliezer says — A bad eye; R. Yehoshua
says — A bad friend; R. Yose says — A bad
neighbor; R. Shimon says — One who borrows
and does not repay. One who borrows from a
person is as one who borrows from the Omnipresent, as it is said: "The wicked person borrows and never repays, but the righteous person is
gracious and gives" (Tehillim 37:21); R. Elazar
says — A bad heart. He [Rabban Yochanan] said
to them: I prefer the words of Elazar the son of
Arach to yours, for your words are included in his
words.

Here Rabban Yochanan asks the students to define *the evil*

way which should be avoided. The students, true to their nature, respond in a way which closely parallels their answers to the first question.

Rabbi Eliezer, who is compared to a *plastered cistern* and advocates a *good eye,* sees a *bad eye* as that which must be avoided. A bad eye sees bad in everything, projects a negative view, and brings out the worst in everyone.

Rabbi Yehoshua (*happy is she who bore him*), who recommended the *good friend* policy, suggests that being a *bad friend* is the evil which should be avoided. The bad friend alienates those who need help, denigrates those in need, and spreads a poisoned atmosphere in the community.

Rabbi Yose, the *pious man,* who exalts being a *good neighbor,* condemns being a *bad neighbor.* A bad neighbor is unmindful of others, shows no concern for their property and dignity, and thus creates an atmosphere of hate.

Rabbi Shimon, the *sin-fearing man,* who ennobles *one who foresees that which will be,* denounces *one who borrows and does not repay.* He first equates borrowing from a person with borrowing from God, as the money pool is really God's money entrusted to people to help uplift one another. One who borrows and does not repay (literally — will not repay) assumes that money is not God's, that the individual has a personal claim on it, and can thus keep it. This is the mark of a wicked person, as opposed to the r ghteous one who is *gracious and gives.* The righteous person appreciates that any wealth is God's material entrusted to people, and the will of God is best realized in being gracious and giving. One who borrows and does not repay, besides being blind to the fact that such action is a distortion of God's will, also is insensitive to the consequences of such action. Borrowing with no intention to repay (will not repay) is the antithesis of foreseeing *that which will be.* It shows a total obliviousness to what will be. It matters not that not repaying may bring poverty to the lender, or a hesitancy to lend again, thus bringing unwarranted suffering to the needy. Such wickedness can destroy the cooperative basis of society.

Rabbi Elazar, the *spring which continually increases its flow,* and who espouses the value of a *good heart,* sees *a bad heart* as the way to be shunned. The bad heart is callous, insensitive, unresponsive, and cruel.

Rabban Yochanan, again appreciating the different views of his students, accepts Rabbi Elazar's view as most all-embracing. A person with a bad heart has a bad eye, is a bad friend and neighbor, and ignores the consequences of any action.

טו הֵם אָמְרוּ שְׁלֹשָׁה דְבָרִים. רַבִּי אֱלִיעֶזֶר אוֹמֵר, יְהִי כְבוֹד חֲבֵרְךָ חָבִיב עָלֶיךָ כְּשֶׁלָּךְ וְאַל־תְּהִי נוֹחַ לִכְעוֹס וְשׁוּב יוֹם אֶחָד לִפְנֵי מִיתָתְךָ וֶהֱוֵה מִתְחַמֵּם כְּנֶגֶד אוּרָן שֶׁל־חֲכָמִים וֶהֱוֵה זָהִיר בְּגַחַלְתָּן שֶׁלֹּא תִכָּוֶה, שֶׁנְּשִׁיכָתָן נְשִׁיכַת שׁוּעָל וַעֲקִיצָתָן עֲקִיצַת עַקְרָב וּלְחִישָׁתָן לְחִישַׁת שָׂרָף וְכָל־דִּבְרֵיהֶם כְּגַחֲלֵי אֵשׁ:

15 They [the disciples of Rabban Yochanan] each said three things. R. Eliezer says: Let your friend's honor be as dear to you as your own, do not be easily provoked to anger, and repent one day before your death. Be warmed by the fire of the sages but beware of their glowing coals lest you be burned, for their bite is the bite of the fox, their sting the sting of a scorpion, and their hiss is the hiss of the serpent, and all their words are like coals of fire.

Rabbi Eliezer, characterized as a *plastered cistern,* who stresses the importance of a *good eye,* urges the individual to look kindly at others, to see the honor of others as one would see one's personal honor. One who adopts the attitude that a friend's honor is *as dear to you as your own* will thus *not easily be provoked to anger.* One whose goodness is able to see the worth of other people's dignity is unlikely to compromise that dignity by becoming angry and saying or doing things that may be insulting.

As considerate and tempered as one must be to others,

so must one be hard on oneself. To *repent one day before your death* is to repent every day of life, to question the actions of today as to improve tomorrow.

The individual who is hard on others usually is unable to honestly look at the self. Here it is recommended that the process be reversed; that one be easy with others but very demanding of the self.

The *plastered cistern* appreciates the full worth of the Rabbis' teachings, and heartily recommends that people be *warmed by the fire of the sages,* but also warns that like fire, if not properly approached, it can result in being burned rather than being warmed.

A wrong decision based on a casual approach to learning can be as destructive as the devouring *bite of the fox.* An idea which penetrates half-heartedly because of light-headedness in approach to study can become as painful and destructive as the *sting of a scorpion.* A lackadaisical attitude to learning can be as ominous as the *hiss of the serpent. All their words are like coals of fire,* which can singe as well as warm. And like the coals, each one of which would expire if left alone but glows when grouped with the whole, so the words of the sages, *all* the words, are like coal. They must all be carefully nurtured and taken as a whole. The *plastered cistern which does not lose a drop* is thus not merely a student with a good memory, but one with a good appreciation of the value of Torah.

מֵז רַבִּי יְהוֹשֻׁעַ אוֹמֵר, עַיִן הָרַע וְיֵצֶר הָרַע
וְשִׂנְאַת הַבְּרִיּוֹת מוֹצִיאִין אֶת־הָאָדָם מִן־
הָעוֹלָם:

16 Rabbi Yehoshua says: A bad eye, bad passion, and hatred of one's fellow creatures drive a person out of the world.

Rabbi Yehoshua, who made *happy she who bore him,* and espouses being a *good friend,* asserts that certain patterns of behavior remove the individual from human existence, driving the person *out of the world.*

A *bad eye,* which looks negatively at others, and begrudges the happiness and success of others, creates a climate of envy. The bad eye alienates, the bad eye disparages, the bad eye destroys the possibilities of friendship.

The bad eye envies what others have. This envy is at the same time an expression of what the envious one desires. An envious person with a bad eye thus would also have a *bad passion,* a strong desire for sensual pleasures. Life is seen as the pursuit of pleasure and material gain, and people are used and ab-used to achieve these goals. Even the most exalted of human expressions, love, becomes a tool, a means toward an end. There are no friends, just instruments to be manipulated.

Naturally, such an attitude to life can easily cause *hatred of one's fellow creatures,* as such an attitude reduces all people to chattel. In the end, those who are so used and manipulated rebel vehemently at their dehumanization and at their dehumanizers. The hatred that develops is merely the by-product of a lifestyle which is devoid of love. The absence of true love eventually becomes hate, and is

יז רַבִּי יוֹסֵי אוֹמֵר, יְהִי מָמוֹן חֲבֵרְךָ חָבִיב
עָלֶיךָ כְּשֶׁלָּךְ וְהַתְקֵן עַצְמְךָ לִלְמוֹד תּוֹרָה
שֶׁאֵינָה יְרֻשָּׁה־לָךְ וְכָל־מַעֲשֶׂיךָ יִהְיוּ לְשֵׁם שָׁמָיִם:

17 Rabbi Yose says: Let your friend's possessions be as dear to you as your own,
prepare yourself for the study of Torah as it does
not come to you by inheritance, and let all your
deeds be for the sake of Heaven.

---

the ultimate bad which emanates from the bad eye and bad
passion.

This drives the person out of the human world.

MISHNA 17

Rabbi Yose, the *pious man* and *good neighbor,* extends the
fusion of piety and good neighborliness into the practical
realm.

LET YOUR FRIEND'S POSSESSIONS BE AS DEAR TO YOU AS
YOUR OWN. A good neighbor respects the property of others
and, in piety, is as scrupulous about protecting the property of others as about protecting personal property. Piety
involves a healthy respect for other people, for what is
important to them. The pious person looks favorably and
trustingly at others, assumes that what they have is really
theirs and deserves to be protected.

Torah, however, is not the same as property. What one
has can readily be transferred to others, and can surely be
given over to the succeeding generation as an inheritance.
But Torah *does not come to you by inheritance:* it is not
automatically bequeathed from parent to child. To be sure,

the child who is fortunate enough to have parents imbued with Torah is lucky and starts with a great advantage. But the child so blessed should not think that parents can guarantee posterity. Regarding this sacred heritage of our people, *prepare yourself for the study of Torah.* Adopt the attitude that it will not be yours automatically, unless you prepare yourself for it, unless you develop the necessary frame of mind to appreciate Torah and be receptive to it.

The essence of piety is the adoption of the proper attitude to all activity, be it the activity relating to people or the activity relating to God. This attitude is best encapsuled in the phrase — *let all your deeds be for the sake of Heaven.* The approach to Torah as well as to neighbors should be for God's sake. It should not be for the sake of fame as a scholar, or for the sake of popularity as being a nice fellow. There is nothing wrong with being a scholar or a nice fellow, but many things can go wrong if these are the ultimate goals. If everything is done for the sake of Heaven, for God's sake, it becomes an unconditional commitment, as valid and alive in private as in public. There is no expectation of reward or praise, no negative feeling from being unappreciated, and no limit to what should be done for others. This is true piety.

רַבִּי שִׁמְעוֹן אוֹמֵר, הֱוֵי זָהִיר בִּקְרִיאַת **יח**
שְׁמַע וּבִתְפִלָּה וּכְשֶׁאַתָּה מִתְפַּלֵּל אַל־
תַּעַשׂ תְּפִלָּתְךָ קֶבַע אֶלָּא רַחֲמִים וְתַחֲנוּנִים לִפְנֵי
הַמָּקוֹם, שֶׁנֶּאֱמַר כִּי־חַנּוּן וְרַחוּם הוּא אֶרֶךְ אַפַּיִם
וְרַב־חֶסֶד וְנִחָם עַל־הָרָעָה. וְאַל־תְּהִי רָשָׁע בִּפְנֵי
עַצְמֶךָ:

18 Rabbi Shimon says: Be careful in the reading of the Shema and in prayer, and when you pray, do not make your prayer a mechanical routine but an appeal for mercy and graciousness before the Omnipresent, as it is said: "For He is gracious and merciful, slow to anger and abounding in loving-kindness, and relenting of the evil" (Yoel 2:13); and do not consider yourself wicked.

Rabbi Shimon, the *sin-fearing man* who lauds *one who foresees that which will be,* here suggests that the best way to avoid sin is by seeing that life is a constant confrontation with God. To *be careful in the reading of the Shema and in prayer* is to fully understand the import of accepting the yoke of Heaven and then speaking with God in prayer.

Shema is the joyous acceptance of God's imperatives for life and the commitment to actualize them. Prayer is the actual direct talk with God, acknowledging God's majesty and power, and asking God to take care of human needs. If this is done carefully, then that which follows it, the daily encounter with life, is sure to be free from sin.

85

However, this is only so if the Shema and prayer are not a *mechanical routine but an appeal for mercy and graciousness before the Omnipresent.* As a mechanical routine, the Shema and prayer lack meaning, and will have no real impact on life itself. If prayer is an appeal for mercy and graciousness, a supplication which follows the authentic placing of God in the role of absolute Lord of the world and Architect of its purpose, then a solid relationship is forged which places God in the forefront of any subsequent activity.

The verse cited, which refers to God as gracious and merciful, is preceded by the exhortation to *tear your hearts, not your clothing, and return unto God.* When return is a true heart-rending process, it is likely to meet a gracious and merciful God. Anything less is an incomplete exercise which cannot expect any reciprocity.

The approach to God is somewhat fraught with difficulties, not the least of which is the possibility that one might not consider the self worthy enough to even approach God. However, *do not consider yourself wicked,* do not see yourself as beyond hope. The mere approach to God, in sincerity, is likely to induce major changes. Moreover, with a negative view of the self one fails to foresee that which will be. The person who sees the self as wicked may embark on a life which will become a self-fulfilling prophecy. The consequence of having a dim view of the self is that such a view will become retroactively validated.

Therefore, one should approach God, in humility, with full awareness of the potential for good with which every person is blessed.

רבִּי אֶלְעָזָר אוֹמֵר, הֱוֵי שָׁקוּד לִלְמוֹד **יט**
תּוֹרָה וְדַע מַה־שֶּׁתָּשִׁיב לְאֶפִּיקוֹרוֹס וְדַע
לִפְנֵי מִי אַתָּה עָמֵל וּמִי הוּא בַּעַל מְלַאכְתְּךָ שֶׁיְּשַׁלֶּם
לָךְ שְׂכַר פְּעֻלָּתֶךָ:

19 Rabbi Elazar says: Be diligent to study Torah, and know what to respond to a heretic; know before Whom you toil and who your Employer is who will pay you the reward of your labor.

Rabbi Elazar, *like a spring which continually increases its flow* and recommending a *good heart*, says that the ability to perceive the needs of a given situation and apply Torah principles comes only from being *diligent to study Torah*. With diligence, one learns again and again, and pores over the learning searchingly, thus being able to perceive the underlying but often hidden ideas that are at work.

Diligence in Torah enables the individual to respond to any eventuality, even one which may not have been anticipated. The diligent student of Torah is rarely caught off guard, and can respond even to those who question the very foundations of Torah itself. To *know what to respond to a heretic*, one has to be prepared for the unlikely. Thorough and profound knowledge is the only guarantor of such preparedness, and diligence is the only means by which to attain thorough and profound knowledge.

At all times, even when confronted by a heretic, the Torah scholar must be careful not to become locked into a personality struggle. The defense of Torah is not the defense of the Torah scholar, but of truth itself. Even in

87

בַּ רַבִּי טַרְפוֹן אוֹמֵר, הַיוֹם קָצֵר וְהַמְּלָאכָה
מְרֻבָּה וְהַפּוֹעֲלִים עֲצֵלִים וְהַשָּׂכָר הַרְבֵּה
וּבַעַל הַבַּיִת דּוֹחֵק:

20 Rabbi Tarfon says: The day is short, the task is great, the workers are lazy, the reward is great, and the Master of the house is insistent.

---

such a confrontation, *know before Whom you toil,* be aware of God's presence and thus ever mindful of the proper perspective in your struggle.

Even more, know *who your Employer is who will pay you the reward of your labor.* Be aware of the fact that you are doing God's work, that this is not a game of personalities. Such awareness should bring with it a commensurate humility at being entrusted with such a lofty responsibility.

If your ability to respond even to the heretic emanates from having a good heart, then your response will not be in the form of insult or invective, but as an understanding person whose love comes through in dialogue and who projects how Torah, properly understood and amalgamated, brings with it spiritual and moral excellence. The projection of such an atmosphere may separate the heretic from the heresy, and bring the dissident gently into better appreciation of what Torah is all about.

MISHNA 20

This is a further elaboration of the notion that life in this world is a fulfillment of God's work.

The day is short and each individual is only allotted a

finite stay in the world, but *the task is great,* the task itself
is an infinite, never ending one. Every moment wasted is a
wasted opportunity which becomes irretrievable. Since the
day is short, nothing can be put off, especially if the task is
so great, even limitless.

Not surprisingly, *the workers are lazy.* Those who toil
in the world and are committed to doing the work of
righteousness and truth are dedicated, no doubt, but
unaware of the great task which awaits fulfillment. Relative
to the great task which must be approached in a short life,
the workers are lazy. Were they truly aware of what must be
achieved, they would not relax from their responsibility.

Added to this, *the reward is great.* Work in the arena of
life is the most rewarding work, for even if it might bring
many frustrations, nevertheless, ultimately, sincere commitment and dedication to the task enhances the quality of
life itself, makes life worth living, and even brings ultimate
rewards.

Because of this, *the Master of the house is insistent.*
God, the Master of the world, is singularly aware of the
nature of the human being. God is cognizant of human
potential and human limitation. God knows the whys and
wherefores of life, and what is needed to legitimize human
existence. God is fully aware of the great task at hand, the
limited time each person has to achieve the task, and
the great rewards such achievement may bring. God is
therefore insistent that each individual dedicate life to the
achievement of the task and the fulfillment of life's purpose. God's insistence is not to increase pressure on people,
but to urge them into the dimension of life most commensurate with their having been created in the first place, and
to bring to these people the multiple rewards from having
lived a full and proper life.

כא הוּא הָיָה אוֹמֵר, לֹא עָלֶיךָ הַמְּלָאכָה
לִגְמוֹר וְלֹא־אַתָּה בֶּן־חוֹרִין לְהִבָּטֵל
מִמֶּנָּה. אִם לָמַדְתָּ תוֹרָה הַרְבֵּה נוֹתְנִין לְךָ שָׂכָר
הַרְבֵּה וְנֶאֱמָן הוּא בַּעַל מְלַאכְתְּךָ שֶׁיְּשַׁלֵּם לְךָ שְׂכַר
פְּעֻלָּתֶךָ וְדַע שֶׁמַּתַּן שְׂכָרָן שֶׁל־צַדִּיקִים לֶעָתִיד
לָבוֹא:

21 He [Rabbi Tarfon] used to say: It is not up to you to complete the task, but you are not free to desist from it. If you have studied much Torah, abundant reward will be given to you, and your Employer is faithful to pay you the reward of your work. But know that the payment of reward to the righteous is in the time to come.

The task is great, and, spread out over a significant but limited life span, is impossible to fully achieve. It is readily acknowledged that no individual can actualize the infinite task. In fact, *it is not up to you to complete the task.* But this infinite task is not of the type which are worse off half done. People are naturally reluctant to assume a task which cannot be fully achieved and thus may desist from the life task for fear of sure failure. However, precisely because total achievement is impossible is failure also a different category. Failure is defined in terms of not even trying, of seeing no culmination and therefore not even starting the task. *You are not free to desist from it.* Life is not a birth and a death, a start and a finish; it is a never ending process in which every little bit contributes to life's ultimate aims.

The mere orientation around life's purpose, even if it

90

does not bring measurable results, is a contribution in itself. Even *if you have studied much Torah, abundant reward will be given to you.* That is, even if your embarking on life's task never reached beyond the stage of Torah study, you never graduated to teaching Torah or sharing its values with others — even in such a case, your life has meaning and value, committed as it was to the real aims of the world. Reward is measured not in terms of quantitative results, but in terms of qualitative living. At all times, *your Employer is faithful to pay you the reward of your work.* The task is infinite, immeasurable, so that appropriate recompense cannot itself be expressed in finite terms, but God, the Employer, who dwells in the realm of the infinite, can adequately gauge proper recompense.

Reward itself may be seen as the anthropomorphic terminology which best expresses the desires of God. What God rewards is what God considers worthwhile and vital. To say that God rewards is to say that God appreciates. To say that God appreciates is to say that it is important and basic to life.

Reward is, in essence, other-worldly. *Know that the payment of reward to the righteous is in the time to come.* It is not of finite, this-worldly quality.

Payment of reward is not this-worldly also because there is no time in this world to bask in glory, as this only sidetracks from the infinite task which beckons. Also, there is no cause and effect relationship to goodness. To reward immediately the good and to punish immediately the bad is to eliminate the ingredient of choice from human activity and to reduce all behavior to a form of lollipop philosophy. People will make choices based only on the anticipated gain, so that even moral behavior is founded on specious motives. Of necessity, reward must be other-worldly, to ensure that all actions for the good are for their own sake, and thus, eminently rewardable.

CHAPTER **3** ❁

The sanctification

of life

אֲ עֲקַבְיָא בֶּן־מַהֲלַלְאֵל אוֹמֵר, הִסְתַּכֵּל
בִּשְׁלֹשָׁה דְבָרִים וְאֵין אַתָּה בָא לִידֵי
עֲבֵרָה, דַּע מֵאַיִן בָּאתָ וּלְאָן אַתָּה הוֹלֵךְ וְלִפְנֵי מִי
אַתָּה עָתִיד לִתֵּן דִּין וְחֶשְׁבּוֹן. מֵאַיִן בָּאתָ מִטִּפָּה
סְרוּחָה, וּלְאָן אַתָּה הוֹלֵךְ לִמְקוֹם עָפָר רִמָּה
וְתוֹלֵעָה, וְלִפְנֵי מִי אַתָּה עָתִיד לִתֵּן דִּין וְחֶשְׁבּוֹן
לִפְנֵי מֶלֶךְ מַלְכֵי הַמְּלָכִים הַקָּדוֹשׁ בָּרוּךְ הוּא:

1 Akavya the son of Mahalalel says: Concentrate on three things and you will
not fall into the grip of sin. Know from where you
came, where you are going, and before Whom you
will have to give account and reckoning. From
where you came — from a putrid drop. Where
you are going — to a place of dust, worms, and
maggots. And before Whom you will have to give
account and reckoning — before the Supreme
King of kings, the Holy One, blessed be He.

The statement made by Akavya starts out similarly to that
made by Rabbi Yehuda haNasi in the beginning of Chapter
Two. However, unlike Rabbi Yehuda haNasi, Akavya's
equation deals with the question of birth, death, and the
period between. R. Yehuda haNasi's advice on how to avoid
sin is to be aware of *a seeing eye, a hearing ear, and all your
deeds are recorded in a book.* Akavya's approach is to be
aware of one's origins, one's destination, and what one will
have to answer for in the period between.

Akavya posits an affirmative approach to the nothingness of the human being; the human being begins in nothingness and ends in nothingness. The person starts off from a *putrid drop* and goes *to a place of dust, worms, and maggots.* One will have to answer for what happens in the interim period.

If one is confronted with the reality of nothingness before and nothingness after, and sees that what one gives to life in terms of meaning is in the interim period, then all sin could not really occur. The deviance that comes from corporeal attachments would be impossible if one were aware that the physical aspect of life ends in nothingness. Being aware and confronted with this, one either rejects this notion of Akavya and ends up with a life of lust and pleasure or else focuses on it consciously, and in this way avoids the deviances as per Akavya's statement.

Perhaps it is possible to theorize that R. Yehuda ha-Nasi is addressing the individual who is concerned about going on the right path. After having recommended the right path, R. Yehuda haNasi gives a model which makes it possible for the individual to constantly be mindful of that path. Akavya is perhaps not addressing the one who is already philosophically attuned, rather one who is being awoken to the meaning of life. Akavya says the starting point is to recognize that one's roots and one's destination, physically, are of insignificance; that the only significance that can be lent to life is in the period between the beginning and the end.

Akavya's statement points in the direction of what may be termed ultimate values; values which transcend even death itself and which give a meaning to life beyond the physical. It is this element, with which one invests one's life in the present, which has an orientation towards a future beyond this world, where *account and reckoning* must be given.

ב רַבִּי חֲנִינָא סְגַן הַכֹּהֲנִים אוֹמֵר, הֱוֵה מִתְפַּלֵּל בִּשְׁלוֹמָהּ שֶׁל־מַלְכוּת שֶׁאִלְמָלֵא מוֹרָאָהּ אִישׁ אֶת־רֵעֵהוּ חַיִּים בְּלָעוֹ:

2 Rabbi Chanina, the Deputy High Priest, says: Pray for the welfare of the government, for were it not for the fear of it, people would swallow each other alive.

As if to anticipate that the statement in *mishna* 1 almost precludes concern for the here and now, this statement by R. Chanina indicates that one should not go towards extremes, that even though it is important to be concerned with ultimate values, nevertheless worldly matters are also important. It is vital to *Pray for the welfare of the government*, so that one can live in the here and now, because without a base in the here and now, it is impossible to have a true future orientation. Concern for the future should not blind one to concern for the present. Quite the contrary, concern for ultimate values should lead to placing greater emphasis on creating a viable present, in order to make such a future possible.

The statement here — *Pray for the welfare of the government* — does not recommend protest. One could even argue that it recommends the reverse, the maintaining of a status quo, a government which inspires fear in the people such that the people are afraid to do that which is wrong. In other words, a strong bad government is better than no government at all, because with no government, there is chaos and with chaos, there is absolutely no present. With no present, it is very difficult to contemplate a future.

97

Certain governments, as has been the pattern in Jewish experience, were fear-inspiring and even tried to interfere with the Jew's attempts to actualize Jewish responsibilities. It would seem that we are praying for something that goes against our theological responsibilities. However, life in all instances is judged by what is possible within given parameters. If one lives in a generation where certain fulfillments are made impossible by the yoke of government, then such individuals are not judged adversely because of this. Conversely, in a generation where the government is more liberal and allows for fulfillment, then the parameters are expanded, and the responsibility to actualize one's Judaism is greater.

ג רַבִּי חֲנַנְיָא בֶּן־תְּרַדְיוֹן אוֹמֵר, שְׁנַיִם שֶׁיּוֹשְׁבִין וְאֵין בֵּינֵיהֶם דִּבְרֵי תוֹרָה הֲרֵי זֶה מוֹשַׁב לֵצִים, שֶׁנֶּאֱמַר וּבְמוֹשַׁב לֵצִים לֹא יָשָׁב. אֲבָל שְׁנַיִם שֶׁיּוֹשְׁבִין וְיֵשׁ בֵּינֵיהֶם דִּבְרֵי תוֹרָה שְׁכִינָה שְׁרוּיָה בֵינֵיהֶם, שֶׁנֶּאֱמַר אָז נִדְבְּרוּ יִרְאֵי יְיָ אִישׁ אֶל־רֵעֵהוּ וַיַּקְשֵׁב יְיָ וַיִּשְׁמָע וַיִּכָּתֵב סֵפֶר זִכָּרוֹן לְפָנָיו לְיִרְאֵי יְיָ וּלְחֹשְׁבֵי שְׁמוֹ. אֵין לִי אֶלָּא שְׁנַיִם, מִנַּיִן אֲפִילוּ אֶחָד שֶׁיּוֹשֵׁב וְעוֹסֵק בַּתּוֹרָה שֶׁהַקָּדוֹשׁ בָּרוּךְ הוּא קוֹבֵעַ לוֹ שָׂכָר, שֶׁנֶּאֱמַר יֵשֵׁב בָּדָד וְיִדֹּם כִּי נָטַל עָלָיו:

3 Rabbi Chananya the son of Teradyon says: Two who sit together and no words of Torah are exchanged between them, this is the company of scorners, as it is said, "and never sat in the company of scorners" (Tehillim 1:1). But two who sit together and words of Torah are exchanged between them, the Divine Presence abides with them, as it is said, "Then they who were filled with awe of God spoke with one another, and God took note and heard, and a book of remembrance was written before Him for those who are in awe of God and dwell upon His name" (Malachi 3:16). This only proves the case of two; from where can it be derived that even one who sits and is occupied with Torah, the Holy One, blessed be He, establishes for that person a reward? Because it is said, "Let him sit alone, and be at rest, for he has received that which was meant for him" (Eicha 3:38).

This *mishna* gets back to the theme of how to fill the middle between birth and death. Within the Judaic context, the manner of fulfillment is linked with Torah, which is the way of life and the way towards meaning in life. We take Torah here in the greater context, not only in terms of learning, but occupying oneself with thoughts that are Torah inspired and deal with the obligations of the individual as enunciated in the Torah.

If two *sit together, and no words of Torah are exchanged between them*, then *this is a company of scorners*. The proof text for this statement, "and never sat in the company of scorners," is followed immediately by the words "but rather has one's desire in God's Torah." That is to say, happy is the person who never sat in the company of scorners, but who has his desire in God's Torah, which establishes that the company of scorners is not concerned with God's Torah, but rejects life's value.

The Divine Presence, however, abides with those *who sit together and words of Torah are exchanged between them* — even as a matter of conversation, not necessarily only in terms of real learning, but in terms of the concerns between them, that their concerns should be Torah-oriented.

Furthermore, the importance of learning Torah and occupying oneself within a Torah framework is so important that even if a single individual is so occupied, a reward is established for that person. It should be noted that the reward in this instance is not necessarily given, but it is set aside — it is reserved — because the individual meditation has not yet fully evolved into its ultimate in terms of dialogue with others and concern for others.

The proof text for this, "Let him sit alone, and be at rest, for he has received that which was meant for him" deals with one who has been afflicted and who should, nevertheless, contemplate the possible good in the future, because if there is affliction in the present, it is obviously what has been meant, deserved and warranted.

This would seem, at first glance, to have nothing to do with the issue of meditation in Torah. However, one can perhaps see in this the hope, the confidence, that if in meditation one can look forward to the future, even though the present is not a very happy one, how much more so can one who meditates on Torah look forward to a future reward, because of the meaning and potential ultimate value of such contemplation.

The fact that for a dialogical encounter, God takes note of everything that is spoken, indicates, from a theological perspective, how much importance is given to these words of meaning that are interchanged between individuals. It is this contemplation which justifies the very existence of the world.

רַבִּי שִׁמְעוֹן אוֹמֵר, שְׁלשָׁה שֶׁאָכְלוּ עַל
שֻׁלְחָן אֶחָד וְלֹא אָמְרוּ עָלָיו דִּבְרֵי תוֹרָה
כְּאִלּוּ אָכְלוּ מִזִּבְחֵי מֵתִים, שֶׁנֶּאֱמַר כִּי כָּל־שֻׁלְחָנוֹת
מָלְאוּ קִיא צֹאָה בְּלִי מָקוֹם. אֲבָל שְׁלשָׁה שֶׁאָכְלוּ
עַל שֻׁלְחָן אֶחָד וְאָמְרוּ עָלָיו דִּבְרֵי תוֹרָה כְּאִלּוּ
אָכְלוּ מִשֻּׁלְחָנוֹ שֶׁל־מָקוֹם, שֶׁנֶּאֱמַר וַיְדַבֵּר אֵלַי זֶה
הַשֻּׁלְחָן אֲשֶׁר לִפְנֵי יְיָ:

4 Rabbi Shimon says: Three who have
eaten at a table and have spoken there
no words of Torah, it is as if they had eaten from
offerings to the dead, as it is said: "For all their
tables are full of vomit and filth with no space"
(Yeshayahu 28:8). But three who have eaten at a
table and have spoken there words of Torah, it is
as if they had eaten at the table of the Omnipresent, as it is said: "And He said to me: this is
the table that is before the Lord" (Yechezkel
41:22).

Continuing the theme of how to fill the middle between
birth and death with meaning, this *mishna* indicates that
even the materialistic, physical, consumptive aspects of life
can be hallowed. Three who eat at a table are chosen,
perhaps, because three indicates a special attempt to enjoy
company together; it is more than just eating quickly in
order to get on with other things. It establishes a presence
and therefore is singled out as the minimum for the
observation that if no words of Torah are shared at such a

table, it is as if the individuals eating at this table had eaten from sacrifices offered to the dead.

The proof text is "For all their tables are full of vomit and filth with no space." Literally, this indicates that those who are idolaters have their tables so full of vomit and filth that there is no space free of it. At the same time, the words "with no space" seem to refer also to the identification of Makom with God, who is the place of the world. There is no place left on the table for holiness. If people have made no room for God and Torah at their tables it is as if they have eaten from sacrifices to idols which have no life, no power or thrust.

However, three who have eaten at a table and have spoken words of Torah, it is as if they have eaten at God's table. The proof text for this is "And He said to me: this is the table that is before the Lord." This is the last part of a verse, the first part of which deals with the measurements of the altar in the Temple to be built in the future by God and shown in a vision to Yechezkel. Yechezkel did not see, in this vision, a table; he was shown an altar. After having been shown the altar, its measurements, and the substance from which it would be made, Yechezkel says, "And he said to me: this is the table that is before the Lord."

In other words, the table conforms to the measurements of the altar, but it is *in front* of God even after the destruction of the Temple. Unlike the altar itself, which is non-existent in exile, the table itself is existent. The table is the altar in the era subsequent to the destruction of the Temple. Since there are no sacrifices after the destruction of the Temple, it must be that this table is for those who eat, but who eat in a Godly atmosphere; they share words of Torah at the table. This becomes God's table, or the surrogate altar in the exilic era.

ה רַבִּי חֲנִינָא בֶּן־חֲכִינַאי אוֹמֵר, הַנֵּעוֹר
בַּלַיְלָה וְהַמְהַלֵּךְ בַּדֶּרֶךְ יְחִידִי וּמְפַנֶּה לִבּוֹ
לְבַטָּלָה הֲרֵי זֶה מִתְחַיֵּב בְּנַפְשׁוֹ:

5 Rabbi Chanina, the son of Chachinai
says: One who keeps awake at night,
and one who goes on the way alone, and makes
room in the heart for idleness, forfeits one's soul.

In a word, one can exalt even mundane daily activity
by raising it into a cause for further serving God and for
promulgating the Torah.

MISHNA 5

This *mishna* continues the theme of investing life with
meaning. There are possibilities for having one's conversation occupied with Torah-oriented themes or even for
investing the eating enterprise with a more noble purpose.
However, there are individuals who, because of the work
cycle, are not afforded the opportunity for learning or for
finding meaning. These individuals are of the type who,
hopefully, given a time when the opportunity would be
available, would use this opportunity to full advantage.

The telltale sign that such individuals are sincere
about the "if I only had the time" claim is when, in fact,
they do have the time. Two such instances are where one is
awake at night unable to sleep, and therefore has a free
period which is available for contemplation oriented
around Torah; and when one is alone *on the way,* when one
has much time to meditate and to concentrate on things
which are important.

The individual who, caught up in the work cycle and

וֹ רַבִּי נְחוּנְיָא בֶּן־הַקָּנָה אוֹמֵר, כָּל־הַמְקַבֵּל
עָלָיו עוֹל תּוֹרָה מַעֲבִירִין מִמֶּנּוּ עוֹל
מַלְכוּת וְעוֹל דֶּרֶךְ אֶרֶץ וְכָל־הַפּוֹרֵק מִמֶּנּוּ עוֹל
תּוֹרָה נוֹתְנִין עָלָיו עוֹל מַלְכוּת וְעוֹל דֶּרֶךְ אֶרֶץ:

6 Rabbi Nechunya the son of HaKana says: Whoever accepts upon the self the yoke of the Torah, the yoke of worldly occupation is removed from him. But whoever casts off from the self the yoke of Torah, the yoke of the kingdom and the yoke of a worldly occupation are placed upon him.

---

therefore unable to incorporate meaningful aspects into the everyday, squanders the opportunity for fulfillment which is made available by being *awake at night* or being *on the way alone,* and who instead *makes room in the heart for idleness* and thinks idle thoughts, that individual forfeits the soul. If we see suicide as one's drastically doing away with life, then one can see suicide in two forms, both along the person-time continuum. There is a suicide of killing the person, the self, and there is the suicide of killing time. It is relative to this type of suicide that the *mishna* brands one who kills such time as forfeiting one's soul, for indeed one has killed away the precious opportunity which was made available; one has committed suicide in installments.

MISHNA 6

If the previous *mishna* spoke about the work cycle relative to Torah pursuits, this *mishna* indicates that the priorities one chooses greatly affect the type of lifestyle one will lead.

105

Thus, if one places primacy on the Torah, that is, accepts upon oneself *the yoke of the Torah,* that type of primacy has a cycle of its own. The Torah becomes primary, everything else is secondary and thus, recedes into insignificance. Such an individual, who places primacy on Torah, will make anxieties about Torah fulfillment the primary preoccupation in life, such that everything else is subordinated to this pursuit. It thus makes eminent sense that such an individual will have removed from the self *the yoke of the kingdom and the yoke of worldly occupation.* These simply will pale into insignificance relative to the primary pursuit of Torah.

However, *one who casts off from the self the yoke of Torah* will have placed upon the self *the yoke of the kingdom and the yoke of a worldly occupation.* An individual who is not anxious to fulfill the obligations and responsibilities inherent in Torah will have other anxieties instead, the anxieties of making a living, the anxieties of fulfilling the dictates of another power. There are always forces which drive the individual, and anxieties which confront the individual who is faced with negotiating these forces. It is up to the individual to choose which anxiety will be the primary one. If the anxiety is one which does not involve Torah, then it will most logically involve daily living and coming to grips with the forces that govern one's life in a secular sense, namely government. However, one who takes upon the self the primacy of Torah, will, by definition, make that an all encompassing lifestyle, such that everything else will just have to fit into the Torah framework.

ז רַבִּי חֲלַפְתָּא בֶּן־דּוֹסָא אִישׁ כְּפַר חֲנַנְיָא
אוֹמֵר, עֲשָׂרָה שֶׁיּוֹשְׁבִין וְעוֹסְקִין בַּתּוֹרָה
שְׁכִינָה שְׁרוּיָה בֵּינֵיהֶם, שֶׁנֶּאֱמַר אֱלֹהִים נִצָּב
בַּעֲדַת־אֵל. וּמִנַּיִן אֲפִילוּ חֲמִשָּׁה, שֶׁנֶּאֱמַר וַאֲגֻדָּתוֹ
עַל־אֶרֶץ יְסָדָהּ. וּמִנַּיִן אֲפִילוּ שְׁלֹשָׁה, שֶׁנֶּאֱמַר
בְּקֶרֶב אֱלֹהִים יִשְׁפֹּט. וּמִנַּיִן אֲפִילוּ שְׁנַיִם, שֶׁנֶּאֱמַר
אָז נִדְבְּרוּ יִרְאֵי יְיָ אִישׁ אֶל־רֵעֵהוּ וַיַּקְשֵׁב יְיָ וַיִּשְׁמָע.
וּמִנַּיִן אֲפִילוּ אֶחָד, שֶׁנֶּאֱמַר בְּכָל־הַמָּקוֹם אֲשֶׁר
אַזְכִּיר אֶת־שְׁמִי אָבֹא אֵלֶיךָ וּבֵרַכְתִּיךָ:

7 Rabbi Chalafta the son of Dosa of the
village of Chananya says: Ten who sit
together and occupy themselves with the Torah,
the Divine Presence abides with them, as it is
said: "God stands in the congregation of the
Almighty" (Tehillim 82:1). And from where can it
be derived that this applies even in the case of
five? As it is said: "He has founded His band
upon earth" (Amos 9:6). And from where can it be
derived that this applies even in the case of
three? As it is said: "In the midst of judges, He
judges" (Tehillim 82:1). And from where can it be
derived that this applies even in the case of two?
As it is said: "Then they who were in awe of God
spoke to each other and God listened and heard"
(Malachi 3:16). And from where can it be derived
that this applies even in the case of one? As it is

107

said: "In every place where I cause My Name to
be remembered I will come to you and bless you"
(Shemoth 20:21).

Continuing the theme of placing one's primary thrust in
Torah orientation, this *mishna* indicates how God relates
with enthusiasm to such pursuits; a group of ten who gather
together to study Torah actually have the Divine Presence
abiding with them. "God stands in the congregation (a
congregation involves a minimum of ten) of the Almighty"
— of those who are occupied with the word of the Almighty.
This applies even to half of a congregation, to five, as it is
said, "He has founded His band upon the earth." The word
"aguda" referring to band is identified with the five fingers
of the hand, which form a band. This refers to the righteous
who are the foundation, the band, of the earth.

Even for three, the minimum for a court, who occupy
themselves with Torah, "In the midst of judges, He
judges." God descends and spends time with those who are
attempting to render Torah judgment on matters brought
to their attention. This obtains even in the case of two,
which is the minimum for a dialogue. God is concerned
about those who are in awe of God and who speak to each
other concerning God's word — God hears and listens to
what they have to say.

It even applies to one — "In every place where I cause
My Name to be remembered, I will come to you and bless
you" — the Divine Presence rests in any place. God causes
His Name to be remembered, which is a way of saying that
all individuals are obliged to look upon the entire world as
being permeated with God's presence, so that the mention
of God in any place, or the attentiveness to God's word in
any place, is *caused* by this Omnipresence. But, in spite of
the fact that this is caused by God's Omnipresence, the free

choice of the individual to so affirm God in individual locations, such as in the home, or in study, will cause Divine blessing to descend upon that place. This is an indication of the value of even the single individual who meditates on God's word, and it goes beyond the view previously expressed in Chapter 3, *mishna* 3, that for the one who is occupied with Torah God *establishes a reward*. Here, emphasis is given to the fact that the Divine Presence resides even with the lone individual who learns.

Mishna 5 and *mishna* 6, though seemingly unrelated and intervening between the common theme of *mishna* 3 and *mishna* 7, nevertheless relate to the importance of the individual and the individual's meditation on Torah. They build up to the culminating point of *mishna* 7, which is that even the *one* who meditates on Torah is considered vital enough. Such an individual merits the Divine Presence. Of course, *mishna* 4 also intervenes between *mishna* 3 and *mishna* 7, but it deals with the dialogue in hallowing even the mundane aspects of life, such as the meal, so that it relates directly to the dialogical framework of *mishna* 3. *Mishna* 5 and *mishna* 6 appear to be out of place, but in the context of building up the importance of individual endeavor, even though it may be in private, even isolated, they seem to be the preparatory ground for the crescendo in *mishna* 7.

ח רַבִּי אֶלְעָזָר אִישׁ בַּרְתּוֹתָא אוֹמֵר, תֶּן־לוֹ
מִשֶּׁלוֹ שָׁאַתָּה וְשֶׁלְּךָ שֶׁלּוֹ, וְכֵן בְּדָוִד הוּא
אוֹמֵר כִּי־מִמְּךָ הַכֹּל וּמִיָּדְךָ נָתַנּוּ לָךְ:

8 Rabbi Elazar of Bartotha says: Give Him from what is His, because you and all that you have are His. And thus is it said of David: "for all things come from You and of Your own we have given to You" (I Divrey Hayamim 29:14).

All the emphasis on spending time in Torah obviously leads to the question, "What about me?" With all the time spent on the pursuits involved in Torah, what time is there left for the individual? Aside from the fact that Torah pursuits are obviously predicated on bringing out the best in the individual, the fact is that in terms of mere possessiveness, as an aspect of human endeavor, it should be clear that what we are doing is giving God from what is His, because we and all that we have are His. Not only our wealth, our health and all our possessions, but even the time that we have at our disposal is God's gift entrusted to us. It should not be considered as anything special if we give this time to God's word, because we are giving this time to God's word from God's own time.

God is the trustee of all; our transcending the self toward the world of values and investing our energies and time in it is merely giving back to God what belongs to God. The verse cited from David, "for all things come from You and of Your own we have given to You," is not an absolute proof of this statement, such that the words introduced here are *And thus is it said of David.* David said this in

מ רַבִּי יַעֲקֹב אוֹמֵר, הַמְהַלֵּךְ בַּדֶּרֶךְ וְשׁוֹנֶה
וּמַפְסִיק מִמִּשְׁנָתוֹ וְאוֹמֵר מַה־נָּאֶה אִילָן
זֶה מַה־נָּאֶה נִיר זֶה, מַעֲלֶה עָלָיו הַכָּתוּב כְּאִלּוּ
מִתְחַיֵּב בְּנַפְשׁוֹ:

9 Rabbi Yaakov says: One who is walking
by the way in study and interrupts the
study to exclaim "How beautiful is this tree!"
"How beautiful is this field!" is regarded by
Scripture as having forfeited one's soul.

---

regard to material wealth. However, reading the implications of the statement and its radical generality would
indicate that David was referring not only to material
possessions, but to all that which is ours and which is
available for our use in this world.

MISHNA 9

If, as has been posited in the previous *mishna*, all is God's,
this would include the heavens and the earth, nature, the
trees, the fields. One can see in all of this the greatness and
majesty of God. Nevertheless, this should not develop into
an equation of sameness. There is profound significance in
everything, but not everything is the same. There is a scale
of values; there are priorities and levels of importance. One
who is walking by the way in study and interrupts the study
to admire nature by saying "*How beautiful is this tree!*" or
another such statement which affirms the majesty of God
in the world, has made a priority substitution which is
distorted. This distortion inheres in that such an individual
has seen fit to interrupt Torah study to admire nature.

111

Admiring nature is part of appreciating the beauty of the world, but not a priority when juxtaposed with Torah study. Nature is God's work, but the Torah is God's formula for life. Interrupting Torah to admire nature is a value distortion.

The *mishna* ends by saying that the individual who makes this value distortion *is regarded by Scripture as having forfeited one's soul.* It is unclear which verse in Scripture is the proof text for this. In all probability, it would seem that Scripture in general makes this observation. It is in the very nature of the importance of Scripture. One who denies Scripture's importance by placing primacy on nature, by interrupting Torah meditation to admire nature, Scripture itself sees this as a rejection of the very notion of Scripture's being so vital to life, and being the most crucial of all human pursuits. Placing this pursuit in a subordinate position to admiring nature denies the primary importance of Scripture. It is as if one has forfeited one's soul, because in the process of placing Torah and its values in a secondary position, one has denied its essentiality to life and has thus compromised the value actualization which is so vital for a meaningful life.

רַבִּי דּוֹסְתַּאי בַּר יַנַּאי מִשּׁוּם רַבִּי מֵאִיר
אוֹמֵר, כָּל־הַשּׁוֹכֵחַ דָּבָר אֶחָד מִמִּשְׁנָתוֹ
מַעֲלֶה עָלָיו הַכָּתוּב כְּאִלּוּ מִתְחַיֵּב בְּנַפְשׁוֹ, שֶׁנֶּאֱמַר
רַק הִשָּׁמֶר לְךָ וּשְׁמֹר נַפְשְׁךָ מְאֹד פֶּן־תִּשְׁכַּח אֶת־
הַדְּבָרִים אֲשֶׁר־רָאוּ עֵינֶיךָ. יָכוֹל אֲפִילוּ תָּקְפָה עָלָיו
מִשְׁנָתוֹ, תַּלְמוּד לוֹמַר וּפֶן־יָסוּרוּ מִלְּבָבְךָ כֹּל יְמֵי
חַיֶּיךָ, הָא אֵינוּ מִתְחַיֵּב בְּנַפְשׁוֹ עַד שֶׁיֵּשֵׁב וִיסִירֵם
מִלִּבּוֹ:

10 Rabbi Dostai the son of Yannai said in the name of Rabbi Meir: Whoever forgets one word of study is regarded by Scripture as having forfeited one's soul, as it is said: "Only take heed of yourself, and guard your soul diligently lest you forget the things which your eyes have seen" (Devarim 4:9). It might be assumed that this applies even in a case where study was too hard; against this the Torah adds: "and lest they depart from your heart all the days of your life" (Devarim 4:9). That is, one does not forfeit one's soul unless one sits and deliberately removes them [the teachings] from the heart.

The primacy of Torah is evident not only in that it is of highest priority, but also in terms of how one approaches Torah study. It should not be considered as a subject for which one crams in order to pass an exam, after which one can summarily forget all that has been absorbed; rather, it

113

is a formula for life. One is constantly confronted with value actualization in life, such that forgetting Torah means that one has forgotten about the essentials of life.

It therefore follows that one who forgets obviously has not approached Torah seriously enough, has not seen Torah as so crucial that every word is critical, and therefore, should be vibrantly remembered. Scripture admonishes that one take heed of oneself and guard the soul diligently to prevent the forgetting of things which the eyes have seen, which refers to the experience of revelation and all that it contained. The terminology "guard your soul" indicates that forgetting is detrimental to the soul; or, in terms of the *mishna,* an individual who forgets is regarded as *having forfeited one's soul.*

Obviously, in situations of forgetfulness one has to distinguish between forgetfulness which emanates from a lack of serious approach and forgetfulness which emanates from inability to properly comprehend that which is projected. Accordingly, the *mishna* concludes that the forfeiture of soul associated with forgetfulness applies only if one forgets it all the days of one's life; that is to say, there was a conscious effort to remove what was studied from the heart.

This conscious effort does not necessarily come from saying "I will forget." Obviously, motivated forgetting is the best way to remember. It comes from willfully ignoring the import of the message. Those who would like to incorporate an element of knowledge into one's person, but cannot because it has not been properly comprehended, have not ignored, and have even tried to do the reverse. Those who have absorbed this knowledge but have failed to incorporate it are guilty of having an improper approach to the vital nature of Torah.

רַבִּי חֲנִינָא בֶּן־דּוֹסָא אוֹמֵר, כֹּל שֶׁיִּרְאַת
חֶטְאוֹ קוֹדֶמֶת לְחָכְמָתוֹ חָכְמָתוֹ
מִתְקַיֶּמֶת וְכֹל שֶׁחָכְמָתוֹ קוֹדֶמֶת לְיִרְאַת חֶטְאוֹ אֵין
חָכְמָתוֹ מִתְקַיֶּמֶת:

11 Rabbi Chanina the son of Dosa says: One in whom the fear of sin comes before wisdom, that person's wisdom endures. But one in whom wisdom comes before the fear of sin, that person's wisdom does not endure.

In emphasizing the importance of Torah endeavor, it is important to place the learning process into proper context. The proper context is one in which *the fear of sin comes before wisdom*. Only by establishing the fear of sin and the awesomeness of doing wrong as the primary motivational factor in accelerating the study of Torah, such that it is not seen as simply the aggrandizement of knowledge, but rather as the essential life system, is wisdom based on a scrupulous life. The wisdom has its proper roots and will be properly interpreted in the context of avoiding that which must be avoided.

However, in a contrary situation, where *wisdom comes before the fear of sin*, where wisdom is seen as a value in and of itself and with a priority of its own, such wisdom remains disconnected from life. It is something which one has, rather than something which one is, and it really has no anchor in human experience. It is a subject, rather than an awe inspiring learning process. Ultimately, such wisdom, uprooted as it is from human experience, will not endure. It will recede into the insignificance which is

יב הוּא הָיָה אוֹמֵר, כֹּל שֶׁמַּעֲשָׂיו מְרֻבִּים מֵחָכְמָתוֹ חָכְמָתוֹ מִתְקַיֶּמֶת וְכֹל שֶׁחָכְמָתוֹ מְרֻבָּה מִמַּעֲשָׂיו אֵין חָכְמָתוֹ מִתְקַיֶּמֶת:

12 He [Rabbi Chanina the son of Dosa] used to say: One whose deeds exceed the person's wisdom, that person's wisdom endures. But one whose wisdom exceeds the person's deeds, that person's wisdom does not endure.

---

attached to it by virtue of its being viewed as just a mere subject.

MISHNA 12

This *mishna* cautions, in a manner similar to the previous *mishna*, against the rootlessness of Torah wisdom. Here the point made is that whatever wisdom one gains should be directed futuristically towards fulfillment. The previous *mishna* dealt with the motivation for acquiring the wisdom, namely to avoid doing that which is wrong. This *mishna* deals with the outgrowth of the acquisition of the wisdom, namely, doing that which is right.

In a word, the knowledge which one acquires from Torah study should be knowledge which can be actualized in deed. *One whose deeds exceed the person's wisdom, that person's wisdom endures* because that knowledge is not an abstraction but is rooted in life, is reinforced by experience, and therefore continues to live. However, *one whose wisdom exceeds the person's deeds, that person's wisdom will not endure*, as the actions do not reinforce the learning. The learning remains an abstraction which does not relate

116

רג הוא הָיָה אוֹמֵר, כֹּל שֶׁרוּחַ הַבְּרִיּוֹת נוֹחָה
הֵימֶנּוּ רוּחַ הַמָּקוֹם נוֹחָה הֵימֶנּוּ וְכֹל
שֶׁאֵין רוּחַ הַבְּרִיּוֹת נוֹחָה הֵימֶנּוּ אֵין רוּחַ הַמָּקוֹם
נוֹחָה הֵימֶנּוּ:

13 He [Rabbi Chanina the son of Dosa] used to say: One in whom the spirit of humankind takes delight, the spirit of the Omnipresent takes delight. But one in whom the spirit of humankind takes no delight, the spirit of the Omnipresent takes no delight.

---

to life, is not identified with life, and therefore dies the natural death of all things which are not perceived as being significant.

MISHNA 13

The previous statements dealt with how to incorporate wisdom in the proper context, motivationally and once having acquired the wisdom. The integration of wisdom into one's lifestyle is the basic theme that evolves. Here the *mishna* indicates that there is a telltale sign of how one has integrated the religious imperative implied in Torah. It is, very simply, whether the religious quest has integrated the theological and the social context. If an individual has met with the acceptance of the *spirit of humankind* then such an individual can be guaranteed acceptance by the spirit of God. On the other hand, if one has not met with the acceptance of the *spirit of humankind*, then it is likely that one has not met with acceptance by the spirit of God.

This is the true test. Whether an individual has

יך רַבִּי דוֹסָא בֶּן הָרְכִּינַס אוֹמֵר, שֵׁנָה שֶׁל-
שַׁחֲרִית וְיַיִן שֶׁל-צָהֳרַיִם וְשִׂיחַת הַיְלָדִים
וִישִׁיבַת בָּתֵּי כְנֵסִיּוֹת שֶׁל-עַמֵּי הָאָרֶץ מוֹצִיאִין אֶת-
הָאָדָם מִן-הָעוֹלָם:

14 Rabbi Dosa the son of Harkinas says: Morning sleep, midday wine, children's talk, and sitting in the assembly houses of the ignorant drive a person out of the world.

---

integrated Torah properly is measured in terms of whether it has excited others, whether it has given others a positive stance towards life, and alerted them to the great value possibilities that are inherent in Torah. It should be emphasized that we are dealing here not with the acceptance of a general, amorphous public but rather with the "spirit of humankind." It is not vital to be popular with the materialistic, pleasure-seeking crowd. Instead, success is gauged by the impact one has with the serious, spiritually-oriented folk. It is they, not the majority in numbers, but the majority in terms of commitment and proper orientation, who are the final arbiters over the question whether one has successfully integrated Torah in one's lifestyle.

MISHNA 14

This *mishna* further develops the social context within which one's Torah expression must be integrated. It cautions against taking social acceptance to an extreme by saying that there are four things which can *drive a person out of the world*, out of the meaningful world which is so inextricably linked with Torah. *Morning sleep*, which would come from too much indulgence in night activity and indicates a form of bodily laziness, is one such element. A second element is *midday wine*, a spiritual laziness which allows for the wasting of precious hours and the achieving of highs, not by what one does for others, but rather artificially, by taking wine or other related intoxicants. Then there is *children's talk*, or intellectual laziness, the concern about trivial, insignificant matters and the involvement in an atmosphere which deals with "baby topics," subjects which are not worthy of adult concern.

Finally, there is the *sitting in the assembly houses of the ignorant*, being stultified in a time-wasting ambience, rather than trying to upgrade oneself. The assembly halls of the ignorant imply a fulfillment laziness which is part of the syndrome of staying up late, involving oneself in idle baby chatter, sleeping late in the morning, and bringing on the emptiness which would necessitate midday wine, and so on, ad infinitum. These all form part of a pattern, one leading to the other, completing a vicious cycle. It turns the individual away from the upward thrust towards meaning which should be one's real endeavor in the world.

טן רַבִּי אֶלְעָזָר הַמּוֹדָעִי אוֹמֵר, הַמְחַלֵּל אֶת־
הַקְּדָשִׁים וְהַמְבַזֶּה אֶת־הַמּוֹעֲדוֹת
וְהַמַּלְבִּין פְּנֵי חֲבֵרוֹ בָּרַבִּים וְהַמֵּפֵר בְּרִיתוֹ שֶׁל־
אַבְרָהָם אָבִינוּ וְהַמְגַלֶּה פָנִים בַּתּוֹרָה שֶׁלֹּא
כַהֲלָכָה, אַף עַל פִּי שֶׁיֶּשׁ בְּיָדוֹ תּוֹרָה וּמַעֲשִׂים
טוֹבִים, אֵין לוֹ חֵלֶק לָעוֹלָם הַבָּא:

15 Rabbi Elazar of Modin says: One who profanes sacred things, who despises the appointed festivals, who humiliates a fellow being in public, who rejects the covenant of Avraham our father, and who interprets the Torah in a way which contradicts the Halacha, even though in possession of Torah knowledge and good deeds, has no share in the world to come.

The assembly halls of the ignorant are implicitly reductionist in that they do not affirm the important things in life and regard them as unworthy of their attention. There is another form of reductionism perhaps even more dangerous, one which is aware of vital notions in life but rejects these notions out of hand. This is the primary thrust of this *mishna*, which concerns itself with those who reject basic concepts sharing one common ingredient, that of specialness.

There is the specialness of *sacred things*, things which have been set aside for hallowed purposes which may seem from the external view to be the same as any other things, but because they have been relegated for sacred purposes assume a sanctity of their own.

There are the *appointed festivals*, which could be seen by an outsider as days like any other days, but are specifically relegated for unique fulfillments.

There are *fellow beings*. They may appear to be merely two-legged animals, but they are sacred; they have been created in God's image, and their very existence must be treated with the delicate care which comes with the sanctity of the individual.

There is the uniqueness and sanctity of Israel, as is evident in the covenantal relationship of circumcision which binds the Jew to fulfilling the dictates of the Torah. A Jew outwardly looks like any other individual, yet the responsibilities assumed by the Jew are uniquely different.

Then there is the sanctity of the *Torah*, which is not like any other philosophical doctrine, to be manipulated and interpreted as one would want, poetically or otherwise. Rather, it has a specific framework of interpretation which must be adhered to strictly or else the very notions of Torah could be distorted and turned upside down.

An individual who rejects the specialness of sacred things, who neglects and shames the appointed festivals, who denies the sanctity of the individual by humiliating the individual publicly, who does not accept the specialness of Israel—thus rejecting the covenant with Avraham—or who goes about extending the Torah into halachic pronouncements based on individual perceptions which are totally divorced from the hallowed approach to Torah so crucial to proper Torah knowledge, such an individual forfeits eternality. Such an individual misleads the self and others into thinking that Judaism can exist without the notion of sanctity, that it can be a regular, steady life pattern which does not have its sacred and its mundane. This, in reality, cannot be. Such an individual, who strikes one as

רַבִּי יִשְׁמָעֵאל אוֹמֵר, הֱוֵה קַל לְרֹאשׁ
וְנוֹחַ לְתִשְׁחֹרֶת וֶהֱוֵה מְקַבֵּל אֶת־כָּל־
הָאָדָם בְּשִׂמְחָה:

16 Rabbi Yishmael says: Be amenable with a superior, co-operative with youth, and receive all people with cheerfulness.

---

being an ethical humanist, might have *Torah knowledge* and may even have *good deeds*, but cuts the self off from the spiritual dimension and projects the self as an example that the spiritual dimension is totally unnecessary, that the uniquely Judaic expression of the spirit as is involved in Torah is not sacrosanct. By so doing, one has taken the sacred out of life, robbed it of its meaning potential, and thus denied the self and others the possibility of gaining eternal life.

MISHNA 16

The previous *mishna* dealt with one's rejecting the notion of sanctity and being oblivious to the implications of such rejection for the self and for others. Such an individual disregards the implications of this approach for the community. The present *mishna* deals with ego difficulties relative to communal functioning. Primarily, they may be said to focus around individuals who have not reached the position of prominence in the community they felt was appropriate for them. The general tendency of such individuals is to downgrade those who have superseded them and to discourage those who would in the future gain the very positions they have failed to attain.

The advice in this *mishna* is to conquer this ego

difficulty, not to destroy the very structure of community. In other words, do not envy or covet another individual's position and show this envy by not co-operating with leadership. Rather, *Be amenable with a superior.* Do not ask why that individual is better than you and why you should follow. Rather, say that this is a position of responsibility, and the only way that responsibility can be realized is if the public co-operates.

Then there is the matter of the attitude to those who are on the way towards gaining positions of prominence and becoming superiors, the youth of the community. Do not let the disappointment and frustration with your stunted growth lead you to discourage those who are on the way up the communal ladder. Your melancholy at not having made it should not be employed in discouraging those younger than you who will realize and achieve what you failed to achieve. Rather, *be co-operative with youth.*

Finally, *receive all people with cheerfulness.* You may have a chip on the shoulder from what you perceive has been denied to you. Nevertheless, it is up to you not to spread your melancholy to others and to deny them the excitement that they feel towards their work or towards life in general. Receive all people with cheerfulness. Transcend yourself, transcend your frustration, and allow the community to function in the way that is necessary so that all individuals may benefit from leadership and their wisdom.

יז רַבִּי עֲקִיבָא אוֹמֵר, שְׂחוֹק וְקַלּוּת רֹאשׁ מַרְגִּילִין אֶת־הָאָדָם לְעֶרְוָה. מַסֹרֶת סְיָג לַתּוֹרָה, מַעְשְׂרוֹת סְיָג לָעֹשֶׁר, נְדָרִים סְיָג לִפְרִישׁוּת, סְיָג לַחָכְמָה שְׁתִיקָה:

17 Rabbi Akiva says: Jesting and levity accustom a person to lewdness. The transmitted tradition is a fence around the Torah; tithes are a fence for riches; vows are a fence for abstinence; a fence for wisdom is silence.

The matter of frustration with not having realized whatever position one felt one deserved can turn one off from society in general, such that it is not unlikely that an attitude of *jesting and levity* should evolve. Jesting may be seen as a form of sarcasm directed at something or at someone, perhaps at a position or a particular leader. Levity is a general lack of seriousness not directed at any individual. Both are expressions of one who is not attuned to the importance of community.

This attitude of jesting and levity can affect the individual in that the individual will deny, as a form of defence mechanism, the very things which were previously perceived as important and desirable. The ultimate objectives which previously could have been reached in involvement with the community are now denied. Instead, what is affirmed is a this-worldly accent on pleasure and a retreat into the exercise of passion. This is to compensate with momentary fulfillment for the lack of real, ultimate fulfillment. In a word, *Jesting and levity accustom a person to lewdness.*

How does one maintain perspective, such that stepping out of the bounds of concern will be unlikely to occur? First, the tradition surrounding the Torah puts the Torah into proper perspective. It raises it up from being just a collection of legislation into an intense application to all aspects of life; it hones in on the parameters of life. The giving of 10% of one's wealth keeps a perspective on what one has obtained, in that it is not there to be owned, but is entrusted to be shared and to be the focus for value realization.

Every individual has instincts. Those who are properly attuned will try to control these instincts. The instinct to self-aggrandizement is well checked by the sharing with the poor, by giving 10%; the tradition helps to place into proper perspective the Torah legislations and thus mediate the passions of an individual. But sometimes passion has a strength of its own, which forces extraordinary measures such as vowing to abstain from even getting close to a situation where the passions might be excited.

These deal with placing in perspective that which one has, or has already acquired. The final statement deals with a methodology which enhances the acquisition of that which one does not yet have, namely wisdom. *A fence for wisdom is silence.*

To acquire wisdom, one should be silent or contemplative in absorbing realities, rather than be eager to challenge those realities. The over-eagerness to challenge and to debate makes it likely that one has not really absorbed the wisdom in the first place. The primary focus should be on learning and trying to understand.

Once having understood, one can start wrestling with what one has digested. If one is not silent, but rather vocal in challenging before learning, then one's knowledge will be

יח הוּא הָיָה אוֹמֵר, חָבִיב אָדָם שֶׁנִּבְרָא
בְּצֶלֶם, חִבָּה יְתֵרָה נוֹדַעַת לוֹ שֶׁנִּבְרָא
בְּצֶלֶם, שֶׁנֶּאֱמַר כִּי בְּצֶלֶם אֱלֹהִים עָשָׂה אֶת־הָאָדָם.
חֲבִיבִין יִשְׂרָאֵל שֶׁנִּקְרְאוּ בָנִים לַמָּקוֹם, חִבָּה יְתֵרָה
נוֹדַעַת לָהֶם שֶׁנִּקְרְאוּ בָנִים לַמָּקוֹם, שֶׁנֶּאֱמַר בָּנִים
אַתֶּם לַיָי אֱלֹהֵיכֶם. חֲבִיבִין יִשְׂרָאֵל שֶׁנִּתַּן לָהֶם כְּלִי
חֶמְדָּה, חִבָּה יְתֵרָה נוֹדַעַת לָהֶם שֶׁנִּתַּן לָהֶם כְּלִי
חֶמְדָּה שֶׁבּוֹ נִבְרָא הָעוֹלָם שֶׁנֶּאֱמַר כִּי לֶקַח טוֹב
נָתַתִּי לָכֶם תּוֹרָתִי אַל־תַּעֲזֹבוּ:

18 He [Rabbi Akiva] used to say: Beloved is the human being, since he was created in God's image. Greater is that love in that it was made known to him that he was created in God's image, as it is said: "In the image of God did God make the person" (Bereshith 9:6). Beloved are Israel, since they are called children of the Omnipresent. Greater is

---

superficial and will bring the very sarcasm and levity which comes from having superficial knowledge.

To maintain the parameters of seriousness and directedness towards real fulfillment, one must always place a check around that which one has absorbed, be it knowledge, be it wealth, be it even the passions with which an individual must wrestle.

that love in that it was made known to them that they are called the children of the Omnipresent, as it is said: "You are children to God, your God" (Devarim 14:1). Beloved are Israel, since a precious instrument was given to them. Greater is that love in that it was made known to them that a precious instrument was given to them through which the world was created, as it is said: "For I give you good doctrine, forsake not My Torah" (Mishley 4:2).

An aid to the seriousness with which one must approach life and the best way to avoid sarcasm is to appreciate the importance with which God has invested life. First, God has created individuals in the Divine image; all individuals are extensions of the Godly and thus may legitimately aspire to Godly heights within the context of human potentiality. God did not make the individual as just another animal, but rather created the individual with Divine propensities, such that a transcending level of fulfillment can be expected. Moreover, this was not a secret kept from the individual. The love of God for humankind is all the greater in that the human being was made aware of the height to which one can legitimately aspire.

In a more precise dimension, the people of Israel, over and above having been created, like all other human beings, in the Divine image, are also perceived as children of God. They have been given the tools, and have accepted those tools, for following the design of the Father. These tools are the Torah, which is the third great gift.

Not only were all the Israelite people perceived as God's children, but it was made known to them that they were

יט הַכֹּל צָפוּי וְהָרְשׁוּת נְתוּנָה. וּבְטוֹב
הָעוֹלָם נָדוֹן. וְהַכֹּל לְפִי רֹב הַמַּעֲשֶׂה:

19 All is foreseen yet freedom [of choice] is given, the world is judged according to the good, and everything is measured according to the multitude of deeds.

---

so thought of. This very knowledge is seen as an inspiration towards actualizing the type of responsibilities that a child has towards a father.

Finally, the belovedness of Israel is seen in the fact that the exercise of their filial responsibilities was not left to their whims, which would leave it open-ended and therefore dangerously elusive, but rather, the very instrument by which they were to actualize their responsibilities was given to them. Even more, it was revealed to them that the Torah is that instrument.

Obviously, all this adds to one's responsibility. The weight of having been created in God's image, the weight of being considered God's children, the burden of having to live along the lines of Torah responsibility, are all tremendous challenges. But they were given out of love and they are expressions of love, for they give the compass by which to orient life and make it possible for the individual to invest life with its transcending direction. Anyone who is aware of these realities cannot help but avoid sarcasm and become seriously committed to the importance of life — to nothing less than the importance God has given to it.

MISHNA 19

Having just stated what should be the directional thrust of life and the focus of one's value orientation, the Mishna proceeds to indicate that all individuals must choose towards this very goal, yet the very choice of this lofty ideal is an act in freedom of choice. Paradoxically, this freedom is one which is granted in spite of the fact that everything is foreseen.

This is, at first glance, a contradiction. How can things be foreseen and freedom of choice still exist? Nevertheless, the mere fact that praise and blame are incurred for acts which are performed by the individual indicates that choice is assumed.

Even if there would seem to be a theological contradiction, since God judges the individual in terms of choice, the affirmation of faith would include the assurance that God would not judge an individual favorably or adversely if the choice did not exist. If such judgment is made, then obviously such choice exists. How that choice exists is beyond human ken, but it is no more beyond human ken than the perception of God or the notion of God's foreknowledge. We incorporate the notion of free choice into the very dilemma of faith itself.

Without choice, praise and blame are impossible. The world is judged by the orientation around and the actualization of the good, *according to the multitude of deeds.* An individual is judged by how the freedom toward the ultimate goal is actually lived. Even then, the primary judgmental element is the multitude of deeds. On the balance scale, the decisions about the worthwhileness of life in general and of individual lives in particular reside in the preponderance of deeds, good vs. bad, whether the life lived and the values realized are affirmative in their nature, such that life itself is affirmative.

כ הוּא הָיָה אוֹמֵר, הַכּל נָתוּן בְּעֵרָבוֹן.
וּמְצוּדָה פְרוּשָׂה עַל־כָּל־הַחַיִּים. הֶחָנוּת
פְתוּחָה וְהַחֶנְוָנִי מַקִּיף, וְהַפִּנְקֶס פָּתוּחַ וְהַיָּד
כּוֹתֶבֶת, וְכָל הָרוֹצֶה לִלְווֹת יָבֹא וְיִלְוֶה. וְהַגַּבָּאִין
מַחֲזִירִין תָּדִיר בְּכָל־יוֹם וְנִפְרָעִין מִן־הָאָדָם מִדַּעְתּוֹ
וְשֶׁלֹּא מִדַּעְתּוֹ וְיֵשׁ לָהֶם עַל מַה שֶׁיִּסְמֹכוּ. וְהַדִּין דִּין
אֱמֶת וְהַכֹּל מְתֻקָּן לִסְעוּדָה:

20 He [Rabbi Akiva] used to say: Everything is given on pledge, and a net is spread out over all the living. The shop is open, the merchant extends credit, the ledger is open and the hand writes. Whoever wishes to borrow may come and borrow. The collectors regularly make their rounds each day, and they exact payment from the person whether with or without that person's knowledge. They have what to rely upon, the judgment is a true judgment, and all is ready for the banquet.

In affirming the notion of freedom toward the actualization of values, one should see oneself as a confronted individual. But confrontation should not assume the mercifulness of God, because once such an assumption is made, it is quite likely that laxity will set in and one will rely on this mercy. Rather, one should view life on a strict credit/debit basis so laxity will not set in. One should see that all that we have and all that we are is the security for the deeds that we perform in life, and the Divine response to human action is all-encompassing and spreads over the entire world.

One can spend one's life in overindulgence and increase one's debit, the consequences for that indulgence. This consequence does not necessarily come immediately. The consequence can come long after the debt has been contracted, so much after that one loses sight of the fact that the consequence is a direct result of the action.

Nevertheless, one should realize that this element of justice guarantees that there will never be an overstepping of the boundaries of justice, but everything will be in conformity with the debit; judgment is exacted in keeping with the rule that there is *what to rely upon* [to collect from] and *the judgment is a true judgment.*

Yet it is not adverse judgment that is desired, but rather that the individual, seeing the self as confronted, behave in such a way that adverse judgment is unnecessary and that the final destination for the individual be the experiencing of the great banquet which comes from leading a meritorious life. It is only in perceiving life as based on strict justice that one will, on one's merit, gain eternal life.

רַבִּי אֶלְעָזָר בֶּן־עֲזַרְיָה אוֹמֵר. אִם אֵין
תּוֹרָה אֵין דֶּרֶךְ אֶרֶץ, אִם אֵין דֶּרֶךְ אֶרֶץ
אֵין תּוֹרָה. אִם אֵין חָכְמָה אֵין יִרְאָה, אִם אֵין יִרְאָה
אֵין חָכְמָה. אִם אֵין דַּעַת אֵין בִּינָה, אִם אֵין בִּינָה
אֵין דַּעַת. אִם אֵין קֶמַח אֵין תּוֹרָה, אִם אֵין תּוֹרָה
אֵין קֶמַח:

21 Rabbi Elazar the son of Azaria says: If
there is no Torah, there is no proper
conduct; if there is no proper conduct, there is no
Torah. If there is no wisdom, there is no awe; if
there is no awe, there is no wisdom. If there is no
knowledge, there is no understanding; if there is
no understanding, there is no knowledge. If there
is no sustenance, there is no Torah; if there is no
Torah, there is no sustenance.

The choices that one makes in life and the ability to
perceive that the choices made are the right ones, are made
easier by the reflexive nature of life.

The affirmation of one value is linked to its comple-
mentary value; one can judge the proper fulfillment by
whether it brings the anticipated response. Thus, *if there is
no Torah, there is no proper conduct.* Torah is the basis of a
profound and sensitive human encounter. Without it there
can be no proper human encounter. Also, *if there is no
proper conduct, there is no Torah,* because if there is Torah
then that proper conduct would come responsively. *If there
is no wisdom, there is no awe; if there is no awe, there is no
wisdom.* One cannot really appreciate in meticulous detail

the value of life if one has not absorbed all the wisdom which incorporates this meticulousness. If there is no true wisdom, there cannot be this appreciation, and if there is no appreciation, no awareness of the awe of life, then there obviously is no wisdom. The true absorbing of this would bring with it a proper appreciation of the awesomeness and majesty of this world.

If there is no knowledge, there is no understanding; if there is no understanding, there is no knowledge. The knowledge of facts is a prelude to being able to make judgments, to being able to understand, to being able to perceive based on the knowledge. Without the knowledge, one makes decisions in ignorance. If there is no understanding, then it is because the knowledge has not been properly amalgamated into the self. One cannot have the one without the other.

Finally, *if there is no sustenance, there is no Torah; if there is no Torah, there is no sustenance.* If one does not have the wherewithal to live, then one cannot actualize all the dictates of Torah. One is so preoccupied with avoiding starvation that Torah values remain distant from human preoccupation. On the other hand, if there is no Torah, then there is no sustenance in the ultimate sense. Without Torah, there is no real value to sustaining oneself. It just becomes an exercise in survival. Real sustenance, sustenance which sustains in the spiritual sense, is seen as that which comes from a Torah lifestyle, a lifestyle oriented around the ultimate meaning which Judaism attaches to life. Without Torah, and without the meaning which it brings, one simply feels that one exists, not that one really is sustained and accelerated along the path of life.

In all of these elements, there is the reflexive reinforcement of the two sides of the spectrum. One can readily perceive whether one has gone along the proper way simply by gauging whether this reflexive reinforcement exists.

כב הוּא הָיָה אוֹמֵר, כֹּל שֶׁחָכְמָתוֹ מְרֻבָּה
מִמַּעֲשָׂיו לְמָה הוּא דוֹמֶה, לְאִילָן
שֶׁעֲנָפָיו מְרֻבִּין וְשָׁרָשָׁיו מֻעָטִין וְהָרוּחַ בָּאָה
וְעוֹקַרְתּוֹ וְהוֹפַכְתּוֹ עַל פָּנָיו, שֶׁנֶּאֱמַר וְהָיָה כְּעַרְעָר
בָּעֲרָבָה וְלֹא יִרְאֶה כִּי־יָבוֹא טוֹב וְשָׁכַן חֲרֵרִים
בַּמִּדְבָּר אֶרֶץ מְלֵחָה וְלֹא תֵשֵׁב. אֲבָל כֹּל שֶׁמַּעֲשָׂיו
מְרֻבִּים מֵחָכְמָתוֹ לְמָה הוּא דוֹמֶה, לְאִילָן שֶׁעֲנָפָיו
מֻעָטִין וְשָׁרָשָׁיו מְרֻבִּין, שֶׁאֲפִילוּ כָּל־הָרוּחוֹת
שֶׁבָּעוֹלָם בָּאוֹת וְנוֹשְׁבוֹת בּוֹ אֵין מְזִיזִין אוֹתוֹ
מִמְּקוֹמוֹ, שֶׁנֶּאֱמַר וְהָיָה כְּעֵץ שָׁתוּל עַל־מַיִם וְעַל־
יוּבַל יְשַׁלַּח שָׁרָשָׁיו וְלֹא יִרְאֶה כִּי־יָבֹא חֹם וְהָיָה
עָלֵהוּ רַעֲנָן וּבִשְׁנַת בַּצֹּרֶת לֹא יִדְאָג וְלֹא יָמִישׁ
מֵעֲשׂוֹת פֶּרִי:

22 He [Rabbi Elazar the son of Azaria] used to say: One whose wisdom exceeds one's deeds, what is that person like? Like a tree whose branches are many but whose roots are few; the wind comes and uproots it and overturns it upon its face, as it is said: "And he shall be like a lonely juniper tree in the wasteland and shall not see when good comes, but shall inhabit the parched places of the wilderness, a salt-filled land which is uninhabitable" (Yirmiyahu 17:6). But one whose deeds exceed one's wisdom, what is that person like? Like a tree whose branches are few but whose roots are many; even if all the winds in the world were to come and blow upon it, they would not move it from its place, as it is said: "He shall be like a tree planted by the waters, which spreads out its roots by the river, and shall not perceive when heat comes but its leaf shall remain fresh; and it will not be troubled in the year of drought, nor will it cease to bear fruit" (Yirmiyahu 17:8).

This *mishna* further develops the theme of the reinforcement of values and deals specifically with wisdom and deeds. It asserts that an individual whose wisdom exceeds the individual's deeds is like a tree with many branches but few roots, which is vulnerable to wind that can uproot it and overturn it on its face. The proof text used deals with individuals who trust in other people and are blown away by the wind and fall on their faces. Knowledge which is not reinforced with deed is vulnerable to the winds of challenge. If the knowledge is not firmly anchored in fulfillment, then that knowledge can be questioned and can even be knocked off its moorings totally. In the encounter with the faddish trends of society, the lack of the proper reinforcement of wisdom can place that wisdom on very shaky ground.

On the other hand, an individual whose deeds exceed that individual's wisdom is comparable to a tree with few branches but many roots, which can withstand all the winds. The proof text for this refers to an individual who places trust in God and cannot be shaken from that trust no matter how strong the pressures may be. In a similar manner, an individual who has actualized more than the wisdom absorbed has placed that wisdom on a firm footing, because such an individual has experienced that the

כג רַבִּי אֶלְעָזָר (בֶּן־) חִסְמָא אוֹמֵר, קִנִּין
וּפִתְחֵי נִדָּה הֵן הֵן גוּפֵי הֲלָכוֹת. תְּקוּפוֹת
וְגֵמַטְרִיָּאוֹת פַּרְפְּרָאוֹת לַחָכְמָה:

23 Rabbi Elazar Chisma says: The laws concerning bird sacrifices and the onset of menstruation are important ordinances of the law. Astronomy and geometry are aftercourses of wisdom.

---

wisdom is not abstract, but has real value in life. Once having seen the fulfillment of the deeds which are recommended by the acquired wisdom, such an individual would be able to laugh at all of society's challenges. The skeptical and the scornful who say that the wisdom is useless and that one should not waste one's time with it can be decisively and pointedly countered with the experiential knowledge of what that wisdom really does for the self and for others in life. No abstract system can challenge or negate this.

MISHNA 23

This *mishna* extends further the theme of reacting to pressures that may be brought to bear on an individual by society at large. The individual who wants to put knowledge to good use is likely to measure the utility aspect of that knowledge — how much of it can actually be applied to life. As such, astronomy and geometry, which are seen as important by society, would seem to rate as of greater importance than the laws concerning bird sacrifices and the onset of menstruation. The *mishna*, however, indicates that the Torah's laws of bird sacrifices and the onset of menstruation, as complex and remote as they may seem, nevertheless are important ordinances of the law.

Whether or not they apply in the here and now, whether or not their application may be abstract for the individual who studies them, they are important for the protection of the dignity of specific sacrifices or the calculation of the menstruation period. They are applications, however remote from immediate concern, of vital principles in life, and thus important ordinances of Torah law. They are part and parcel of the very intricacies which serve to show how sacred the law is, in that even the most minute and particular details of it are protected by complex calculations and intricate judgments. They may seem to be removed from the world scene, but they are essential.

Astronomy and geometry, on the other hand, are merely aftercourses. They are condiments. They are not as critically important as the laws of bird sacrifices and of the onset of menstruation. They are not, to be sure, unimportant, but they cannot rank in the same dimension as Torah law.

In a word, one is not to learn only that which leads to immediate application, but even that which seems remote. In the long run, if it is part of the Torah, then it is, by definition, not remote, because the Torah would not have included it in its system if it was irrelevant to life itself.

CHAPTER **4** ❀

Integration

of values

א בֶּן־זוֹמָא אוֹמֵר, אֵיזֶהוּ חָכָם, הַלּוֹמֵד
מִכָּל־אָדָם, שֶׁנֶּאֱמַר מִכָּל מְלַמְּדַי
הִשְׂכַּלְתִּי כִּי עֵדוֹתֶיךָ שִׂיחָה לִי. אֵיזֶהוּ גִבּוֹר,
הַכּוֹבֵשׁ אֶת־יִצְרוֹ, שֶׁנֶּאֱמַר טוֹב אֶרֶךְ אַפַּיִם מִגִּבּוֹר
וּמֹשֵׁל בְּרוּחוֹ מִלֹּכֵד עִיר. אֵיזֶהוּ עָשִׁיר, הַשָּׂמֵחַ
בְּחֶלְקוֹ, שֶׁנֶּאֱמַר יְגִיעַ כַּפֶּיךָ כִּי תֹאכֵל אַשְׁרֶיךָ וְטוֹב
לָךְ. אַשְׁרֶיךָ בָּעוֹלָם הַזֶּה וְטוֹב לָךְ לָעוֹלָם הַבָּא.
אֵיזֶהוּ מְכֻבָּד, הַמְכַבֵּד אֶת הַבְּרִיּוֹת, שֶׁנֶּאֱמַר כִּי
מְכַבְּדַי אֲכַבֵּד וּבֹזַי יֵקָלּוּ׃

1 Ben Zoma says: Who is wise? One who learns from all people, as it is said, "From all those who have taught me I have obtained understanding for your testimonies are my pursuits" (Tehillim 119:99). Who is mighty? One who conquers one's passions, as it is said: "One who is slow to anger is better than the mighty, and one who rules over one's spirit is better than one who conquers a city" (Mishley 16:32). Who is rich? One who rejoices in one's portion, as it is said: "When you eat of the labor of your hands you shall be happy and it shall be well with you" (Tehillim 128:2). "You shall be happy" — in this world; "and it shall be well with you" — in the world to come. Who is honored? One who honors humankind, as it is said, "For those who honor Me, I will honor, and those who

despise Me shall be held in contempt" (I Shmuel 2:30).

This chapter begins with a statement concerning the individual's mental capacities, physical capacities, wealth, and social station. They are elements of one's life which, more or less, form the totality of one's existence — what one does with one's body, with one's mind, with one's possessions, and how the individual interacts with society at large. In all of these, the valuational judgment is one which is not materialistically oriented. The *mishna* introduces a totally different perspective to these categories. The concern is not with what one has, but rather with what one is, not with a static, materialistic possessiveness, but rather with an active, humanistic process orientation; not a concern with facts, but with attitudes. It posits the notion that life is a process, that those who are involved in the process have affirmed the vitality of life. Those who see themselves as having completed the process are out of the picture. Thus, who is the wise person? The *one who learns from all people*, one who continuously is learning, who feels that there is always more to learn. The proof text is one which indicates that the learning process is a continuous one. "From all those who have taught me I have obtained understanding for your testimonies are my pursuits" or, my normal conversation. In other words, it is natural to pursue knowledge because that is what life is all about.

The mighty individual is the one who conquers one's passions; not the one who is blessed with a good physique, rather one who is able to overcome whatever instinctual drives might incline the individual towards undesirable forms of behavior. The rich person is not one who has much money, but rather one who is satisfied with one's possessions. The proof text for this is "When you eat of the labor of your hands, you shall be happy and it shall be well with you." If you are not interested in laboring so that you have more than you need, but rather you eat of the labor of your hands, this implies that you work just long enough in order to be sustained. You see the work process as only a means towards enabling you to sustain yourself and therefore subsequently indulge in the meaning dimension of Torah. Then you will be happy because you will find the meaning in Torah, and it will have an ultimate, lasting value even in the world to come.

The individual who is honored is not one who seeks honor or demands respect, but one who bestows honor on others. The model for this in the proof text is God saying that honor will only be bestowed on those who honor God, but those who despise God will be held in contempt. This God model also applies to people.

An individual who honors others has a high regard for others. This initiates a reflexive process in which those who are the beneficiaries of this high regard will reciprocate, because they will be flattered. They will be sincerely ennobled by the image that others project about them, and they will bestow honor on others in turn. Conversely, if one looks with scorn and derision on others, that will be reciprocated in kind, because one who looks contemptuously on others will generate that very same contempt on the rebound.

Whether it be wisdom, might, wealth, or one's honored station in life, all of these are active processes; one must continuously learn, one must continuously fight against one's own inner inclinations, one must continually have the attitude of satisfaction with what one has, and one must continually bestow honor on others. In this process, we gain fulfillment of the values of wisdom, might, wealth, and honor.

בֶּן־עַזַּאי אוֹמֵר, הֱוֵה רָץ לְמִצְוָה קַלָּה
וּבוֹרֵחַ מִן־הָעֲבֵרָה, שֶׁמִּצְוָה גּוֹרֶרֶת
מִצְוָה וַעֲבֵרָה גּוֹרֶרֶת עֲבֵרָה שֶׁשְּׂכַר מִצְוָה מִצְוָה
וּשְׂכַר עֲבֵרָה עֲבֵרָה:

2 Ben Azzai says: Hasten to fulfill even a light precept, and flee from all sin, for one good deed generates another good deed and one sin generates another sin; for the payment for a good deed is a good deed and the payment for a sin is a sin.

Continuing further along the theme of life being a process, this *mishna* indicates that in stasis the individual would stagnate. The normal pattern for a fulfilling life should be one that involves the hastening *to fulfill even a light precept* and the fleeing *from all sin.* If one remains static and takes no action towards self-betterment, then that individual will be overpowered by the temptations that surround him. So there must be a fleeing from that which could overcome the individual. And, even those fulfillments which seem so easy that they would always be readiy at hand, are elusive. They do not just fall into place, they must be pursued.

In a word, human life must be directional. There must be the element of process, the recognition that things do not evolve on their own, that things are not given to the individual by birthright or by fortune.

As has been established in the previous *mishna*, it is not wealth per se that is vital, it is the attitude one takes to one's possessions that is the crucial element. That can only

גהוּא הָיָה אוֹמֵר, אַל־תְּהִי בָז לְכָל־אָדָם
וְאַל־תְּהִי מַפְלִיג לְכָל־דָּבָר, שֶׁאֵין לְךָ
אָדָם שֶׁאֵין לוֹ שָׁעָה וְאֵין לְךָ דָּבָר שֶׁאֵין לוֹ מָקוֹם:

3 He used to say: Do not despise any person, and do not consider anything impossible, for there is no person who does not have an hour and no thing that does not have its place.

---

happen when one works at it. It cannot happen on its own. Once one becomes involved in choice, in making a conscious decision to flee from the bad and to embrace the good, this sets into motion a syndrome of behavior where one good deed and its fulfillment excites the individual towards the next good deed and its fulfillment, and so on, ad infinitum. The reverse, however, in terms of momentary pleasure of sinfulness, is also true. It is up to the individual to make the first choice, the initial lifestyle choice, in the correct manner. Otherwise it can set into motion a syndrome which may be very difficult to surmount.

MISHNA 3

This *mishna*, continuing along the theme of attitudes and syndromes of behavior, deals not with attitude towards deeds, but rather with attitude towards people and things. It asserts that one should *not despise any person* and that one should *not consider anything as impossible* or unnecessary, *for there is no person who does not have an hour and no thing that does not have its place.* Everything in life has its purpose, every individual has a potential meaning possibility, however distant and remote it might seem from

רַבִּי לְוִיטַס אִישׁ יַבְנֶה אוֹמֵר, מְאֹד מְאֹד
הֱוֵה שְׁפַל רוּחַ שֶׁתִּקְוַת אֱנוֹשׁ רִמָּה:

4 Rabbi Levitas of Yavneh said: Be of an exceedingly humble spirit, for the hope of the human being is decay.

---

the superficial view. It is obligatory upon each individual to see the good and the potential of other individuals.

The sarcastic syndrome is one which would condemn an individual entirely for possessing one flaw. This *mishna* recommends the reverse, that even if one can see just a little virtue one must look positively on the individual. There is always the potentiality for repentance. There is always the possibility that an individual's meaning of life might be condensed into one very meritorious action. There is a possibility that what seems to be useless and of no value can come in very handy on one occasion or another; and so an individual is obliged to look positively on life, to affirm life, to try to emphasize the positive in others. In all likelihood, such emphasis will elicit from others the positive.

MISHNA 4

In dealing with the attitude towards others, like the previous *mishna*, this *mishna* advises how one can take an affirmative attitude towards others and see the positive in others. This is best achieved by being *exceedingly humble of spirit* in front of individuals. The individual who is humble, who sees all the flaws within the self, will be very unlikely to see flaws in others. Human experience shows that those who are analytical and critical of others are usually neglectful of the self and those who are very critical

146

of the self do not look critically upon others. Therefore, it is advised to be *exceedingly* humble. In a word, a half way measure in humility is not sufficient. In humility, one must go the total route. Once an individual sees there is so much to improve upon, the individual will become involved in self-improvement and will project publicly the idea of self-introspection and critical analysis which is inner rather than outer directed. This will inspire others to do the same, such that this attitude becomes a model for others to emulate.

It is not asked that an individual preach modesty, but rather that one be modest. All this modesty is justified, because if the ultimate destiny of individuals is decay, in the physical sense, then there is nothing one can do to save the physical. Rather, one should emphasize that which is eternal, the soul aspects of human existence. Humility is in order and self-improvement and self-betterment the obligation of the hour.

הַ רַבִּי יוֹחָנָן בֶּן־בְּרוֹקָה אוֹמֵר, כָּל־הַמְחַלֵּל
שֵׁם שָׁמַיִם בְּסֵתֶר נִפְרָעִין מִמֶּנּוּ בְּגָלוּי,
אֶחָד שׁוֹגֵג וְאֶחָד מֵזִיד בְּחִלּוּל הַשֵּׁם:

5 Rabbi Yochanan the son of Beroka
says: One who desecrates the Name of
God in secret will suffer the penalty through
being exposed in public. Whether unwittingly or
intentionally, it is the same concerning desecration of the Name.

The previous *mishna* dealt with the perspective one should
project towards others. This *mishna* deals with the consis-
tency of one's public image and one's private behavior. It
asserts that one who desecrates the name of God in secret
will be exposed in public. An individual who purports to
stand for that which the community assumes to be vital,
but privately totally rejects these values and has only used
piety in order to gain position and influence, such an individual will eventually lose sight of the difference between
the private and the public dimension. What is the normative, private behavior will soon be unabashedly public and
thus, such an individual will be exposed.

Desecration of God's name is considered the ultimate
deviance. It is a deviance which cannot come from an
individual who is concerned and sincere. The fact that such
deviance exists is an indication of a lack of sincerity, of a
feigned concern, of a life which is a lie, one which eventually will explode in infamy. It is the ultimate in hypocrisy. In
terms of desecration of God's name, there can be no distinction between willful and unwitting. Even the unwitting
is willful, for the sincere individual can never desecrate.

‏רַבִּי יִשְׁמָעֵאל בַּר רַבִּי יוֹסֵי אוֹמֵר,‏
‏הַלּוֹמֵד עַל־מְנָת לְלַמֵּד מַסְפִּיקִים בְּיָדוֹ‏
‏לִלְמוֹד וּלְלַמֵּד, וְהַלּוֹמֵד עַל־מְנָת לַעֲשׂוֹת מַסְפִּיקִים‏
‏בְּיָדוֹ לִלְמוֹד וּלְלַמֵּד לִשְׁמוֹר וְלַעֲשׂוֹת:‏

6 Rabbi Yishmael the son of Rabbi Yose says: One who learns in order to teach others will be granted the opportunity to learn and to teach, and one who learns in order to practice will be granted the opportunity to learn and to teach, to observe and to fulfill.

This *mishna* continues along the lines of individual pursuits relative to the public arena. It deals here with the concern that an individual expresses towards the public in the educational process. *One who learns in order to teach others*, who has the ultimate goal of being a teacher of what has been studied, *will be granted the opportunity to learn and to teach*. The individual who *learns in order to practice*, and practice includes teaching others, performing the deeds, and eliciting from others the response to the deeds, *will be granted the opportunity to learn and to teach*, which are included in practice, and also *to observe* the prohibitive commandments *and to fulfill* the positive commandments.

The *mishna* indicates that in terms of ultimate goals, limited horizons bring limited fulfillment, while grand visions are somewhat akin to self-fulfilling dreams. They create a momentum of their own which brings the desired result. If one desires to serve the community one should aspire to the ultimate, because, by so doing, the concentra-

149

ז רַבִּי צָדוֹק אוֹמֵר, אַל־תִּפְרוֹשׁ מִן־הַצִּבּוּר
וְאַל־תַּעַשׂ עַצְמְךָ כְּעוֹרְכֵי הַדַּיָּנִין וְאַל־
תַּעֲשֶׂה עֲטָרָה לְהִתְגַּדֶּל־בָּהּ וְלֹא קַרְדּוֹם לַחְפָּר־
בָּהּ, וְכַךְ הָיָה הִלֵּל אוֹמֵר וּדְאִשְׁתַּמֵּשׁ בְּתָגָא חֲלָף,
הָא לָמַדְתָּ כָּל־הַנֶּהֱנֶה מִדִּבְרֵי תוֹרָה נוֹטֵל חַיָּיו מִן־
הָעוֹלָם:

7 Rabbi Zadok says: Do not separate
yourself from the community; in the
office of judge do not act as counsel; do not make
of the Torah a crown for self-aggrandizement, nor
a spade wherewith to dig. And thus Hillel used to
say — "One who makes use of the crown will
die." Thus you may derive that one who reaps
personal profit from the words of the Torah takes
one's own life from the world.

---

tion on study is better honed and of a higher quality. The
individual who studies in order to perform, knowing that
everything which has been studied must be translated into
deed, will be more attentive than one who restricts the self
to the four walls of study.

MISHNA 7

Continuing along the theme of orientation around community, this *mishna* asserts that communal concerns should
be foremost, that even if one is not a giver towards the
community, at least one should be a receiver, one should
not separate oneself from the community. However, there is
always the danger that wanting to satisfy communal needs

can clash with other values, which momentarily, at least, demand more scrupulousness. Communal concern should not interfere with an appointed task. For example, a judge should not act as a counsel — a judge should not employ concern for community when it compromises the position of judge. Do not advise those you would normally like to help when, as a judge, you have to give a strictly legal decision.

In the pursuit of community position, which is normally gained by acquisition of superior knowledge, there is a caution that the knowledge gained should of its own bring the recognition, but one should not project that knowledge either to catapult the self or to downgrade others. It should not be *for self-aggrandizement* or *a spade wherewith to dig*, as per the statement by Hillel. The individual *who reaps personal profit from the words of Torah takes one's own life from the world*, takes away the life fulfillment which is available through Torah by making it a means for profit, a tool rather than a life orientation. Such an individual strips the Torah of its beauty and thus denies the self the real opportunity for meaningful expression.

ח רַבִּי יוֹסֵי אוֹמֵר, כָּל־הַמְכַבֵּד אֶת־הַתּוֹרָה
גּוּפוֹ מְכֻבָּד עַל־הַבְּרִיוֹת וְכָל־הַמְחַלֵּל
אֶת־הַתּוֹרָה גוּפוֹ מְחֻלָּל עַל־הַבְּרִיוֹת:

8 Rabbi Yose says: One who honors the
Torah will be honored by humankind,
but one who dishonors the Torah will be dishon-
ored by humankind.

Instead of using Torah in order to gain honor, against which
the previous *mishna* cautioned us, one should rather
indulge in the reverse procedure, namely to honor the
Torah. Paradoxically, the individual who honors the Torah,
who shows how vital and meaningful it is and who thus
alerts and excites others to the fulfillments available, will
so enrich society that society, in its gratitude, cannot help
but honor that individual. This is implicit in the terminology "honored by humankind," which would better be
translated as "that individual's personage is the manifes-
tation of honor on society." The reverse is true for the one
who dishonors, who will become debased by the scorn for
Torah, and project that debasement onto society. That very
debasement which has been projected will boomerang back
onto the individual.

רַבִּי יִשְׁמָעֵאל בְּנוֹ אוֹמֵר, הַחוֹשֵׂךְ עַצְמוֹ
מִן־הַדִּין פּוֹרֵק מִמֶּנּוּ אֵיבָה וְגָזֵל וּשְׁבוּעַת
שָׁוְא, וְהַגַּס לִבּוֹ בְּהוֹרָאָה שׁוֹטֶה רָשָׁע וְגַס רוּחַ:

9 Rabbi Yishmael, his son, says: One who avoids assuming judicial office rids the self of hatred, robbery, and vain swearing. But one who renders decisions presumptuously is foolish, wicked, and arrogant.

Continuing along the theme of honoring Torah, this *mishna* asserts that the honor of Torah is achieved not through forcing Torah down another individual's throat or forcing judgment upon other individuals. It is necessary to avoid being presumptuous when acting as a judge. In so doing, one avoids the bitterness that usually becomes apparent between the litigants, each of whom wants to win the case; the hatred being directed by the litigants either towards each other or towards the common enemy, the judge. This also avoids *robbery*, the stealing that can accrue from an individual wanting so much to be the victor in a case that chicanery is used. The ultimate could be vain swearing, false oaths made by either of the litigants in order to win the case.

The greatest advantage of not being in judicial office is that one is not party to this type of behavior. The individual who renders decisions presumptuously, who is so excited about the idea of being a sanctified judge who can sit in judgment over society, is *foolish* for participating in and, in some instances, even inducing *hatred*; *wicked* for being party to the *robbery*, and *arrogant* for being unmindful of the *vain swearing*, that can arise.

י הוּא הָיָה אוֹמֵר, אַל־תְּהִי דָן יְחִידִי שֶׁאֵין
דָן יְחִידִי אֶלָּא אֶחָד, וְאַל־תֹּאמַר קַבְּלוּ
דַעְתִּי שֶׁהֵם רַשָׁאִים וְלֹא אָתָּה:

10 He [Rabbi Yishmael] used to say: Do not judge alone, for none may judge alone save One, and do not say "Accept my view," for it is their choice, not yours.

It should be stated that this *mishna* is not recommending that there be no judges. Obviously society needs judges in order to adequately administer the system of justice. The *mishna* is asserting that the one who chases after the position of judge is more concerned with the position than with the responsibility attached to it and is, therefore, likely to be irresponsible. The best judge is the one who initially seeks to flee from the position. Such an individual fully understands the import of judging and its consequences, and thus makes a much better judge.

MISHNA 10

Further in the concerns that should occupy a judge, this *mishna* asserts that any judge who is placed in a position of responsibility, most likely because the community appreciates the individual's expertise, should not be carried away by this acknowledgment, should not ever try to be a singlehanded judge. Rather the judge is best served and justice similarly best served when the judge works in consultation, when a judge is never so self-assured that there is an assumption of independence and an "I don't need others" attitude. None may judge alone save One, namely God, Who is the source of all wisdom and Who, thus, is the independent Judge of all.

154

יא רַבִּי יוֹנָתָן אוֹמֵר, כָּל־הַמְקַיֵּם אֶת־הַתּוֹרָה מֵעֹנִי סוֹפוֹ לְקַיְּמָהּ מֵעֹשֶׁר. וְכָל־הַמְבַטֵּל אֶת־הַתּוֹרָה מֵעֹשֶׁר סוֹפוֹ לְבַטְּלָהּ מֵעֹנִי:

11 Rabbi Yonathan says: One who fulfills the Torah out of poverty will ultimately fulfill it out of wealth, but one who neglects the Torah out of wealth will eventually neglect the Torah out of poverty.

Even where the judge assumes the position not of a decider, but of an arbitrator, it is vital that the judge not impose the self upon others by saying *"Accept my view."* The nature of arbitration is such that it cannot be imposed upon the parties; it is something that is *their choice*, not the choice of the judges. The position of arbitrator is gained by request, not by demand. In a word, the fact that a community has accepted an individual as an expert should not induce in the expert the self-appointed right to impose the self upon the accepting community.

MISHNA 11

If the previous statements concerned individuals who have climbed the social ladder into prominence, this *mishna* asserts that a Torah lifestyle is independent of circumstance, independent of position and station in life. One who fulfills the Torah out of poverty would ultimately fulfill the Torah out of wealth and one who neglects the Torah out of wealth, would neglect the Torah out of poverty. There is no cause and effect relationship between financial position and spiritual commitment. The financial position is the context, but not the content of life. Torah, itself, can and

155

יב רַבִּי מֵאִיר אוֹמֵר, הֱוֵה מְמַעֵט בְּעֵסֶק
וַעֲסֹק בַּתּוֹרָה וֶהֱוֵה שְׁפַל־רוּחַ בִּפְנֵי כָל־
אָדָם וְאִם־בָּטַלְתָּ מִן־הַתּוֹרָה יֶשׁ־לְךָ בְּטֵלִים הַרְבֵּה
כְּנֶגְדֶּךָ וְאִם־עָמַלְתָּ בַתּוֹרָה יֶשׁ־לוֹ שָׂכָר הַרְבֵּה לִתֶּן
לָךְ:

12 Rabbi Meir says: Minimize your
business activities and occupy yourself
with Torah, and be of humble spirit before all
people. If you neglect the Torah many causes for
neglecting the Torah will present themselves to
you, but if you toil in Torah, God has great
reward to give to you.

---

should surmount the challenges of both plenty and poverty.
It can exist in all circumstances. The key factor is the
human acceptance, the attitude an individual takes
towards circumstance. The individual who affirms Torah,
affirms the Torah unconditionally; the individual who
rejects the Torah makes a rejection which, as a matter of
course, would become unconditional.

MISHNA 12

Although the previous *mishna* disconnected financial
position from affirmation of Torah, this does not mean that
attitudes towards finance do not affect the intensity with
which one might approach Torah. It is advisable to
minimize business activity and occupy oneself with Torah.
Too much business activity, the desire to accumulate
wealth, is an assault on an individual's time, such that
there would be no available period to concentrate on Torah

activity, which is the more vital and has the highest priority. It is, therefore, recommended that one cut down on business pursuits, to make just that which is necessary so that the balance of the day is free towards affirming the essential elements of Torah in one's lifestyle.

It is with a sense of pride that an individual can make such a major decision — to minimize business activity. Normally, such a decision would bring with it a boastful attitude of "See what I have done." For this, the *mishna* recommends that even though one may make this major and most meaningful decision, nevertheless, one should not boast about it but still *be of humble spirit before all people*. Those who did not share another individual's farsightedness may have had other circumstances. One may have done the right thing, but doing the right thing does not give the individual the privilege to broadcast and project the self over other people.

Regarding the basic decision to curtail business activity in favor of Torah, individuals can always find rationalizations for continually neglecting the Torah and for not being able to curtail business activity. For those who neglect the Torah, *many causes for neglecting the Torah will present themselves*. There are a multitude of excuses. However, if you decide in favor of Torah, then there is a great reward in store for you; the fulfillments of Torah bring with them the necessary benefits. It is these benefits with which one should be content; one need not gain extra attention by broadcasting how good one is or what a nice decision one has made.

רַבִּי אֱלִיעֶזֶר בֶּן־יַעֲקֹב אוֹמֵר, הָעוֹשֶׂה
מִצְוָה אַחַת קוֹנֶה לוֹ פְּרַקְלִיט אֶחָד
וְהָעוֹבֵר עֲבֵרָה אַחַת קוֹנֶה לוֹ קַטֵּגוֹר אֶחָד, תְּשׁוּבָה
וּמַעֲשִׂים טוֹבִים כִּתְרֵיס בִּפְנֵי הַפּוּרְעָנוּת:

13 Rabbi Eliezer the son of Yaakov says: One who fulfills one precept gains for the self one advocate, and one who commits one transgression gets for the self one accuser. Repentance and good deeds are as a shield against calamity.

The fulfillment of deeds, like the fulfillment of Torah itself, has its rewards. Every precept affirms the validity of one's sojourn in life and justifies creation. *One who fulfills one precept gains for the self one advocate*, and an argument in favor of the whole process of creation. One who transgresses *gets for the self one accuser*. Each transgression brings with it an accusation that creation was a useless exercise and a futile endeavor. The best *shield* against the *calamity* of a worthless life, one which proliferates with accusers, is *repentance and good deeds*; *repentance* to erase a previously transgression-filled life, and *good deeds*, a future which is filled with affirmations of precepts. Repentance erases past failures and good deeds chart a positive course for the future. Both of these are endeavors which manifest life's worthwhileness and the validity of the act of creation.

יד רַבִּי יוֹחָנָן הַסַּנְדְּלָר אוֹמֵר, כָּל־כְּנֵסִיָּה
שֶׁהִיא לְשֵׁם שָׁמַיִם סוֹפָהּ לְהִתְקַיֵּם
וְשֶׁאֵינָהּ לְשֵׁם שָׁמַיִם אֵין סוֹפָהּ לְהִתְקַיֵּם:

14 Rabbi Yochanan the sandal maker says: Every assembly which is for the sake of Heaven will ultimately endure, but that which is not for the sake of Heaven will ultimately not endure.

The previous *mishna* dealt with the charting of a course in life which is a shield against calamity. There is a shield against calamity in the personal dimension and a shield against calamity in the public dimension. In the public dimension, the shields would be projected in conventions or assemblies which are gathered for the sake of Heaven, gathered to discuss what has gone wrong within society and within the individual and how to put society and the individual back on track. Such assemblies, as they are oriented around ultimate concerns, will ultimately endure. The noble purposes for convening such assemblies will, by their very nature, ensure perpetuation. However, that which is not for the sake of Heaven, that which is only concerned with the moment and with the transitory, will fade into the irrelevance that is normally associated with transitoriness.

רַבִּי אֶלְעָזָר בֶּן שַׁמּוּעַ אוֹמֵר, יְהִי כְּבוֹד
תַּלְמִידְךָ חָבִיב עָלֶיךָ כְּשֶׁלָּךְ וּכְבוֹד חֲבֵרְךָ
כְּמוֹרָא רַבָּךְ וּמוֹרָא רַבָּךְ כְּמוֹרָא שָׁמָיִם:

15 Rabbi Elazar the son of Shammua says: Let the honor of your disciple be as dear to you as your own, the honor of your colleague as dear as the reverence for your teacher, and the reverence for your teacher as dear as the awe of Heaven.

The classic assembly which is for the sake of Heaven is the assembly of teacher with students. Any assembly which is for noble purposes involves teachers and students, those who can transmit of their knowledge and those who are there to digest and gain benefit from that knowledge. In terms of such assembly and in terms of the concerns for the betterment of community, the teacher must be vitally involved and attuned to the students' dignity. A teacher who does not appreciate the dignity of a student will not apply the self seriously to putting the student on the right track. Any educational endeavor demands a high image of those who are learning or else there would be a natural laxity toward the very process. Therefore, *Let the honor of your disciple be as dear to you as your own.*

The learning process involves not only teaching students but also learning from colleagues. So it is obligatory that the honor of one's colleague be as dear as the reverence for one's teacher. The teacher, who is the source of one's knowledge, is to be revered. The colleague, with whom one shares knowledge and who shares knowledge with the in-

רַבִּי יְהוּדָה אוֹמֵר, הֱוֵי זָהִיר בְּתַלְמוּד **טז**
שֶׁשִּׁגְגַת תַּלְמוּד עוֹלָה זָדוֹן:

16 Rabbi Yehuda says: Be cautious in study, for error in study is considered intentional sin.

---

dividual, is therefore to be honored equally; thus the intensity of honor towards a colleague should be equivalent to the intensity of reverence towards a teacher.

Finally, the teacher, who is the source of an individual's knowledge, is acting on God's behalf — God being the source of all knowledge, in transmitting God's word to the individual. It is vital that the individual have as much reverence for the teacher as one is in awe of Heaven. Simply put, the teacher is God's agency towards eliciting the capacity for actualizing the Divine responsibilities placed upon an individual.

MISHNA 16

The previous *mishna* is concerned with the dignity of disciples and cautions that one must approach disciples with dignity. This *mishna* is concerned with the caution with which one must approach the subject matter itself — the learning. It advocates that one *Be cautious in study, for error in study is considered intentional sin.* The teacher who intends to impart knowledge has a great responsibility. The educational responsibility is one which must weigh heavily on the individual when the individual is learning, because the learning itself is the beginning of the teaching process.

Any mistake which comes from superficially approaching the learning is one which is founded on an

161

רַבִּי שִׁמְעוֹן אוֹמֵר, שְׁלֹשָׁה כְתָרִים הֵן, **יז**
כֶּתֶר תּוֹרָה וְכֶתֶר כְּהֻנָּה וְכֶתֶר מַלְכוּת.
וְכֶתֶר שֵׁם טוֹב עוֹלֶה עַל גַּבֵּיהֶן:

17 Rabbi Shimon says: There are three
crowns: the crown of Torah, the crown
of priesthood, and the crown of royalty, but the
crown of a good name is superimposed on them
all.

---

incomplete appreciation of the full import of the teaching
position. This is a brazen misrepresentation of a sacred
calling. Anything which emanates from such a misrepresentation is considered an intentional sin, because it
comes from an inexcusable failure to understand that
which should be obvious — that a teacher forms the personality of the student and has a sacred, inviolable, and
uncompromising responsibility to be meticulous and
scrupulous in study, so that what is imparted in the
learning process is absolutely correct.

MISHNA 17

Whether it be as a teacher or in any other profession, an
individual acquires a good name and a good reputation as
an outgrowth of living according to the perceived responsibility of the occupational context. There are, therefore,
different crowns of achievement. There is the *crown of
Torah* knowledge, which is a real achievement, but, to a
certain extent, is dependent upon natural and environ-
mental factors. It is dependent on whether the individual
has been blessed with a superior intellect and whether one
has been afforded the opportunity to study with those who

can bring out the best in the individual. The *crown of priesthood* is a crown which has been ennobled in Jewish society, but is a blessing of parentage, although the fact that one's father is a *kohen* does not guarantee that the individual will be admired, respected, and loved as a priest. But at least it catapults such an individual into eligibility for such adulation. There is the *crown of royalty*, which is a direct result of birth. Royalty has its own legal mechanisms for deciding who will be the leader of a country.

These three crowns — of Torah, of priesthood, and of royalty — are, to one extent or another, achievements which are not totally one's own. They come with varying degrees of ordained, inherited blessing that make such achievements and crowns possible. What overarches these attainments is the *crown of a good name*. The crown of a good name is *superimposed* upon all these crowns. An individual who has attained Torah but does not have a good reputation, or a priest without a good reputation, or even a monarch without a good reputation, has a deficient crown. Any crown that an individual achieves, any crown that a person gains, must have on top of it the crown of a good name — the crown of a true human achievement, the crown of having used the natural capacities with which an individual has been blessed to the fullest; the crown of having gained the acceptance of a not so fortunately blessed public for the achievements that one has attained in life.

רַבִּי נְהוֹרַאי אוֹמֵר, הֱוֵה גוֹלֶה לִמְקוֹם יח
תּוֹרָה וְאַל־תֹּאמַר שֶׁהִיא תָבוֹא אַחֲרֶיךָ
שֶׁחֲבֵרֶיךָ יְקַיְּמוּהָ בְיָדֶיךָ וְאֶל־בִּינָתְךָ אַל־תִּשָּׁעֵן:

18 Rabbi Nehorai says: Transport yourself
to a place of Torah, and do not say that
it will follow you, for it is your colleagues who will
firmly establish it for you, and do not rely on your
own understanding.

The crown of a good name is desirable, but adulation, the
natural outgrowth of a good name, should not be the key
element of an individual's choice of locale. Rather, one
should transport oneself *to a place of Torah* where one
would absorb from the ambience of the place and from the
individuals who have created this ambience. No matter
how good one's name is, one should not say it will follow the
individual. One can never be so self-sufficient as to think
the entire world revolves around oneself, no matter how
much the individual is adored or how much recognition the
individual has received.

The Torah will only be firmly entrenched within the
individual because of the individual's colleagues, *who will
firmly establish it* for the individual. Therefore, one should
not rely on one's *own understanding* and do it alone, but
rather recognize that no matter how lofty are the attainments of the individual, the individual will always need the
reinforcement of one's colleagues.

יט רַבִּי יַנַּאי אוֹמֵר, אֵין בְּיָדֵינוּ לֹא מִשַּׁלְוַת
הָרְשָׁעִים וְאַף לֹא מִיִּסּוּרֵי הַצַּדִּיקִים:

19 Rabbi Yannai says: It is not within our grasp to explain the tranquility of the wicked or even the suffering of the righteous.

This *mishna* is a good illustration of why it is impossible for us to rely on our own understanding. It is an instance where even collective understanding cannot achieve satisfactory explanation. *It is not within our grasp to explain the tranquility of the wicked or even the suffering of the righteous.* We cannot explain why a certain individual has been plagued with suffering or why another individual has been blessed with tranquility and prosperity. This is beyond human ken.

However, it is possible, in a limited sense, to explain why there is such a reality as the righteous suffering and the wicked prospering. It is simply a basic necessity in order to maintain the dynamics of free will. If one could picture a world in which every righteous individual is prosperous, happy and content, and every wicked individual is melancholy, suffering, and deprived, then all individuals would gladly choose to be righteous, knowing full well that wickedness brings with it such undesirable end results. However, individuals would then choose righteousness not because of the intrinsic worthwhileness of righteousness but because of the materialistic benefits which righteousness brings. Any choice towards righteousness would really not be a choice for anything else but material comfort. This would deny the basic human element of free choice. It therefore becomes essential to the maintenance of free will that there is no cause and effect relationship between

בַּ רַבִּי מַתְיָא בֶּן־חָרָשׁ אוֹמֵר, הֱוֵה מַקְדִּים
בִּשְׁלוֹם כָּל־אָדָם וֶהֱוֵה זָנָב לָאֲרָיוֹת וְאַל־
תְּהִי רֹאשׁ לַשֻׁעָלִים:

20 Rabbi Mathya the son of Charash says: Be the initiator of greetings to all people; be a tail among lions rather than a head among foxes.

---

righteousness and contentedness, or between wickedness and suffering. What remains impossible for the human being to explain is not the general existence of this syndrome but why specific individuals were chosen to be the exceptions for the specific categories.

MISHNA 20

In spite of the fact one might be plagued with the dilemma of existent wickedness, nevertheless, one should not try to erase this dilemma by consciously obliterating the wicked from one's frame of reference. Instead, this *mishna* suggests that one should *Be the initiator of greetings to all people*, one should show concern for all, even the wicked whom we perceive as being a great dilemma for this world. Perhaps by showing such concern, we can lift the wicked individuals out of their self-constructed rut.

Relative to the notion of choosing a place of Torah, this *mishna* further comments on the nature of such a choice. It asserts that it is better to *be a tail among lions rather than a head among foxes*. The head among foxes will have a superior position in terms of honor. The tail among lions will have an inferior position in terms of honor, but a superior position in terms of self-betterment. The ultimate

כא רַבִּי יַעֲקֹב אוֹמֵר, הָעוֹלָם הַזֶּה דּוֹמֶה לִפְרוֹזְדוֹר בִּפְנֵי הָעוֹלָם הַבָּא. הַתְקֵן עַצְמְךָ בִּפְרוֹזְדוֹר כְּדֵי שֶׁתִּכָּנֵס לִטְרַקְלִין:

21 Rabbi Yaakov says: This world is like a vestibule before the world-to-come. Prepare yourself in the vestibule, so that you will be able to enter the banquet hall.

---

choice of where to live should not be based on how much honor one receives, how much respect one is given, but rather on how conducive the environment is towards the individual's self-improvement. This is the most important variable. The tail among lions, who is obviously gaining much more than even the best among the foxes, is making a choice that honor is secondary and self-improvement primary. Such an individual recognizes that all people have not, even cannot, bridge the gap between what they are and what they ought to be. This perception will make it easier to be *the initiator of greetings to all people*, who share this basic aspect of the human condition.

MISHNA 21

Since *This world is like a vestibule*, or a preparatory ground, *before the world-to-come*, it is advisable to prepare in the vestibule to be able *to enter the banquet hall*. The awareness of the ultimate goal makes the decision concerning being a tail among lions as opposed to a head among the foxes much easier to negotiate. If this world is considered a realm of preparation, then one must strive to gain the best type of preparation; honor is irrelevant in this context. What becomes most relevant and crucial is which

167

כב

הוּא הָיָה אוֹמֵר, יָפָה שָׁעָה אַחַת
בִּתְשׁוּבָה וּמַעֲשִׂים טוֹבִים בָּעוֹלָם הַזֶּה
מִכֹּל חַיֵּי הָעוֹלָם הַבָּא וְיָפָה שָׁעָה אַחַת שֶׁל־קוֹרַת
רוּחַ בָּעוֹלָם הַבָּא מִכֹּל־חַיֵּי הָעוֹלָם הַזֶּה:

22 He [R. Yaakov] used to say: Better is
one period of repentance and good
deeds in this world than all of life of the world-to-
come; and better is one period of spiritual bliss in
the world-to-come than all of life of this world.

---

way one can best be prepared for the future world.
Becoming the tail among lions is a choice which should
come naturally.

MISHNA 22

Though this world is merely a preparatory for the world-to-
come, there are, nevertheless, benefits in this world which
have no equal in the world-to-come. *Better is one period of
repentance and good deeds in this world than all of life of
the world-to-come.* The transcendent thrust of repentance
and good deeds brings with it a fulfillment which is not
available in the hereafter. The hereafter is essentially the
bliss of having attained, but the process of attaining is
greater than the goal itself.

On the other hand, *better is one period of spiritual bliss
in the world-to-come than all of life of this world.* The
spiritual bliss in the hereafter is unlike any pleasure in this
world. It is both dimensionally different and qualitatively
superior, somewhat akin to the infinite being condensed
into a short time period.

כג רַבִּי שִׁמְעוֹן בֶּן־אֶלְעָזָר אוֹמֵר, אַל־תְּרַצֶּה אֶת־חֲבֵרְךָ בִּשְׁעַת כַּעֲסוֹ וְאַל־תְּנַחֲמֵהוּ בְּשָׁעָה שֶׁמֵּתוֹ מֻטָּל לְפָנָיו וְאַל־תִּשְׁאַל לוֹ בִּשְׁעַת נִדְרוֹ וְאַל־תִּשְׁתַּדֵּל לִרְאוֹתוֹ בִּשְׁעַת קַלְקָלָתוֹ:

23 Rabbi Shimon the son of Elazar says: Do not try to assuage the anger of your friend in the height of your friend's anger; do not try to comfort your friend when your friend's deceased lies before him; do not question your friend at the time your friend makes a vow; and do not seek to see your friend in the time of your friend's humiliation.

The *mishna* does not compare repentance and good deeds in this world with the bliss of the world-to-come. Such comparison is impossible because it is the repentance and good deeds of this world which lead to the bliss of the world-to-come. The one leads to the other, the one depends on the other, the one is caused by the other.

MISHNA 23

This world being the vestibule, or preparatory ground for the future world, there are situations where the individual is thrown off the vestibular track. This can occur either through anger, through agony and sorrow, as in mourning, or through various forms of wrong-doing. One who is a friend would instinctively, for the other's benefit, desire to erase the anger or the hurt almost instantaneously and thus place the other back onto the right track. However, the *mishna* recommends that one should not try to assuage the anger of one's friend in the period of the friend's anger. Assuaging at the wrong time can intensify the anger and harden the individual's stance, causing the anger to become an all-consuming hatred. One does no favor by injecting oneself immediately.

In the same sense, one should not try to comfort one's friend when the deceased is literally before that friend. Condolences at the wrong time can cause the very rejection of the attempts at comforting. An individual must be ready to accept the comfort. When the deceased is before the individual, there is no such readiness. The wound is too fresh, the shock too deep and the receptivity too shallow.

When an individual makes a vow to abstain from something or to do something which the friend perceives to be ill advised, there is obviously an intense feeling against this vow taking. At the moment that the vow is made, the individual who makes the vow has a firm resolve. Any attempt to shake that resolve will be futile and harms the capacity for future renunciation of the vow. Legally, vows can be erased by asking questions which would indicate that, were the individual aware of certain circumstances at the time of the vow, the individual would not have made the vow. But, these questions are not to be asked at the time of the vow. The resolve is so strong that the individual would reject any attempt to absolve him of the vow. Such rejection would make it all the more difficult to use these very crucial openings at a more receptive period.

Finally, *do not seek to see your friend in the time of your friend's humiliation.* When an individual is involved in a wrong-doing, and a friend desires to prevent this wrong-doing, or embarrasses the individual during the wrong-doing so that the wrong is not repeated, the friend will so embarrass the individual that in the future the individual will avoid all contact with the friend, who will become totally unable to help.

כד שְׁמוּאֵל הַקָּטָן אוֹמֵר, בִּנְפֹל אוֹיִבְךָ אַל־
תִּשְׂמָח וּבִכָּשְׁלוֹ אַל־יָגֵל לִבֶּךָ, פֶּן־יִרְאֶה
יְיָ וְרַע בְּעֵינָיו וְהֵשִׁיב מֵעָלָיו אַפּוֹ:

24 Shmuel the Younger says: When your
enemy falls, do not rejoice, and when
your enemy stumbles, let not your heart be glad,
lest God see it and be displeased, and turn away
His wrath from him.

This *mishna* recommends a certain amount of patience
and understanding of the plight of others. One may be
eager to help, but sometimes the eagerness to help involves
a tremendous amount of patience to control that eagerness.
One is obliged to be less concerned with getting things off
one's chest, and more concerned with the results brought
by the reaction.

MISHNA 24

With friends, one's desire is to place those who have veered
off the track back into the vestibule dimension. With
enemies this does not apply. What attitude should one take
toward enemies? This *mishna* recommends that *When your
enemy falls, do not rejoice, and when your enemy stumbles,
let not your heart be glad.*

One would *rejoice* at a *fall* because the fall indicates
that the enemy is finished and will no more be heard from.
A *stumble* only implies a temporary lapse, for which an
explicit demonstration of joy is inappropriate, as the
stumbler might recover and go on to worse things. For
stumbling, the natural reaction is a muted *gladness of the
heart*, but even this is inappropriate. There is a fear that

God will *see it and be displeased, and turn away His wrath* from the enemy.

The *mishna* is not saying that one should avoid joy at an enemy's fall because of the way God may react. Instead, there is a meaning to God's reaction which is implicit in the relationship one has with a so-called enemy. The *mishna* is dealing here with a valuational enemy, one who rejects the meaningfulness of a Torah lifestyle and misleads others. In this circumstance, the enmity attitude is not out of place. However, when the enemy falls, one should be happy not with the enemy's fall, but with the outgrowth and end result of the fall — the benefit which accrues to society in that truth may once again emerge to the fore.

However, if one gloats over the fall, then it would indicate that one has reduced this value fight to a personality clash. God, in turn, seeing this, may turn away wrath from the enemy, and may see the enemy as the victim of a personality clash in which each one is partly to blame. Therefore, in all situations in which one has value conflicts with others, one should make sure that it is not a personality clash in which one is placing one's ego in direct confrontation with another's ego, for then one's gloating reaction will be divorced from the value and merely an affirmation of one's own ego superiority.

כה אֱלִישָׁע בֶּן אֲבוּיָה אוֹמֵר, הַלּוֹמֵד יֶלֶד
לְמָה הוּא דוֹמֶה לִדְיוֹ כְתוּבָה עַל־נְיָר
חָדָשׁ, וְהַלּוֹמֵד זָקֵן לְמָה הוּא דוֹמֶה לִדְיוֹ כְתוּבָה
עַל־נְיָר מָחוּק:

25 Elisha the son of Avuya says: One who learns in one's youth, to what is such a person comparable? — To ink written on fresh paper. But one who learns in one's old age, to what is such a person comparable? — To ink written on used paper.

As an outgrowth of the fact that there may be such a thing as an enemy who distorts society's values, this *mishna* recommends that an ounce of prevention is better than any attempts at eradication as a radical cure. It is recommended that one should be involved in education at as early an age as possible, such that one will be imbued with the proper value orientation and thus, more likely to be an affirmer of life rather than a nihilistic negator of life. The *One who learns in one's youth* is *comparable to ink written on fresh paper*. The young brain is a clean slate and a malleable substance; such education can more easily form a clear and positive pattern for the future.

However, learning in old age is comparable *To ink written on used paper*, paper which has been written upon which now must be erased to make room for the fresh approach which is involved in the Torah. It is not impossible to teach those who are older. In some respects there is a greater challenge, because one has to not only show the worthwhileness of the Torah approach, but must do so in

רַבִּי יוֹסֵי בַּר יְהוּדָה אִישׁ כְּפַר הַבַּבְלִי
אוֹמֵר, הַלּוֹמֵד מִן־הַקְּטַנִּים לְמָה הוּא
דוֹמֶה לְאוֹכֵל עֲנָבִים קֵהוֹת וְשׁוֹתֶה יַיִן מִגִּתּוֹ,
וְהַלּוֹמֵד מִן־הַזְּקֵנִים לְמָה הוּא דוֹמֶה לְאוֹכֵל עֲנָבִים
בְּשׁוּלוֹת וְשׁוֹתֶה יַיִן יָשָׁן:

26 Rabbi Yose the son of Yehuda, from Kfar HaBavli, says: One who learns from the young, to whom is such a person comparable? — To one who eats unripe grapes and drinks wine from the press. But one who learns from the old, to whom is such a person comparable? — To one who eats ripe grapes and drinks aged wine.

---

direct competition with other value stances. There is an obligation to improve the education of people of all ages, but if one has a choice in which area to concentrate, it would obviously be not to wait until the individual reaches an age where erasing is necessary, but rather to start young.

MISHNA 26

Although teaching is most effective with the young set, study is best achieved through learning with those of an older age. In other words, the combination of this *mishna* and the previous *mishna* indicates that a properly functioning, educationally-oriented society is one in which the elders are involved with the destiny of the youngsters. There is no generation gap; by definition, it is this very interaction which makes dialogue and dialectic possible.

כז רַבִּי מֵאִיר אוֹמֵר, אַל־תִּסְתַּכֵּל בַּקַּנְקַן אֶלָּא בְּמָה שֶׁיֶּשׁ־בּוֹ, יֵשׁ קַנְקַן חָדָשׁ מָלֵא יָשָׁן. וְיָשָׁן שֶׁאֲפִילוּ חָדָשׁ אֵין בּוֹ:

27 Rabbi Meir says: Do not look at the jug, but at what it contains. There may be a new jug filled with old wine, and an old jug that does not even contain new wine.

One who learns from the young is like *one who eats unripe grapes and drinks wine from the press*. The young have fruit, but they are not fully developed. That which emanates from the fruit, the wine, is also not ready to be fully appreciated and will not have the desired impact that wine is supposed to have. On the other hand, if *one learns from the old*, this is as if one *eats ripe grapes and drinks aged wine*, as if one eats fruit which is fully developed and thus compatible with one's digestive system, as learning from the old is compatible with one's intellectual system. The fruits of such wisdom are an aged wine which has the desired spiritual impact on the individual and enhances that individual's life orientation.

MISHNA 27

In making a choice of teachers, namely the choice of the teacher who is better imbued with knowledge and is an elder, this *mishna* cautions that one should not look at the external appearance, one should *not look at the jug, but at what it contains. There may be a new jug filled with old wine* — a young teacher who has fully developed knowledge and has tested this knowledge in the field of human experience. There may be *an old jug that does not even*

175

כח

רַבִּי אֶלְעָזָר הַקַּפָּר אוֹמֵר, הַקִּנְאָה
וְהַתַּאֲוָה וְהַכָּבוֹד מוֹצִיאִים אֶת הָאָדָם מִן
הָעוֹלָם:

28 Rabbi Elazar haKappar says: Envy, lust, and thirst for honor drive the person out of the world.

---

contain new wine — an individual who looks older, but has knowledge which is still raw and unripe.

It is not the age which is the key in terms of deciding who the teacher should be, it is the individual who has amalgamated the wisdom most cogently. This statement is made of teachers, but it is true of the meaning of life in general. One cannot judge the worthwhileness of life by the years that have been lived, but rather, one must judge the worthwhileness of life by the meaning with which the years allotted have been invested. Sometimes there is more quality and meaning in a short life than there is in a life which is of significant quantity.

MISHNA 28

In the vestibule dimension of life, it is natural for each individual to desire to become a jug filled with old wine, an individual well saturated with knowledge which is integrated into the personality and thus helps to forge the complete human being, the ideal for which all individuals should strive. There are, however, certain pitfalls in life which must be avoided if the individual is to attain these goals, or at least come close.

In the focus on values, it is vital not to *envy* others' achievements but rather to strive to do one's best, because it is within that context that one is primarily obligated. The exercise of passion is an enterprise which, if not properly channelled, can lead the individual astray from true fulfillment.

Finally, the primary goal of one's value orientation should be self-betterment through transcending the self towards the world of Torah values. These values should be actualized for their own sake, not for the honor which one may gain from being admired as a value actualizer.

Eventually, reducing values to a vehicle for honor, the envy of others' achievements, and the exercising of one's passion, *drive the person out of the world*. They take the individual off the vestibule track, off the orientation around values towards the envy of others' values, towards the expression of the instinctual rather than the spiritual, and towards reducing values to a tool for self-aggrandizement.

כ הוּא הָיָה אוֹמֵר, הַיִּלוֹדִים לָמוּת וְהַמֵּתִים
לְהֵחָיוֹת וְהַחַיִּים לִדּוֹן, לֵידַע וּלְהוֹדִיעַ
וּלְהִנָּדַע, שֶׁהוּא אֵל הוּא הַיּוֹצֵר הוּא הַבּוֹרֵא הוּא
הַמֵּבִין הוּא הַדַּיָּן הוּא הָעֵד הוּא בַּעַל דִּין הוּא עָתִיד
לָדוֹן. בָּרוּךְ הוּא, שֶׁאֵין לְפָנָיו לֹא עַוְלָה וְלֹא שִׁכְחָה
וְלֹא מַשּׂוֹא פָנִים וְלֹא מִקַּח שֹׁחַד, שֶׁהַכֹּל שֶׁלּוֹ. וְדַע
שֶׁהַכֹּל לְפִי הַחֶשְׁבּוֹן, וְאַל־יַבְטִיחֲךָ יִצְרְךָ שֶׁהַשְּׁאוֹל
בֵּית מָנוֹס לָךְ, שֶׁעַל כָּרְחֲךָ אַתָּה נוֹצָר וְעַל כָּרְחֲךָ
אַתָּה נוֹלָד וְעַל כָּרְחֲךָ אַתָּה חַי וְעַל כָּרְחֲךָ אַתָּה מֵת
וְעַל כָּרְחֲךָ אַתָּה עָתִיד לִתֵּן דִּין וְחֶשְׁבּוֹן לִפְנֵי מֶלֶךְ
מַלְכֵי הַמְּלָכִים הַקָּדוֹשׁ בָּרוּךְ הוּא:

29 He [Rabbi Elazar haKappar] used to say: Those who are born are destined to die, and those who die are destined to be brought back to life; the living, to be judged; to know, to teach, and to make known that He is God, He is the Designer, He is the Creator, He is the Discerner, He is the Judge, He is the Witness, He is the Plaintiff, He is destined to judge; blessed be He, before Whom there is no wrong, no forgetfulness, no partiality, and no taking of bribes, for all is God's. And know that all is according to the reckoning. And let not your impulse convince you that the grave will be a place of refuge for you, for against your will are you formed, against your will are you born, against your will do you live,

178

against your will do you die, and against your will are you destined to give account and reckoning before the Supreme King of kings, the Holy One, blessed be He.

This life is the vestibule for a future life, but entry into a future life is not an automatic result of living in this world. There is a phase intervening between the two worlds, the phase of death, which is a momentary respite between the two worlds. In the next phase, there is a preparatory period in which the individual is judged as to whether this world was firmly and absolutely used as a vestibule to prepare for the future world. The individuals who die *are destined to be brought back to life* and then *to be judged* on the worth-whileness of their vestibule dimension, *to know, to teach, and to make known the majesty of God*. The judgment will concern whether one learned (*to know*), whether one taught (*to teach*), and whether one was a living example (*to make known*) revealing the omnipotence and majesty of God, the Source of all being. God, Who is the ultimate Judge, an-alyzes each individual's life with precision and takes into account everything that has transpired in one's life. There is no way to avoid this judgment, there is no way to compromise this judgment, there is no *forgetfulness, no partiality, no taking of bribes*. The judgment is a fair judg-ment, *all is according to the reckoning*. This is not a court of justice which has to contend with the moods of intem-perate judges, or which must cater to the materialistic desires of those who seek to benefit from the unfortunate. This is a court which is absolutely truthful and absolutely fair.

An individual should not think that the end of life signals the end of responsibility. This is the normal pattern of the suicide, who "jumps to the conclusion" that leaving life means ridding the self of all the problems and discontents which life may bring. Suicide only exacerbates these problems and creates an even greater accusation than the wastage of a few moments. The suicide projects the real question of why life was squandered so radically? For this and for the wastage of precious moments, one will have to give *account and reckoning* before God. There is no choice in terms of having to give this reckoning, and there is no escape from this reckoning, because the forces of life are stronger than any individual. There is, however, one choice — what that account and reckoning will be. This is in nobody's hands but the individual's.

The emphasis on ultimate judgment as a recurring ethical theme is constantly brought to the fore because it places individuals on their eternal ethical toes, by forcing the recognition that every act, every deed performed, and every transgression avoided has ultimate value and will ultimately be weighed. The individual sees that everything has consequence. It is the individual who sees consequence in every action who is most likely to be ethically attuned.

CHAPTER **5** ❁

Torah, history

and nature

אבַּעֲשָׂרָה מַאֲמָרוֹת נִבְרָא הָעוֹלָם. וּמַה
תַּלְמוּד לוֹמַר וַהֲלֹא בְּמַאֲמָר אֶחָד יָכוֹל
לְהִבָּרְאוֹת, אֶלָּא לְהִפָּרַע מִן־הָרְשָׁעִים שֶׁמְּאַבְּדִים
אֶת־הָעוֹלָם שֶׁנִּבְרָא בַּעֲשָׂרָה מַאֲמָרוֹת וְלִתֵּן שָׂכָר
טוֹב לַצַּדִּיקִים שֶׁמְּקַיְּמִין אֶת־הָעוֹלָם שֶׁנִּבְרָא
בַּעֲשָׂרָה מַאֲמָרוֹת:

1 Through ten utterances was the world
created. What does this teach us?
Could it not have been created through one
utterance? Rather this is to exact payment from
the wicked who destroy the world which was
created through ten utterances, and to give rich
reward to the righteous who sustain the world
which was created through ten utterances.

This chapter launches a discussion of the historical perspective in regard to the importance of the individual and
the community of Israel in the Divine plan; it seeks to show
how all the principles enunciated in this tractate were co-
ordinated through history.

The world was created through ten utterances. Surely
the world could have been created with one utterance. The
miracle of creation is the creation of something out of
nothing. God, in Omnipotence, could just as easily have
instantaneously created the world which was expressed in
the final blueprint. Why did God make ten utterances, i.e.
the first — ex-nihilo — and then nine other utterances to
make the world complete?

Simply speaking, the progression of creation reaches its

crescendo with the crown of creation, the human being. Had the human being been created simultaneously with animals, human beings could then legitimately see themselves as on par with animals, as being nothing more than animals. The ten utterances show the meticulous care and detail with which God made the world and completed it, so that when the human being came on the scene, everything was ready to serve the human being.

This meticulous detail inherent in the world and the obvious placing of the human being in the position of prime importance should detract from any attempt to nihilistically reject the importance of the human being. The wicked who explicitly reject this importance, by downgrading the values of life and the importance of the human being, destroy the entire purpose of creation. Creation was specifically made with such care to avoid the possibility of wickedness. A haphazard creation would have legitimized a haphazard approach to life, but it was precisely to prevent the legitimacy of haphazardness that the world was created with such detail and with such a progression. The righteous who affirm the importance of the human being and the values that the human being is to actualize do so unequivocally, and thus corroborate the original design of God, God's master plan for the world.

בּ עֲשָׂרָה דוֹרוֹת מֵאָדָם וְעַד נֹחַ לְהוֹדִיעַ
כַּמָּה אֶרֶךְ אַפַּיִם לְפָנָיו שֶׁכָּל הַדּוֹרוֹת הָיוּ
מַכְעִיסִים לְפָנָיו עַד שֶׁהֵבִיא עֲלֵיהֶם אֶת־מֵי הַמַּבּוּל:

2 There were ten generations from Adam
to Noach, to make known how long-
suffering God is, for all these generations evoked
God's anger until God brought upon them the
waters of the flood.

Although the previous *mishna* asserted that those who
deviate from the master plan for the world and for the
human being will have payment exacted from them, this
mishna indicates quite clearly that the payment is not
exacted instantaneously. One should not think that
deviance is met with a spontaneous, immediate punish-
ment. Though human beings may deviate from what God
perceived to be the human purpose, God is very patient.
There were ten generations from Adam to Noach. These
generations deviated quite radically from what God had in
mind for the world, but as long as there was legitimate
hope, God persevered. However, when there was no hope,
God had to give up and more or less start again by bringing
the deluge and creating a clean slate.

ג עֲשָׂרָה דוֹרוֹת מִנֹּחַ וְעַד אַבְרָהָם, לְהוֹדִיעַ
כַּמָּה אֶרֶךְ אַפַּיִם לְפָנָיו, שֶׁכָּל־הַדּוֹרוֹת
הָיוּ מַכְעִיסִים לְפָנָיו עַד שֶׁבָּא אַבְרָהָם אָבִינוּ וְקִבֵּל
שְׂכַר כֻּלָּם:

3 There were ten generations from Noach
to Avraham, to make known how long-
suffering God is, for all these generations evoked
God's anger until our father Avraham came and
received the reward of them all.

God is patient and waits for what may be termed the
culminating moment, that moment in time when it is
obvious that one has reached the abyss of futility or the
potential peak of fulfillment. The ten generations between
Adam and Noach led to the abyss of futility. However, the
ten generations from Noach to Avraham, again deviating
from God's master plan for the world, culminated in the
personage of Avraham, who, by his devotion to God's
purpose, was a shining example to the world and the potential catalyst for raising and ennobling all of humankind
towards God's purpose. Here, God's patience for ten generations culminates in a more positive moment, a moment
in which is born the real possibility that the damage of
previous generations can be erased, even transcended.

עֲשָׂרָה נִסְיוֹנוֹת נִתְנַסָּה אַבְרָהָם אָבִינוּ
וְעָמַד בְּכֻלָּם לְהוֹדִיעַ כַּמָּה חִבָּתוֹ שֶׁל־
אַבְרָהָם אָבִינוּ:

4 With ten trials was our father Avraham tried and he stood steadfastly through all of them, to make known how great was the love of our father Avraham.

God was singularly aware of the greatness of Avraham. It was not necessary for God to test Avraham since God obviously knew what the results of these tests would be. However, these tests were given to Avraham in order that his devotion, dedication and commitment should become salient for all the rest of civilization. The salvational dimension of Avraham was realized by showing the world his true, abiding love, thus making Avraham a model for the potential rehabilitation of the previous, deviant generations.

It was to make known how great was the love of our father Avraham that Avraham himself was tested. If Avraham was to serve as the catalyst for society, it was incumbent upon God to show to the world the true greatness of Avraham, who, perhaps by his own modesty, would not have broadcast this impression to his contemporaries.

עֲשָׂרָה נִסִּים נַעֲשׂוּ לַאֲבוֹתֵינוּ בְּמִצְרַיִם
וַעֲשָׂרָה עַל הַיָּם:

5 Ten miracles were wrought for our fathers in Egypt, and ten at the sea.

If the previous *mishna* dealt with the individual greatness of Avraham and his covenantal commitment to God's purpose, this *mishna* focuses on the covenantal community of Israel, the commitments which they brought in a societal dimension as a people, as a community, and as a country, towards being a model of what human behavior should be like in all its multi-faceted dimensions. The special relationship with the people of Israel was made manifest by the miracles wrought for them, both in Egypt and at the sea. These were miracles which showed God's great care for them, in that He nurtured those who would carry His word into society. Israel did not assume this position by accident; nor did God allow a haphazard evolution of this societal dimension of Torah commitment.

עֶשֶׂר מַכּוֹת הֵבִיא הַקָּדוֹשׁ בָּרוּךְ הוּא עַל הַמִּצְרִיִּים בְּמִצְרַיִם וְעֶשֶׂר עַל הַיָּם:

6 Ten plagues did the Holy One, blessed be He, bring upon the Egyptians in Egypt, and ten at the sea.

There were ten miracles wrought for the Israelites in Egypt and ten at the sea. Concomitantly, there were ten plagues visited upon the Egyptians in Egypt and ten at the sea. Perhaps the miracles wrought for the Israelites were that the plagues visited upon the Egyptians were localized for the Egyptians only. The miracles in Egypt were necessary so that the Israelites could become slowly detached from their oppressors, leaving, in stages, the slave mentality that had been foisted upon them, so that they could now refocus their inclination to servitude toward a higher purpose and towards the supreme Being, God.

זַ עֲשָׂרָה נִסְיוֹנוֹת נִסּוּ אֲבוֹתֵינוּ אֶת־
הַקָּדוֹשׁ בָּרוּךְ הוּא בַּמִּדְבָּר, שֶׁנֶּאֱמַר
וַיְנַסּוּ אֹתִי זֶה עֶשֶׂר פְּעָמִים וְלֹא שָׁמְעוּ בְּקוֹלִי:

7 Ten times did our fathers try the Holy
One, blessed be He, in the wilderness,
as it is said: "They have tried Me these ten times,
and have not listened to My voice" (Bamidbar
14:22).

It would be assumed that having received all this special
treatment by God, these people, who had chosen to live by
God's word, should reciprocate the great deliverances that
had been wrought for them. It would even be natural for
God to expect that such would be the reaction. Instead we
are told that ten times did our fathers try God in the
wilderness. There was not this anticipated reciprocity —
quite the reverse, there was a testing of God, a questioning
of why all this had been done for them. Nevertheless, in the
same way that God did not exercise anger upon generations
until ten had passed, here, too, God showed patience,
waiting and nurturing the people until the rebelliousness
would creep out of the system, to allow for the total sub-
servience to the higher purposes for which the people had
been brought together.

חֵ עֲשָׂרָה נִסִים נַעֲשׂוּ לַאֲבוֹתֵינוּ בְּבֵית
הַמִּקְדָּשׁ. לֹא הִפִּילָה אִשָּׁה מֵרֵיחַ בְּשַׂר
הַקֹּדֶשׁ, וְלֹא הִסְרִיחַ בְּשַׂר הַקֹּדֶשׁ מֵעוֹלָם, וְלֹא
נִרְאָה זְבוּב בְּבֵית הַמִּטְבָּחַיִם, וְלֹא אֵירַע קֶרִי לְכֹהֵן
גָּדוֹל בְּיוֹם הַכִּפּוּרִים, וְלֹא כִבּוּ הַגְּשָׁמִים אֵשׁ שֶׁל־
עֲצֵי הַמַּעֲרָכָה, וְלֹא נִצְּחָה הָרוּחַ אֶת־עַמּוּד הֶעָשָׁן,
וְלֹא נִמְצָא פְסוּל בָּעֹמֶר וּבִשְׁתֵּי הַלֶּחֶם וּבְלֶחֶם
הַפָּנִים, עוֹמְדִים צְפוּפִים וּמִשְׁתַּחֲוִים רְוָחִים וְלֹא
הִזִּיק נָחָשׁ וְעַקְרָב בִּירוּשָׁלַיִם מֵעוֹלָם, וְלֹא אָמַר
אָדָם לַחֲבֵרוֹ צַר לִי הַמָּקוֹם שֶׁאָלִין בִּירוּשָׁלַיִם:

8 Ten miracles were wrought for our
ancestors in the Temple. 1) No woman
ever miscarried because of the smell of sacred
meat; 2) The sacred meat never became putrid;
3) No fly was ever seen in the slaughter house;
4) Never did the High Priest suffer from un-
cleanness on the Day of Atonement; 5) The rain
never extinguished the fire of the altar wood-pile;
6) The wind never overcame the smoke column
arising from the altar; 7) Never was a disquali-
fying defect found in the Omer, the Two Loaves,
or the Show-breads; 8) The people stood closely
pressed together but had ample room for bowing
down; 9) No snake or scorpion ever inflicted
harm in Jerusalem; 10) No one ever said to a

fellow — "The place is too crowded for me that I should lodge in Jerusalem."

All the effort expended by God in order for the people to express their life's responsibilities in proper orientation around God's word found its response in the Israelites' act of establishing the religious center in Jerusalem, the Temple. This *mishna* tells us that God, in concern that this objective be realizable and attainable, made sure that nothing would impede the Divine service. The ten miracles enumerated here are of a different nature than an active miracle. Active miracles are extraordinary events which occur. These were miracles which were extraordinary in that they did not occur, and over an extended period of time. There is nothing extraordinary about one piece of meat not becoming putrid, but there is something extraordinary about meat never becoming putrid over a long period of time.

This indicates the extraordinary protection and care afforded by God to enable the spiritual expression of the Israelites to continue unimpeded. One could not claim that poor conditions made it impossible to fulfill God's dictates or to express oneself religiously as one would have liked. There were never spoilages, there were never accidents, there were never impediments to the sacred expression, and it was never too difficult to find one's way comfortably towards that expression.

מ עֲשָׂרָה דְבָרִים נִבְרְאוּ בְּעֶרֶב שַׁבָּת בֵּין
הַשְּׁמָשׁוֹת וְאֵלּוּ הֵן. פִּי הָאָרֶץ, פִּי הַבְּאֵר,
פִּי הָאָתוֹן, הַקֶּשֶׁת וְהַמָּן וְהַמַּטֶּה וְהַשָּׁמִיר, הַכְּתָב
וְהַמִּכְתָּב וְהַלֻּחוֹת. וְיֵשׁ אוֹמְרִים אַף הַמַּזִּיקִין
וּקְבוּרָתוֹ שֶׁל־מֹשֶׁה וְאֵילוֹ שֶׁל־אַבְרָהָם אָבִינוּ. וְיֵשׁ
אוֹמְרִים אַף צְבַת בִּצְבַת עֲשׂוּיָה:

9 Ten things were created on the eve of the Sabbath at twilight. They are — 1) the mouth of the earth; 2) the mouth of the well; 3) the mouth of the donkey; 4) the rainbow; 5) the manna; 6) the rod; 7) the shamir; 8) the written characters; 9) the writing; and 10) the tablets. Some say also the destructive demons, the grave of Moshe, and the ram of Avraham our father. And others say also the tongs made with tongs.

This *mishna* is a further indication of the special extent to which God went to provide the ingredients for maintaining a proper perspective and balance in life. It is expressed through those things that were created on the eve of the Sabbath, at twilight. The Sabbath signifies the cessation of creation, of the six days of creation. Twilight contains both a little bit of the six days and a little bit of the Sabbath. It is a post-creation/pre-Sabbath time zone, somewhat in a different dimension than all else. Similarly, the things that were created in this time zone were not creation itself, natural phenomena, but rather extraordinary and supernatural phenomena, a different dimension.

The *mouth of the earth* swallowed Korach and his

rebellious cohorts and affirmed, in a unique manner, the validity of Moshe as the carrier of God's message to the people. The *mouth of the well*, referring to Miriam's well, was the water which sustained the people in the wilderness, a phenomenon not at all usual in a wilderness. The *mouth of the donkey* opened brazenly and taught Bil'am and all Bil'am types in a supernatural way what one's mouth and one's speech should be used for. The *rainbow*, which appeared after the flood, signified that God would remain forever patient with the world and always strive to give it a chance. The *manna* was the heavenly food which sustained the people in the wilderness, something unprecedented, extraordinary, and showing God's personal care. The *rod* by which the signs and the wonders were launched indicates the special intervention that God made on behalf of the people. The *shamir* is the worm which cut the stones for the building of the Temple. God had, by dictate, forbidden the use of metals, employed to make instruments of war, for this task. It was impossible to cut stones other than in a supernatural manner; thus God established parameters for construction and also gave the proper tools, unique as they were, for accomplishing the job. The *written characters* — the letters themselves, the *writing* — the combination of letters forming the words, and the *tablets* of stone together were unique; they were the expression in God's own language, in God's own script, on God's own instrument, of the messages that were vital for the society to be created by the people of Israel.

Others add the creation of *destructive demons*. These are forces which only come into the fore when the human being does not live properly. They are a warning for the individual to get back on the track. The *grave of Moshe* is unknown, supernatural in that one can never pinpoint and locate it. This was to prevent the possibility of people making it a site of idolatrous worship — again indicating the special care to avoid pitfalls which might exist in the development of the religious community. The *ram of Avraham*, which appeared after the binding of Isaac and which afforded Avraham the opportunity to express his thanks to God through an offering, was made available at that point in time to serve as a prototype for the notion that when an individual wants to serve God, the opportunity will always be there.

Others say also *the tongs made with tongs*. The original instrument which made possible other instruments could not have been made in a natural manner, because one would require an instrument in the first place to make others. This was God's contribution towards giving the human being a headstart in developing the world.

All of these are supernatural ingredients with which the world has been blessed. They are ingredients which allow for the maintenance of a proper balance and remind the individual of what the true path really is; and they are further indications of how God intervened, even at the point of creation, to anticipate occurrences later in history which would be potentially dangerous for the people. It would seem as if these historically oriented expressions are included to show that while God expects a lot from the people, it is not a one-way street. Rather, God showed the people how meticulously creation was formulated and carried out, how much was invested in the world in terms of extra ingredients, care and patience, in order that all that was expected of the people would be realized.

שִׁבְעָה דְבָרִים בְּגֹלֶם וְשִׁבְעָה בְּחָכָם.
חָכָם אֵינוֹ מְדַבֵּר לִפְנֵי מִי שֶׁגָּדוֹל מִמֶּנּוּ
בְּחָכְמָה וּבְמִנְיָן, וְאֵינוֹ נִכְנָס לְתוֹךְ דִּבְרֵי חֲבֵרוֹ,
וְאֵינוֹ נִבְהָל לְהָשִׁיב, שׁוֹאֵל כְּעִנְיָן וּמֵשִׁיב כַּהֲלָכָה,
וְאוֹמֵר עַל־רִאשׁוֹן רִאשׁוֹן וְעַל־אַחֲרוֹן אַחֲרוֹן, וְעַל
מַה־שֶּׁלֹּא שָׁמַע אוֹמֵר לֹא שָׁמַעְתִּי, וּמוֹדֶה עַל־
הָאֱמֶת, וְחִלּוּפֵיהֶן בְּגֹלֶם:

10 Seven qualities characterize the boor and seven the wise person: 1) The wise person does not speak before one who is greater in wisdom and experience; 2) does not break into another person's speech; 3) is not hasty to answer; 4) questions according to the subject and responds to the point; 5) addresses first things first and last things last; 6) on what he has not learned he says, "I have not learned this"; 7) and acknowledges the truth. The reverse of all this characterizes the boor.

There is so much detail to the world, so much to appreciate, so much of which to be in awe. Yet there are individuals who fail to grasp this, and are too ego-centered to reach out and fully absorb the surrounding environment. There are seven ways in which one can distinguish the properly integrated, wise individual from the *boor* — the individual who has a fragile ego, who needs to assert the self and bring it into prominence. They all deal with the dialogical quality of the individual vis-a-vis others. The wise person appreciates wisdom, is not threatened by the fact that others may be wiser, will not even dare speak but is ready to absorb the wisdom of others. Such a person will not interrupt someone else's speech, does not feel the world will come to an end if what one has to say is not said immediately.

Also, the wise individual, who places things in perspective and sees the greatness of the world as totally surpassing any self-importance, does not feel a need to give hasty answers, as if a moment of contemplation shows a weakness, an incomplete intellect; after all, no one knows everything. Such an individual is well harmonized, is properly and methodically attuned to the issue at hand; he will not be concerned with personal issues but rather with what is being discussed, and will question according to the subject and answer according to what has been asked. Methodically, such an individual will work things out in progression, so that the emphasis will be on making sure others get a complete picture, in a proper progression, which correlates with the questions and evolves logically. This ensures that others may fully comprehend, remember, and even question. Such an individual is not hesitant to say, "I have not learned this," and is not threatened by the fact that others will find his knowledge incomplete. There is always more to learn and it is not shameful to admit the limitations of finite abilities.

Finally, if such an individual makes a mistake, that individual, concerned about the majesty of the world and the need for maintaining truth in the world, will gladly subserviate the self to the truth and admit, "I am wrong." The boor, however, who is concerned solely about the self, finds it quite impossible to restrain the self, and will speak out even in the presence of those who are smarter, because such an individual thinks there is no one smarter. The boor will consider it legitimate to interrupt conversations because there could be nothing more important than what the boor has to say. The boor will give answers instantaneously to give the impression that all knowledge is at the fingertips, will answer basically according to what the boor feels is important — not according to what the questioner wants to know, and will do it in a haphazard manner. A boor will feign knowledge of a subject because saying "I don't know" is impossible. And finally, the boor will never be able to see the possibility of making mistakes.

The wise person, then, is the individual who perceives the greatness of the world, the insignificance of the human being relative to the majesty of the world, and the truths which should be lived in the world. The boor, on the other hand, is too self-centered and too concerned with the ego to bother with such abstractions as truth and the world's majesty.

The boor, who is an insecure individual, resorts to the overcompensation of projecting the self as being the most vital contribution to the world and the focal point upon which all else centers.

יא שִׁבְעָה מִינֵי פוּרְעָנִיּוֹת בָּאִין לָעוֹלָם עַל־
שִׁבְעָה גוּפֵי עֲבֵרָה. מִקְצָתָן מְעַשְּׂרִין
וּמִקְצָתָן אֵינָן מְעַשְּׂרִין רָעָב שֶׁל־בַּצֹּרֶת בָּא מִקְצָתָן
רְעֵבִים וּמִקְצָתָן שְׂבֵעִים, גָּמְרוּ שֶׁלֹּא לְעַשֵּׂר רָעָב
שֶׁל מְהוּמָה וְשֶׁל־בַּצֹּרֶת בָּא, וְשֶׁלֹּא לִטוֹל אֶת־
הַחַלָּה רָעָב שֶׁל־כְּלָיָה בָּא. דֶּבֶר בָּא לָעוֹלָם עַל
מִיתוֹת הָאֲמוּרוֹת בַּתּוֹרָה שֶׁלֹּא נִמְסְרוּ לְבֵית דִּין
וְעַל פֵּרוֹת שְׁבִיעִית. חֶרֶב בָּאָה לָעוֹלָם עַל עִנּוּי
הַדִּין וְעַל עִוּוּת הַדִּין וְעַל־הַמּוֹרִים בַּתּוֹרָה שֶׁלֹּא
כַהֲלָכָה. חַיָּה רָעָה בָּאָה לָעוֹלָם עַל שְׁבוּעַת שָׁוְא
וְעַל־חִלּוּל הַשֵּׁם. גָּלוּת בָּאָה לָעוֹלָם עַל־עֲבוֹדָה
זָרָה וְעַל־גִּלּוּי עֲרָיוֹת וְעַל־שְׁפִיכוּת דָּמִים וְעַל־
שְׁמִטַּת הָאָרֶץ:

11 Seven kinds of calamity come upon the world for seven types of transgression: 1) If some give their tithes and others do not, famine from drought ensues, some suffer hunger while some are satiated; 2) If all decide not to give tithes, famine through panic and drought ensues; 3) If all decide not to set apart the dough-offering, an all-consuming famine ensues; 4) Pestilence comes upon the world for the commission of those capital crimes enumerated in the Torah, the punishments for which were not turned over to a human court, and for violations of the law concerning produce of the Sabbatical year; 5) The sword comes upon the world for the delay of justice, for the perversion of justice, and for those who teach the Torah inconsistent with its true interpretation; 6) Wild beasts come upon the world because of vain swearing and the desecration of God's Name; 7) Exile comes upon the world because of idolatry, immorality, murder, and violation of the law concerning the rest for the soil in the Sabbatical year.

The previous *mishna* dealt with the incompleteness of the individual who knows it all and fails to see beyond the self. This *mishna* deals with those who are concerned with materialistic matters and overextend in their attempts to gain wealth. The *mishna* indicates that there is an element of consequence to all human action, especially when dealing with the denial of responsibility towards others. This usually bounces back on the perpetrators of the crime of miserliness.

If some give their tithes and others do not, there is the mirrorlike reaction in which there is a drought famine where some go hungry but others do not. Those who refuse to give their tithes are too stingy, unwilling to share with the Levites and the poor. Their tendency towards material possessions will result in hoarding, in over-working the earth, in too much expectation. Even in the simple natural order of things, this leads to a destruction of the earth's propensities.

If all decide not to give tithes, then a worse type of famine ensues, which involves panic. Those who are dependent upon the tithes obviously do not have what they need and those who have refused to give them are constantly searching for more. This leads to a panic situation.

If all decide not to set apart the dough-offering, then the famine which ensues is an all-consuming one. *Challah* is a minute amount; if there is stinginess even towards the giving of the *challah*, then obviously the individuals who are so miserly are probably working the land to death, and, by their insensitivity, bringing about the starvation of those who are in need of their help.

Pestilence comes upon the world for those crimes committed which are not given to a human court to punish. The individuals who perpetrate such crimes know full well that no human court can judge them. They feel free to challenge the enforcibility of the law. In fact, they are right; the law cannot be enforced. In the same sense, they can claim that the fruits of the seventh year were collected legitimately when, in reality, they did not leave them for everyone else as they were supposed to. All these are transgressions where it might be assumed that there is no ultimate court which can exact payment and bring to justice those who have perpetrated these elusive crimes. However, the *mishna* indicates that pestilence will evolve from the proliferation of these actions; pestilence being a type of hidden disease which consumes and wreaks damage in a way commensurate with the nature of the crimes. The crimes were performed stealthily, in an attempt to elude the force of law. The force of law shows itself to be stronger than all that and sends the type of plague from which one cannot escape.

The delay of justice, the perversion of justice, and the existence of those who teach the Torah *inconsistent with its true interpretation*, distorting the instrument of the Jewish legal system: all of these contribute to a chaos which is possible only when the rule of justice and the comprehension of the law are not given their proper expression. In chaos, individuals will lift up *swords*; there will be a destruction that comes from the nonenforcement of the legal statutes.

Vain swearing and the desecration of God's Name bring *wild beasts* upon the world. The human being has many responsibilities, but the most basic is to acknowledge God's having created the world and God's sanctity. Vain swearing, which is the unnecessary use of God's Name and its desecration, are base expressions of depraved individuals who have rejected even this fundamental notion of God's sanctity. They have, by so doing, reduced human beings to animals. They do not subscribe to the idea of the sanctity of God; there is no sanctity of creation, and hence, no uniqueness of the human being. People are simply two-legged animals; commensurately, they will be visited by their brethren, the wild beasts.

The land of Israel, given to the people of Israel, was seen as the breeding ground for a higher system of ethics, one in which idolatry would be impossible, immorality non-existent and murder unheard of. The land was to be treated differently from other lands, it was to be seen as God's and therefore, a rest was to be given to it on the seventh year. These are the basic ingredients which justify existence in the land of Israel. When these conditions do not obtain, then *exile* is the result, because there is no legitimate spiritual lifestyle which justifies the granting of the land in the first place.

יב בְּאַרְבָּעָה פְּרָקִים הַדֶּבֶר מִתְרַבֶּה,
בָּרְבִיעִית וּבַשְּׁבִיעִית וּבְמוֹצָאֵי שְׁבִיעִית
וּבְמוֹצָאֵי הֶחָג שֶׁבְּכָל־שָׁנָה וְשָׁנָה. בָּרְבִיעִית מִפְּנֵי
מַעְשַׂר עָנִי שֶׁבַּשְּׁלִישִׁית, בַּשְּׁבִיעִית מִפְּנֵי מַעְשַׂר
עָנִי שֶׁבַּשִּׁשִּׁית, בְּמוֹצָאֵי שְׁבִיעִית מִפְּנֵי פֵּרוֹת
שְׁבִיעִית, בְּמוֹצָאֵי הֶחָג שֶׁבְּכָל־שָׁנָה וְשָׁנָה מִפְּנֵי גֶּזֶל
מַתְּנוֹת עֲנִיִּים:

12 During four periods pestilence proliferates — in the fourth year, in the
seventh year, at the conclusion of the seventh
year, and at the conclusion of the Tabernacles
feast every year. "In the fourth year" — for
neglecting the tithe for the poor in the third year;
"in the seventh year" — for neglecting the tithe
for the poor in the sixth year; "at the conclusion
of the seventh year" — for neglecting the law
concerning produce of the Sabbatical year; "at
the conclusion of the Tabernacles feast every
year" — for robbing the poor of their prescribed
gifts.

This *mishna* warns with regard to one specific area,
namely, the obligation of the well-off for the poor. There are
specific periods of time in which the poor are singled out for
special attention. The neglect of the poor in these periods
brings with it the visitation of plagues which are the direct
result of taking away sustenance from them. Those who

take away this sustenance jeopardize the lives of the poor; there is an equal and opposite reaction in that their very lives are taken away.

One could probably give a naturalistic explanation for this; when the poor remain hungry and disappointed, their health deteriorates, leaving them open to all kinds of germs. These germs can be fatal to them, but they also spread to others.

Therefore, the following four periods are ones in which pestilence can possibly proliferate; in the fourth year because of the neglect of the tithe that belongs to the poor in the third year. The consequences of neglecting the poor are only felt subsequent to the time of obligation. There is also an obligation to give a tithe to the poor in the sixth year. The consequences of the failure to give would be made manifest in the seventh year. There is the obligation, in the seventh year, to leave the fields available for the poor to come and collect the yield. The failure to do so will have its consequences at the conclusion of the seventh year. Finally, at harvest time, there is an obligation to leave certain parts of the field unharvested and sheaves which have been dropped and forgotten, for the poor to harvest. These are the *gifts* which belong to the poor; the poor rely on them. The consequences of the poor being disappointed are felt after the harvest festival concludes, after the Tabernacles Feast.

This *mishna* indicates, in perhaps naturalistic, but also in transcendental perspective, that the consequences of failure to live an ethically sensitive life are reflected back on the very individuals who have failed to live up to their responsibilities. No one can escape this pattern. It turns out to be in the best interests of those who are wealthy to share their wealth, not only for moral and spiritual reasons, but for physical reasons as well.

רג אַרְבַּע מִדּוֹת בָּאָדָם. הָאוֹמֵר שֶׁלִּי שֶׁלִּי
וְשֶׁלְּךָ שֶׁלָּךְ זוֹ מִדָּה בֵּינוֹנִית וְיֵשׁ אוֹמְרִים
זוֹ מִדַּת סְדוֹם, שֶׁלִּי שֶׁלָּךְ וְשֶׁלְּךָ שֶׁלִּי עַם הָאָרֶץ,
שֶׁלִּי (שֶׁלָּךְ) וְשֶׁלְּךָ שֶׁלָּךְ חָסִיד, שֶׁלְּךָ (שֶׁלִּי) וְשֶׁלִּי
שֶׁלִּי רָשָׁע:

13 There are four character types among
people: One who says "What is mine is
mine and what is yours is yours" is of average
character, and others say this is the characteristic
of Sodom; one who says "What is mine is yours
and what is yours is mine" is an ignoramus; one
who says "What is mine is yours and what is
yours is yours" is a pious person; one who says
"What is yours is mine and what is mine is mine"
is a wicked person.

This *mishna* continues along the theme of possession by
indicating the various reactions toward material possession. The one who says *What is mine is mine and what is
yours is yours* is of average character. Such an individual
does not expect anything from others but does not desire
that others should expect anything from him either. There
are those, however, who equate this with the Sodom-like
character, for the exactitude with which such a statement
is made and the insistence that there can never be sharing
— that what is mine must always be mine, what is yours
must always be yours, I will not give to you and you do not
give to me — can create a syndrome of insensitivity, of non-
communication, of non-concern, which eventually leads to

206 Chapters of the Sages

hardness, callousness, and total disregard of the other individual, even producing the inability to help — and eventually the desire to harm. The attitude of *What is mine is mine and what is yours is yours* creates a progression of depersonalization from which all types of human cruelty can emanate.

An individual who says *What is mine is yours and what is yours is mine* is an ignoramus. Such an individual goes to the opposite extreme and would desire to create a society in which there is no such entity as possession. But there must be such an entity, or else society could not function; there would be total chaos. To go to such an extreme is potentially dangerous; it can undermine the very roots of societal responsibility. All robbery could be condoned with such a philosophy; there would be no security for an individual, no knowing what tomorrow would bring. Everyone would become vulnerable and society itself would be in danger of collapse.

The person who says *What is mine is yours and what is yours is yours* is a pious person. Such an individual acknowledges the notion of possession, but acknowledges it only for others, saying that others need not fear that their possessions will be taken from them and can rest secure that what they have, they really have. However, such an individual, in a legitimate gesture of sensitivity, says that all his personal possessions are available for others to use. If they can be of help the individual will not exercise the rights of title, but would be glad to share. This is the mark of true piety, where one is balanced, does not go overboard, but rather relinquishes what is within his power, while affirming the integrity of what is outside his power.

The reverse is true of the wicked person, who says *What is yours is mine and what is mine is mine*. Such an individual affirms the notion of possession, but only for the self, and rejects the notion of possession for others, saying that

יד אַרְבַּע מִדּוֹת בְּדֵעוֹת. נוֹחַ לִכְעוֹס וְנוֹחַ
לִרְצוֹת יָצָא הֶפְסֵדוֹ בִּשְׂכָרוֹ, קָשֶׁה
לִכְעוֹס וְקָשֶׁה לִרְצוֹת יָצָא שְׂכָרוֹ בְּהֶפְסֵדוֹ, קָשֶׁה
לִכְעוֹס וְנוֹחַ לִרְצוֹת חָסִיד, נוֹחַ לִכְעוֹס וְקָשֶׁה
לִרְצוֹת רָשָׁע:

14 There are four types of disposition:
Easy to provoke and easy to pacify —
the loss disappears in that person's gain; difficult
to provoke and difficult to pacify — the gain
disappears in that person's loss; difficult to
provoke and easy to pacify — this characterizes
the pious person; easy to provoke and difficult to
pacify — this characterizes the wicked person.

---

whatever else exists in society is fair game, and can be
taken at personal whim. Such an individual distorts the
balance, relinquishes what is beyond his power, and
behaves possessively toward that which should be shared.

MISHNA 14

The *mishna* moves from attitudes towards one's material
wealth to attitudes towards one's disposition, the dis-
positions that are a reflection of individual attitudes. The
individual who is *Easy to provoke and easy to pacify* will
not remain angry for long. The loss that is felt through being
easily provoked is more than compensated for by the gain
in having the provocation assuaged quite quickly. Such an
individual might have a trigger temper but really possesses

a good nature. Once the anger has been expressed, the good nature takes over.

The individual who is *difficult to provoke and difficult to pacify* is a little less heated and intense than the first character-type. It takes a lot to excite such an individual, which in itself is indicative of a detached personality type. Once having been excited, that individual is almost impossible to influence. The gain disappears in that person's loss, because obviously the end result of such an equation is an individual who is not pacified, who carries a grudge, who is not willing to forgive. This is the ego-centered type whose expectations have not been met and who, therefore, feels a legitimate right to sulk. This is a personality aberration which is non-desirable.

There are other combinations. An individual who is very hard to provoke but is easy to pacify, is one who can make a quick adjustment, who can easily avoid or subside from intensity. Such a person has formulated within the self an attitude that there are not many important things in life which can cause provocation. Once having been subjected to provocation, one can always find an excuse for forgiving and for alleviating that provocation. This is the pious person.

The wicked person needs no excuse for being provoked; is so concerned about the self and about personal desire that the slightest thing provokes, and is so so idly entrenched in that self-centeredness that it is difficult to pacify him.

These attitudes of temperament are all outgrowths of attitudes towards living. They are laudable and contemptible as they express the essence of individual choice.

טז אַרְבַּע מִדּוֹת בְּתַלְמִידִים. מָהִיר לִשְׁמוֹעַ
וּמָהִיר לְאַבֵּד יָצָא שְׂכָרוֹ בְּהֶפְסֵדוֹ, קָשֶׁה
לִשְׁמוֹעַ וְקָשֶׁה לְאַבֵּד יָצָא הֶפְסֵדוֹ בִּשְׂכָרוֹ, מָהִיר
לִשְׁמוֹעַ וְקָשֶׁה לְאַבֵּד זוֹ חֵלֶק טוֹב, קָשֶׁה לִשְׁמוֹעַ
וּמָהִיר לְאַבֵּד זוֹ חֵלֶק רַע:

15 There are four types among students:
Quick to learn and quick to forget —
the gain disappears in that person's loss; slow
to understand and slow to forget — the loss
disappears in that person's gain; quick to learn
and slow to forget — this is the best portion; slow
to learn and quick to forget — this is the worst
portion.

There are slow and quick reactions in individual
disposition. There are also slow and quick reactions to
study. The individual who absorbs quickly but forgets
quickly has made education a futile exercise because
everything that is learned is forgotten. The individual who
is slow to understand and slow to forget must, by nature, be
more methodical and must concentrate more carefully on
the study, as opposed to the one who learns quickly and
probably, by so doing, learns superficially. The slow learner
has absorbed much better and therefore will be less likely to
forget. Whatever is lost in terms of the time it takes to learn
is more than compensated for by the fact that what has
been learned will be retained.

An individual who is quick to learn and slow to forget
has a talent combination which is really a blessing. His is

the best portion. It is not something which one can normally attribute to effort, but rather is the indication of a special gift. It is branded not as an achievement, but as the best portion.

The reverse is true of the individual who takes much time to learn, but nevertheless is still quick to forget. This is *the worst portion.* One cannot attribute blame to such an individual, one should not look with contempt upon such an individual. This is not necessarily in the element of choice; it might just be that a natural gift for learning has not been granted. This is the worst portion, but this is not the worst individual.

טז אַרְבַּע מִדּוֹת בְּנוֹתְנֵי צְדָקָה. הָרוֹצֶה
שֶׁיִּתֵּן וְלֹא יִתְּנוּ אֲחֵרִים עֵינוֹ רָעָה בְּשֶׁל־
אֲחֵרִים, יִתְּנוּ אֲחֵרִים וְהוּא לֹא יִתֵּן עֵינוֹ רָעָה
בְּשֶׁלּוֹ, יִתֵּן וְיִתְּנוּ אֲחֵרִים חָסִיד, לֹא יִתֵּן וְלֹא יִתְּנוּ
אֲחֵרִים רָשָׁע:

16 There are four types among givers of
charity: One who desires to give but
that others should not give — begrudges what
belongs to others; one who desires that others
should give but he not give — begrudges what
belongs to himself; one who desires to give and
that others should give — this characterizes the
pious person; one who does not give and desires
that others should not give — this characterizes
the wicked person.

The individual who has been blessed with a good portion is
likely to be envied by the one who has not been blessed with
such capacities. In learning, the envy of another's capacities can be a positive force, as it may lead one to seek out
the talented intellect and learn from that individual.
However, with regard to the giving of charity, the envy of
the philanthropic capacities of others is not recommended.
There are four types amongst givers of charity.

One who would like to give but would like that others
should not give *begrudges what belongs to others*,
begrudges them the possibility of performing good deeds,
would like all of the good in the world to focus around the

self, and does not allow others to take part in the world's value expression.

The individual who desires that only others should give *begrudges what belongs to himself*. This is the reverse syndrome, where one says that one can be free from involvement with the world. If there are problems which demand philanthropic expression, let others do it. Such an individual has divorced the self from the sharing endeavor.

The individual *who desires to give and that others should give* sees the world as one big entity and all individuals as belonging to a collective community. Everyone is obligated, everyone is eligible to be involved in this value expression. Such an individual is a pious person.

Then, there is the other extreme, the individual *who does not give and desires that others should not give*, who does not want to be embarrassed by the fact that others are better and who denies the idea that wealth is given in order to share. Such an individual affirms the idea that what an individual has should be kept and not given to others. This is characteristic of the wicked person.

רז אַרְבַּע מִדּוֹת בְּהוֹלְכֵי בֵית הַמִּדְרָשׁ.
הוֹלֵךְ וְאֵינוֹ עֹשֶׂה שְׂכַר הֲלִיכָה בְּיָדוֹ,
עֹשֶׂה וְאֵינוֹ הוֹלֵךְ שְׂכַר מַעֲשֶׂה בְּיָדוֹ, הוֹלֵךְ וְעֹשֶׂה
חָסִיד, לֹא הוֹלֵךְ וְלֹא עֹשֶׂה רָשָׁע:

17 There are four types among those who
attend the house of study: One who
goes but does not practice secures the reward for
attending; one who practices but does not go
secures the reward for practicing; one who goes
and practices is a pious person; one who neither
attends nor practices is a wicked person.

The collectivity of the universal community finds its
viability most enhanced when individuals properly appreciate the responsibility they have towards others, are
concerned with the betterment of society, and are willing to
give of themselves for it. Concurrent with this attitude is
the requirement of individuals toward self-betterment. To
the extent that one betters the self, one is capable of better
serving others, of helping in the self-betterment of others.
There are four types amongst those who attend the house
of study. There are four attitudes towards the element of
self-betterment, which can only be accelerated through
continuous study.

One who goes but does not practice merely has *the
reward for attending.* Mere attendance has an ambience of
its own which obviously uplifts and inspires a person but
such an attitude does not translate itself into real life. The
individual *who practices but does not go* has only *the
reward for practicing,* but it is a stultified form of practicing

213

which will never be uplifted by increasing awareness and expanding knowledge. The individual who *goes and practices is a pious person*. Such an individual dedicates the self to a serious application towards life, is never satisfied with today, and desires that tomorrow be better. The pious person is involved in study so that the practice will be on a higher level, a more profound expression. The individual whose attitude towards self-betterment is one which involves neither attendance nor practice is a wicked person. Such an individual has cut the self off from the element of self-betterment and is, in all likelihood, also not interested in the betterment of others.

יח אַרְבַּע מִדּוֹת בְּיוֹשְׁבִים לִפְנֵי חֲכָמִים,
סְפוֹג וּמַשְׁפֵּךְ מְשַׁמֶּרֶת וְנָפָה. סְפוֹג
שֶׁהוּא סוֹפֵג אֶת־הַכֹּל, וּמַשְׁפֵּךְ שֶׁמַּכְנִיס בְּזוֹ וּמוֹצִיא
בְּזוֹ, מְשַׁמֶּרֶת שֶׁמּוֹצִיאָה אֶת־הַיַּיִן וְקוֹלֶטֶת אֶת
הַשְּׁמָרִים, וְנָפָה שֶׁמּוֹצִיאָה אֶת־הַקֶּמַח וְקוֹלֶטֶת
אֶת־הַסֹּלֶת:

18 There are four types among those who sit before the sages: the sponge, the funnel, the strainer, and the sieve. The sponge — because it absorbs everything; the funnel — because it lets in at one end and out at the other; the strainer — because it lets the wine out and retains the sediment; the sieve — because it lets out the bran and retains the fine flour.

There are different types amongst those who sit regularly before the sages in an attempt to better the self. There are those who are like the *sponge*, which advantageously absorbs everything but is not able to sift out from what has been absorbed that which demands immediate application. There is the *funnel*, the opposite of the sponge, which lets everything in at one end, but out at the other. The knowledge is digested but it is immediately ejected from the system. It is not integrated into the self.

Then there is the *strainer* which lets out the wine and retains the sediment. This is the prototype of the individual who unfortunately is likely to distort the meaning of what has been taught, deriving erroneous implications from the knowledge that is imparted. Finally, the opposite of the

רטז כָּל־אַהֲבָה שֶׁהִיא־תְלוּיָה בְדָבָר בָּטֵל
דָּבָר בָּטְלָה אַהֲבָה, וְשֶׁאֵינָה תְלוּיָה
בְדָבָר אֵינָה בְּטֵלָה לְעוֹלָם. אֵיזוֹ הִיא אַהֲבָה שֶׁהִיא־
תְלוּיָה בְדָבָר זוֹ אַהֲבַת אַמְנוֹן וְתָמָר, וְשֶׁאֵינָה
תְלוּיָה בְדָבָר זוֹ אַהֲבַת דָּוִד וִיהוֹנָתָן:

19 Any love which is contingent on a
thing, when the thing is nullified the
love disintegrates; but a love which is independent of any thing will never disintegrate. What is
the prototype of a love which is contingent on a
thing? — this is the love of Amnon and Tamar.
And what is the prototype of a love which is
independent of any thing? — this is the love of
David and Yonathan.

---

strainer is the *sieve*, because it lets out the bran and retains
the fine flour. The sieve, like the strainer, is able to draw
implications. However, the sieve-type student draws the
proper implications, is able to separate the crucial and to
project it onto the human scene in an appropriate manner.

MISHNA 19

This *mishna* moves from the love of Torah to love of people.
It asserts, in a very simple but profound statement, that
*Any love which is contingent on a thing, when the thing is
nullified the love disintegrates; but a love which is
independent of any thing will never disintegrate.* True love,
it turns out, is a relationship which is not based on the
needs that are fulfilled by a partner, nor by what the

partner has which is the object of desire. In such situations, it is quite natural that the thrill of receiving what one needs will eventually evaporate once the needs have been satisfied. Then, the love which is contingent on the thing will naturally fade away.

True love is a human expression of appreciation and admiration for what the other individual "is." It is a valuational relationship which appreciates the goodness, the warmth, the kindness, the ethical posture of the partner. In such a situation that love is linked with infinite values and has an infinite quality of its own which will never disintegrate. The love of Amnon and Tamar is a prototype of love which is contingent on physical attraction, on beauty which elicits a passionate desire to embrace and experience together. But, once that thrill of embrace and experience has gone, the basis for the relationship is no longer solid. Whatever passions have been aroused have already gained their expression.

The love of David and Yonathan is a good example of a love independent of anything. It is a love of two individuals committed to the growth of the community of Israel, dedicated selflessly to the enhancement of the community. It is not a love which is in any way related to sensual pursuits, but is rather a love which expresses a sharing of values.

בְּ כָּל מַחֲלֹקֶת שֶׁהִיא לְשֵׁם שָׁמַיִם סוֹפָהּ
לְהִתְקַיֵּם וְשֶׁאֵינָהּ לְשֵׁם שָׁמַיִם אֵין סוֹפָהּ
לְהִתְקַיֵּם. אֵיזוֹ הִיא מַחֲלֹקֶת שֶׁהִיא לְשֵׁם שָׁמַיִם זוֹ
מַחֲלֹקֶת הִלֵּל וְשַׁמַּאי, וְשֶׁאֵינָהּ לְשֵׁם שָׁמַיִם זוֹ
מַחֲלֹקֶת קֹרַח וְכָל־עֲדָתוֹ׃

20 Every controversy which is for the sake of Heaven will ultimately endure, but any controversy which is not for the sake of Heaven will ultimately not endure. What is the prototype of a controversy which is for the sake of Heaven? — this is the controversy between Hillel and Shammai. And what is the prototype of a controversy which is not for the sake of Heaven? — this is the controversy of Korach and all his company.

It should not be assumed that a love relationship is necessarily free from argument. Individuals who love in the value-sharing sense often argue, but in such instances, the controversy is *for the sake of Heaven and will ultimately endure.* But a controversy *which is not for the sake of Heaven,* but is based on sensual desires or materialistic pursuits, is as ephemeral as the material itself, and is subject to decay.

Arguments can be rooted in love, where there is a sharing of values but a different approach by individuals with this common commitment. There will be a basic unshakeable respect for the other's motives, but, at the same time, an argument about how best these common motives can reach fruition. The prototype of this is the argumentation between Hillel and Shammai, both of whom took different approaches to various aspects of the law but both of whom respected the fact that the other's intent was for the sake of Heaven.

The prototype of an argument which is for self-aggrandizement, for personal gain, is the controversy of Korach and all his company. The non-durability of such controversy is evidenced in that it is branded as a controversy of *Korach and all his company*, not a controversy between Korach and Moshe. As far as Moshe was concerned, it was not a matter of protecting a position. For Korach it was a matter of gaining position. The controversy is between Korach and his company. Where self gain is the motive, one is hard pressed to keep peace even within one's own ranks.

כָּל־הַמְזַכֶּה אֶת־הָרַבִּים אֵין חֵטְא בָּא עַל־
יָדוֹ וְכָל־הַמַּחֲטִיא אֶת־הָרַבִּים אֵין
מַסְפִּיקִין בְּיָדוֹ לַעֲשׂוֹת תְּשׁוּבָה. מֹשֶׁה זָכָה וְזִכָּה
אֶת־הָרַבִּים זְכוּת הָרַבִּים תָּלוּי בּוֹ שֶׁנֶּאֱמַר צִדְקַת יְיָ
עָשָׂה וּמִשְׁפָּטָיו עִם־יִשְׂרָאֵל. יָרָבְעָם בֶּן־נְבָט חָטָא
וְהֶחֱטִיא אֶת־הָרַבִּים, חֵטְא הָרַבִּים תָּלוּי בּוֹ,
שֶׁנֶּאֱמַר עַל־חַטֹּאות יָרָבְעָם אֲשֶׁר חָטָא וַאֲשֶׁר
הֶחֱטִיא אֶת־יִשְׂרָאֵל:

21 Whoever causes the multitude to be virtuous, no sin shall come through that person, but one who causes the multitude to sin will not be given the opportunity to repent. Moshe was himself virtuous and caused the multitude to be virtuous, therefore the virtuousness of the multitude is ascribed to him, as it is written — "He performed the righteousness of God and His judgments with Israel" (Devarim 33:21); Yerov'am the son of Nevat sinned and caused the multitude to sin, therefore the sin of the multitude is ascribed to him, as it is written — "for the sins of Yerov'am which he sinned, and wherewith he caused Israel to sin" (I Melachim 15:30).

The fact that controversy can legitimately incorporate two opposing views which are both well-intentioned, brings forth a very perplexing question. Obviously, one of the two views must be erroneous; the recommendation of at least one of the protagonists will mislead the public and cause it to err.

The question is — how does one incorporate this possibility and at the same time admire those who are involved in the controversy? This *mishna* indicates that an individual who is properly motivated — this proper motivation being best indicated by the fact that the individual has *caused the multitude to be virtuous*, elevating them through the teaching of Torah — is guaranteed that no sin shall come to him. Too much good has been invested into that public. The public is unlikely to sin on the say-so of that protagonist. There is a guarantee that those who operate within a pure and sincere framework will be protected from deviances which are inconsistent with their own character and commitment. However, those who cause the multitude to sin, who are insincere and oblivious to the needs of the community, will have committed such a gross disservice that atonement will be impossible. Such damage is too overwhelming to ever rectify.

Moshe is the model of one who leads the community towards virtue. *Moshe was himself virtuous and caused the multitude to be virtuous*. Hence to him is ascribed the virtuousness of the multitude. The verse cited is "He performed the righteousness of God and His judgments with Israel." This verse relates to the two points made in the *mishna*. It ascribes the merit of the righteous behavior of Israel to Moshe. It also deals with a potential error, namely the desire of a few tribes — Reuven, Gad, and one-half of the tribe of Menashe — to live in Trans-Jordan. This could have resulted in their not being involved with their brethren in establishing the land; it could have fragmented the community. However, Moshe, who led the people towards the virtues of Torah, took great pains to ensure that this would not happen; that prior to their settling in the Trans-Jordan, these tribes would be involved in the destiny of the people. The virtuousness of Moshe thus served as a guarantee that no harm would evolve from the permission granted to these tribes to settle outside the precise boundaries.

Yerov'am sinned and caused the multitude to sin. He is blamed for the sins of the multitude who followed him thinking he was a legitimate model. Because Yerov'am caused such deviation, he and his posterity were cut off from the community of Israel, "for the sins of Yerov'am which he sinned, and wherewith he caused Israel to sin." The damage was too great and the harm too far-reaching to allow for any repentance on the part of Yerov'am.

כָּל־מִי שֶׁיֶּשׁ־בּוֹ שְׁלֹשָׁה דְבָרִים הַלָּלוּ הוּא מִתַּלְמִידָיו שֶׁל־אַבְרָהָם אָבִינוּ, וּשְׁלֹשָׁה דְבָרִים אֲחֵרִים הוּא מִתַּלְמִידָיו שֶׁל־בִּלְעָם הָרָשָׁע. עַיִן טוֹבָה וְרוּחַ נְמוּכָה וְנֶפֶשׁ שְׁפָלָה מִתַּלְמִידָיו שֶׁל־אַבְרָהָם אָבִינוּ, עַיִן רָעָה וְרוּחַ גְּבוֹהָה וְנֶפֶשׁ רְחָבָה מִתַּלְמִידָיו שֶׁל־בִּלְעָם הָרָשָׁע. מַה בֵּין תַּלְמִידָיו שֶׁל־אַבְרָהָם אָבִינוּ לְתַלְמִידָיו שֶׁל־בִּלְעָם הָרָשָׁע. תַּלְמִידָיו שֶׁל־אַבְרָהָם אָבִינוּ אוֹכְלִין בָּעוֹלָם הַזֶּה וְנוֹחֲלִין הָעוֹלָם הַבָּא, שֶׁנֶּאֱמַר לְהַנְחִיל אֹהֲבַי יֵשׁ וְאוֹצְרֹתֵיהֶם אֲמַלֵּא. תַּלְמִידָיו שֶׁל־בִּלְעָם הָרָשָׁע יוֹרְשִׁין גֵּיהִנֹּם וְיוֹרְדִין לִבְאֵר שַׁחַת, שֶׁנֶּאֱמַר וְאַתָּה אֱלֹהִים תּוֹרִדֵם לִבְאֵר שַׁחַת, אַנְשֵׁי דָמִים וּמִרְמָה לֹא־יֶחֱצוּ יְמֵיהֶם וַאֲנִי אֶבְטַח־בָּךְ:

22 Anyone who possesses these three traits is among the disciples of our father Avraham, but anyone who possesses three other traits is among the disciples of the wicked Bil'am. A good eye, a humble spirit, and a contented soul are the traits of the disciples of our father Avraham; a bad eye, an arrogant spirit, and an insatiable soul are the traits of the disciples of the wicked Bil'am. What is the difference between the disciples of our father Avraham and the disciples of the wicked Bil'am? The disciples of

our father Avraham are sustained in this world
and inherit the world to come, as it is said —
"That I may cause those who love Me to inherit
substance, and that I may fill their treasure-
houses" (Mishley 8:21). But the disciples of the
wicked Bil'am inherit Gehinnom and descend
into the pit of destruction, as it is said — "But
You, God, will bring them down into the pit of
destruction, people of blood and deceit shall not
live out half their days, but I will trust in You"
(Tehillim 55:24).

There are, then, leaders and misleaders. The models of true
leaders and misleaders become apparent through the types
of disciples that each attracts. Another classic model of a
leader is Avraham, who became a leader in a generation
which bordered on moral chaos. The traits exhibited by
Avraham and which, in the personality of others, relate to
the Avrahamic personality, are a *good eye*, which rejoices
sincerely in the achievements of others; a *humble spirit*,
which does not demand glory for the self; and a *contented
soul*, which does not demand any rewards for serving, but is
rather content with being involved in the life dynamic.

On the other hand, the prototype of a misleader is
Bil'am, who possesses a *bad eye* that cannot tolerate the
achievements of others, is envious of them; is *arrogant of
spirit* — demanding all the glory for the self; and is never
satisfied, but always wants more. Those who possess these
traits can trace their spiritual ancestry to Bil'am.

There is a fundamental difference between the disciples
of Avraham and those of Bil'am. Avraham's disciples are
sustained in this world and will inherit the world-to-come,

כג יְהוּדָה בֶּן־תֵּימָא אוֹמֵר, הֱוֵה עַז כַּנָּמֵר
וְקַל כַּנֶּשֶׁר; רָץ כַּצְּבִי וְגִבּוֹר כָּאֲרִי
לַעֲשׂוֹת רְצוֹן אָבִיךָ שֶׁבַּשָּׁמָיִם:

23 Yehuda the son of Tema says: Be strong as a leopard, light as an eagle, swift as a gazelle, and mighty as a lion to do the will of your Father in Heaven.

---

as the verse exclaims — "That I may cause those who love me to inherit substance" (the world-to-come real estate), "and that I may fill their treasure-houses" (sustain them in this world). The disciples of Bil'am descend into a pit of destruction. They are people of blood and deceit who have no scruples against pushing others out of the way, using all forms of chicanery in order to press self-interests to the fore. Such individuals shall not live out half their days. They live in the power syndrome in which whoever is on top is vulnerable to those who envy the position. Ironically, it turns out that it is precisely those who are content and do not run after excess, who will be blessed with plenty, while those who pursue excess will not even have the basics. This is a pattern which finds its fulfillment in everyday life.

MISHNA 23

Humility and contentedness are desirable traits in relation to material concerns. With regard, however, to the exercising of one's spiritual obligations, the flexing of one's muscles and individual assertiveness are the order of the day.

Thus, one should be *strong as a leopard*, aggressive in attaining the good, obstinate and irrepressible in terms of

225

כ הוּא הָיָה אוֹמֵר, עַז פָּנִים לְגֵיהִנֹּם וּבוֹשֶׁת
פָּנִים לְגַן־עֵדֶן. יְהִי רָצוֹן מִלְּפָנֶיךָ יְיָ
אֱלֹהֵינוּ וֵאלֹהֵי אֲבוֹתֵינוּ שֶׁיִּבָּנֶה בֵּית הַמִּקְדָּשׁ
בִּמְהֵרָה בְיָמֵינוּ וְתֵן חֶלְקֵנוּ בְּתוֹרָתֶךָ:

24 He used to say: The arrogant individual is headed for Gehinnom, and
the shamefaced individual is headed for the
Garden of Eden. May it be Your Will, Lord our
God, that the Temple be rebuilt speedily in our
days and grant us our portion in Your Torah.

---

approaching one's obligations. One should be *light as an
eagle*, not feeling the exercise of responsibility as a burden,
but rather as that towards which the individual naturally
flows. The individual should be *swift as a gazelle* who, once
aware of the value possibilities, runs to them with
spontaneity, grace, and urgency.

Finally, the individual who desires to do the will of God
should be *mighty as a lion*. The lion is king of beasts. The
individual, in spiritual activity, is asked to be king over all
internal forces or mechanisms which would detract from
the expression of God's will. The internal strength of the
individual is the lion-like majesty of the human soul.

MISHNA 24

It is important to be strong, even obstinate, but this should
not translate into arrogance. One can be irrepressible in
exercising Divine responsibilities, but one must be careful
not to let this trait evolve into an arrogance which is
stubbornly oblivious to the surrounding environment and

capable of stepping on others, and on all principles, in order to fulfill responsibility. In such a case, the person is simply controlled by his aggressiveness.

It is vital for individuals to exercise control over their attributes. The arrogant individual who has made of the means an end in itself is likely to embark on a process of value distortion, even cruelty in the name of the law, which will lead to a Gehinnom-like existence. The shamefaced individual acts cautiously, is ever careful about harming others, about doing wrong. This built-in check suggests that such an individual is headed in the direction of the Garden of Eden.

However, just as the extreme of arrogance is undesirable, the extreme of bashfulness too has its negative side. The shamefaced will not learn. The virtue of shame-facedness must be tempered by perspective. A bit of strength and aggressiveness is healthy.

We live in a society in which one cannot evolve characteristics towards their extreme. These characteristics must mediate between individual concern and societal reality. The environment itself does not carry the individual towards the end goal. The individual has to constantly be mindful of doing things in proper measure. Hence, the prayer that God should grant that *the Temple be rebuilt speedily in our own days* and that God *grant us our portion in Your Torah*, is a relevant prayer. The rebuilding of the Temple will bring with it a society which is on the right course, where the external conditions and the internal desires will, by definition, be correlated and adequately mediated. One will then be less mindful about the balance and let the social situation carry the individual expression. When this happens there will be less pressure on the individual and the free expression of ultimate purpose will be free to flow unimpeded.

כה הוּא הָיָה אוֹמֵר, בֶּן־חָמֵשׁ שָׁנִים לַמִּקְרָא,
בֶּן־עֶשֶׂר שָׁנִים לַמִּשְׁנָה, בֶּן־שְׁלֹשׁ עֶשְׂרֵה
לַמִּצְוֹת, בֶּן־חֲמֵשׁ עֶשְׂרֵה לַתַּלְמוּד, בֶּן־שְׁמֹנֶה
עֶשְׂרֵה לַחֻפָּה, בֶּן־עֶשְׂרִים לִרְדוֹף, בֶּן־שְׁלֹשִׁים לַכֹּחַ,
בֶּן־אַרְבָּעִים לַבִּינָה, בֶּן־חֲמִשִּׁים לְעֵצָה, בֶּן־שִׁשִּׁים
לְזִקְנָה, בֶּן־שִׁבְעִים לְשֵׂיבָה, בֶּן־שְׁמוֹנִים לִגְבוּרָה,
בֶּן־תִּשְׁעִים לָשׁוּחַ, בֶּן־מֵאָה כְּאִלּוּ מֵת וְעָבַר וּבָטֵל
מִן הָעוֹלָם:

25 He used to say: The age of readiness for the study of Scripture is five years; for the study of Mishna — ten years; for fulfilling the precepts — thirteen years; for the study of Talmud — fifteen years; for marriage — eighteen years; for pursuit of livelihood — twenty years; for strength — thirty years; for understanding — forty years; for counsel — fifty years; for old age — sixty years; for fullness of years — seventy years; for might — eighty years; for being bent — ninety years; for being as if already dead and having passed away from the world — one hundred years.

In the absence of an environment which is consistent with the desired development of the individual, this *mishna* gives the prescription for the way the human being should develop. It is a program for the evolution of the human being in proper chronology. The age of *five* is the age when one should begin the study of the Torah. At *ten* one is ready for the oral expression contained in the Mishna. Having absorbed the Torah and the Mishna, one is aware of the scriptural and rabbinic coordinates of human responsibility. The acceptance of the commandments is then possible. This is done at the age of *thirteen*, normally identified as the Bar Mitzvah age. It is the age when an individual begins to have a sense of self, thinks in terms of the self in a detached manner. The ego identity which comes to the fore at thirteen is thus linked with the responsibility towards actualizing one's religious imperatives. The self and the Torah come simultaneously into prominence.

The Talmud, which is the development of the Mishna and obviously needs the firm foundation of Scripture and Mishna, is recommended for the age of *fifteen*. Marriage is recommended at the age of *eighteen*. This is described as preceding the pursuit of livelihood. The principle involved here is that the individual should have a number of years in which to form a solid relationship with the partner, so that afterwards everything develops in the context of the solid relationship. At *twenty*, having established a solid relationship, one proceeds to the question of identity formation, in the pursuit of a career or the gaining of a livelihood. Support must exist before marriage, but not necessarily career.

Thirty is the age of strength. This is the time which may be called the prime of life. The mental and physical capacities are more or less peaking simultaneously and allow for the expenditure, in strength, of one's energies towards the many aspects of life. By the age of *forty*, the experience one has gained makes one eligible for greater understanding. After having fully honed one's understanding, one reaches the age of being able to give counsel and advice to others, at *fifty*. *Sixty* is seen as the period of old age. One is developing towards the twilight years. *Seventy* is the normally allotted full life span. It is the fullness of years.

Eighty years is considered the age for might. This seems at first glance to be quite peculiar. Eighty-year-olds do not seem to possess might. However, a comparison of this with the notion of thirty as the true age for strength would indicate a very profound idea. At thirty, one possesses an abundance of strength. One is able to extend oneself in so many directions and reach out towards so many causes and ideas. However, through the evolution of the years and the development of greater understanding and wisdom, one is able to distinguish between vital and dispensable commitments. An individual at the age of eighty does not have the energy to expend on so many causes and must make a choice. That choice is which value, which cause, which idea to concentrate on. This process of channeling energy is an expression of might. Strength is the energy of unlimited capacity. Might is the energy of limited capacity which shows a specific form of potency, the potency of having decided that this is vital to the exclusion of so many other things. The eighty-year-old involved in a cause exemplifies might.

At *ninety*, one is bent rather than straight, perhaps burdened by the years, burdened by experiences, burdened by the sorrows and disappointments of life. At *one hundred*, one could not expect new initiatives. The individual is resting on past achievements and coasting along. The individual is not expected to contribute actively to the world and is considered, under normal circumstances, as having passed away from the world.

בֶּן בַּג בַּג אוֹמֵר, הֲפָךְ־בָּה וַהֲפָךְ־בָּה כו
דְּכֹלָּא־בָה, וּבָה תֶּחֱזֵי וְסִיב וּבְלֵה בָּה
וּמִנָּה לָא תָזוּעַ, שֶׁאֵין לְךְ מִדָּה טוֹבָה הֵימֶנָּה:

26 The son of Bag Bag says: Turn it and turn it for everything is in it and through it you will perceive clearly; grow old and gray in it and from it do not depart, for there is no better pursuit for you than it.

If the previous *mishna* is intended as a program for the proper development of the human being, this *mishna* addresses itself to those who would disagree and maintain that there are better avenues for human development, other areas of endeavor which may bring greater fulfillment. To this challenge, the *mishna* indicates that one should *Turn it and turn it for everything is in it*. True enlightenment and broad knowledge of all aspects and dimensions of life can best be attained through Torah study.

Through Torah, one will *perceive clearly*, be better attuned mentally. One's senses will be much sharper. One can *grow old and gray in it*. The wisdom entailed in it can never be totally mastered. There is renewed inspiration and renewed insight all the days of one's life. *From it do not depart, for there is no better pursuit for you than it*. There is nothing better to help one realize one's human obligations than the study and the expression of Torah.

This *mishna* is written in Aramaic perhaps because it is addressed to those who speak the native tongue of Babylon, namely Aramaic, those who are assimilated and claim that Torah is not everything. The *mishna* speaks to these

231

כז בֶּן־הֵא הֵא אוֹמֵר, לְפֻם צַעֲרָא אַגְרָא:

27 The son of Hei Hei says: According to the exertion is the reward.

---

individuals in their language and tells them that there is nothing better for them than the Torah, hoping that by speaking in their language, it will make them understand and focus on the Torah, with its multitude of advantages.

MISHNA 27

There is always the possibility that one might study the Torah and not perceive in it all the fulfillments that are promised in the previous *mishna*. Again addressing the skeptical outsider in Aramaic, this *mishna* exclaims that *According to the exertion is the reward.* It is possible that one may fail to see the glory of the Torah, but this stems from the failure to elicit from the Torah all that is there. However, if one exerts oneself and makes a maximum effort to comprehend and to explore the depths of the Torah, then its manifold applicabilities will become evident. The individual will be convinced, through the maximum effort that has been exerted, that everything is in it.

פרקי אבות

CHAPTER **6**

The acquisition

of Torah

שָׁנוּ חֲכָמִים בִּלְשׁוֹן הַמִּשְׁנָה בָּרוּךְ שֶׁבָּחַר בָּהֶם
וּבְמִשְׁנָתָם:

The Sages taught in the language of the Mishna
— blessed be He Who chose them and their
teaching.

This chapter, is unlike the other five. While the other five
are chapters of *Mishna*, the statements in this chapter are
baraithoth. A *mishna* is that which was taught in the study
hall of Rabbi Yehuda haNasi. *Baraitha* refers to statements
made by Sages in the Tannaitic period, but taught outside
the study hall of Rabbi Yehuda haNasi, who was the
redactor of the Mishna. Nevertheless, the *baraitha*
statements of this chapter are taught in the language of the
Mishna; they are written in the same style, they emanate
from the same personalities and they are part of a unified
whole. Hence the statement, *blessed be He Who chose
them and their teaching*. God has delegated the Sages to
expand on the words of the Torah so that they apply in each
and every generation. This is what is known as the Oral
Law, of which Mishna is an integral part. The Sages are
those who occupy themselves with Torah study on a regular
basis. As this prelude to Chapter Six indicates, God chose
them and their teaching. Even though what is found in
Chapter Six is *baraitha* and not Mishna, it is nevertheless
an integral part of the Chapters of the Sages.

א רַבִּי מֵאִיר אוֹמֵר, כָּל־הָעוֹסֵק בַּתּוֹרָה
לִשְׁמָהּ זוֹכֶה לִדְבָרִים הַרְבֵּה. וְלֹא עוֹד
אֶלָּא שֶׁכָּל־הָעוֹלָם כֻּלּוֹ כְּדַי הוּא לוֹ, נִקְרָא רֵעַ,
אָהוּב, אוֹהֵב אֶת־הַמָּקוֹם, אוֹהֵב אֶת־הַבְּרִיּוֹת,
מְשַׂמֵּחַ אֶת הַמָּקוֹם, מְשַׂמֵּחַ אֶת הַבְּרִיּוֹת.
וּמַלְבַּשְׁתּוֹ עֲנָוָה וְיִרְאָה וּמַכְשַׁרְתּוֹ לִהְיוֹת צַדִּיק
חָסִיד יָשָׁר וְנֶאֱמָן, וּמְרַחַקְתּוֹ מִן־הַחֵטְא וּמְקָרַבְתּוֹ
לִידֵי זְכוּת, וְנֶהֱנִין מִמֶּנּוּ עֵצָה וְתוּשִׁיָּה בִּינָה
וּגְבוּרָה, שֶׁנֶּאֱמַר לִי עֵצָה וְתוּשִׁיָּה אֲנִי בִינָה לִי
גְבוּרָה, וְנוֹתֶנֶת לוֹ מַלְכוּת וּמֶמְשָׁלָה וְחִקּוּר דִּין,
וּמְגַלִּין לוֹ רָזֵי תוֹרָה וְנַעֲשֶׂה כְּמַעְיָן שֶׁאֵינוֹ פוֹסֵק
וּכְנָהָר הַמִּתְגַּבֵּר וְהוֹלֵךְ, וְהֹוֶה צָנוּעַ וְאֶרֶךְ רוּחַ
וּמוֹחֵל עַל־עֶלְבּוֹנוֹ, וּמְגַדַּלְתּוֹ וּמְרוֹמַמְתּוֹ עַל־כָּל
הַמַּעֲשִׂים:

1 Rabbi Meir says: One who is occupied with Torah for its own sake merits many things; moreover, such a person is sufficient reason for the continued existence of the entire world; such a person is called friend, beloved, lover of God, lover of humankind, a bringer of joy to God, a bringer of joy to humankind; the Torah clothes such a person in humility and awe and enables that person to be righteous, pious, upright and faithful; the Torah keeps that person far from sin and brings that person to virtue.

Through that person people benefit in terms of counsel and sound wisdom, understanding and strength, as it is said — "Counsel is Mine and sound wisdom, I am understanding, strength is Mine" (Mishley 8:14). It gives that person sovereignty, dominion, and discerning judgment; the secrets of the Torah are revealed to that person, who becomes like a spring which never fails and a river which gains in strength, and remains modest, patient, and forgiving of insults. The Torah magnifies and exalts that person over all creatures.

This *baraitha* launches an entire chapter dedicated to exploring the ways in which one acquires true Torah knowledge and the benefits that derive therefrom. The first *baraitha*, as if to whet the appetite, deals with the benefits that come from being occupied with Torah for its own sake. An individual thus occupied does not expect any reward, does not contemplate benefits, but nevertheless, as an automatic end result of Torah, receives many benefits; benefits of a meaningful and ultimate nature, as well as those of the immediate moment.

An individual who is occupied with Torah *for its own sake*, who sees the Torah as the vehicle towards actualization of human purpose, justifies the fact of creation. The world was intended as the necessary groundwork, for making possible human approach to the Divine. This approach is made possible through Torah. Those who occupy themselves with this approach justify the creation of the world.

An individual who has integrated the Torah into the self

will fuse personal and social concerns, will be attuned to self-betterment and the betterment of others. The person occupied with Torah for its own sake is called a *friend* of people, who have gained from that individual through having been taught Torah wisdom. Those individuals who gain via Torah will love the teacher who has given them this great benefit in life. Such an individual is a *lover of God*. Once having experienced how Torah enhances life, one cannot help but love God for having made Torah available. The end result of this love is that it is directed towards humankind, who are to be the beneficiaries of the Torah.

An individual who does this brings *joy to God* and *to humankind*. The individual who appreciates the Torah and the majesty of its genius will see the insignificance of human intellect relative to the Torah. The Torah will clothe the individual, will enwrap the individual *in humility*. The humble person is always eager to learn, always eager to achieve, always eager to do the right thing without concern for reward. The individual who is humble and in awe of the Torah will likely be *righteous, pious, upright and faithful*. Such an individual adopts the attitude of wanting to do the right thing. That such an individual is permeated with Torah will act as a guard to keep the individual from doing wrong, and lead him towards that which is virtuous. Often, individuals with proper attitudes do not do the proper things, but being permeated with Torah perspective is a guarantee that wrong will be avoided and right will be exercised.

This individual is a model of the proper attitude and proper behavior. It is not surprising that other people will benefit from the Torah personality in terms of advice and sound wisdom — attitudes and actions for understanding and strength.

The verse cited to prove this is "Counsel is Mine and sound wisdom, I am understanding, strength is Mine." To

God belongs counsel and sound wisdom. God, as the source of all knowledge, knows what is the right approach (counsel) and what is the right behavior (sound wisdom). God is *understanding* and therefore, can give proper counsel. The sound wisdom recommended by God brings with it the *strength* to abide by the wisdom which is projected. There is an equation here linking God and Torah, because the Torah is God's word. The advice which emanates from the Torah is considered as advice emanating from God.

The Torah has within it an innate, majestic bent. It gives the individual *sovereignty, dominion, and discerning judgment*; it gives the individual the capacity to resist external temptations, to rise above societal pressures. It gives the individual the strength to resist whatever forces might seek to steer one from the path of rectitude. To the individual who has placed primacy in the Torah and has made it the focus of the human endeavor will be revealed the intricacies of the Torah. Through constant study and application, one steadily discovers the inner depths of the Torah, the secrets which can only be uncovered through constant application. The individual *becomes like a spring which never fails and a river which gains in strength*. The commitment, like a spring which never fails, is unabated, and the nature of the expression is continuously expanding.

In spite of this, or perhaps because of this, the individual remains *modest* about achievements, knowing full well that they are thanks to God's doctrine. The individual recognizes that being permeated with Torah is a blessing for which one must be grateful. Therefore, one must approach with patience others who are not so blessed. Such an individual sees what is important in life — the actualization of Torah meaning, and will thus be oblivious to insults that are hurled in the way. They cannot detract, cannot inflict any harm on an ego which is Torah centered.

In a word, the individual who occupies the self with Torah for its own sake is magnified and exalted *over all creatures*. Such an individual embraces the ideal of creation and is far above the majority of society, which has not contemplated the purpose of existence. It is within the realm of choice for each individual to become uplifted over all other creatures, and eminently desirable for all individuals to embark upon this path.

ב אָמַר רַבִּי יְהוֹשֻׁעַ בֶּן־לֵוִי, בְּכָל־יוֹם וָיוֹם
בַּת־קוֹל יוֹצֵאת מֵהַר חוֹרֵב וּמַכְרֶזֶת
וְאוֹמֶרֶת אוֹי לָהֶם לַבְּרִיּוֹת מֵעֶלְבּוֹנָהּ שֶׁל־תּוֹרָה,
שֶׁכָּל־מִי שֶׁאֵינוֹ עוֹסֵק בַּתּוֹרָה נִקְרָא נָזוּף, שֶׁנֶּאֱמַר,
נֶזֶם זָהָב בְּאַף חֲזִיר אִשָּׁה יָפָה וְסָרַת טָעַם. וְאוֹמֵר,
וְהַלֻּחֹת מַעֲשֵׂה אֱלֹהִים הֵמָּה וְהַמִּכְתָּב מִכְתַּב
אֱלֹהִים הוּא חָרוּת עַל־הַלֻּחֹת, אַל תִּקְרָא חָרוּת
אֶלָּא חֵרוּת שֶׁאֵין לְךָ בֶּן־חוֹרִין אֶלָּא מִי שֶׁעוֹסֵק
בְּתַלְמוּד תּוֹרָה, וְכָל־מִי שֶׁעוֹסֵק בְּתַלְמוּד תּוֹרָה
הֲרֵי זֶה מִתְעַלֶּה שֶׁנֶּאֱמַר וּמִמַּתָּנָה נַחֲלִיאֵל
וּמִנַּחֲלִיאֵל בָּמוֹת:

2 Rabbi Yehoshua the son of Levi says:
Day after day a Heavenly voice issues
from Mount Horeb proclaiming the following —
"Woe to humankind for their contempt of the
Torah," for whoever is not occupied with the
Torah is considered rebuked, as it is said — "As a
golden ring in a swine's snout, so is a beautiful
woman who deviates from discretion" (Mishley
11:22). And it is said — "And the Tablets are the
work of God and the writing is God's writing,
engraved upon the Tablets" (Shemoth 32:16).
Read not engraved [*charuth*] but freedom
[*cheruth*], for there is none who is free save one
who is occupied with Torah study. And anyone

241

who is occupied with Torah study will become exalted, as it is said — "From God's gift [Mattana] to God's heritage [Nachaliel] and from God's heritage [Nachaliel] to high places [Bamoth]" (Bamidbar 21:19).

There are outstanding individuals who have devoted their lives to Torah for its own sake. There are many others who have forsaken the Torah. This *baraitha* addresses those persons. It asserts that the very existence of Mount Horeb, the mountain on which the Torah was revealed, is a daily challenge to the individual to live up to the responsibilities first broadcast on Horeb, or Mount Sinai. There is a residual call, a *bath-kol*, a challenge to all which says, *"Woe to humankind for their contempt of the Torah."* The mountain of revelation is here referred to as Horeb, implying desolation, perhaps to project the desolate existence that a Torah-less life must become.

On one end of the continuum, an individual who studies Torah for its own sake will eventually become exalted over all other creatures. On the other end, the individual who is in contempt of Torah and willfully rejects the Torah life-style will suffer woefully because of this. An individual who is not occupied with Torah is considered rebuked, removed from the spiritual mainstream of society as envisaged by original creation.

"As a golden ring in a swine's snout, so is a beautiful woman who deviates from discretion." This is the verse which indicates that an individual in contempt of Torah is considered rebuked. A golden ring is a thing of beauty. Placing a thing of beauty in a swine's nose is to link beauty with its very reverse, to employ beauty for purposes which involve filth. In the same sense, the beauty of a woman is a tremendous blessing, but like the golden ring which can be used to gather filth, so can beauty be used in a wayward fashion, which would then distort the beauty and even make it ugly.

Every individual has been given the golden ring, the innate beauty, which is implicit in the potential available from a Torah lifestyle. This very potentiality of the human being is one which, if used properly, can raise the individual onto a transcending level. However, if with beauty one wallows in filth, then one is like the swine with the incongruous golden ring. If the individual did not have potential, it would not be so tragic.

"And the Tablets are the work of God and the writing is God's writing, engraved upon the Tablets." The Tablets are God's work. They are the golden ring, the beauty. They are that which should be inscribed on the human heart. They are the ingredients which should be integrated into the human personality. Just as God's writing is engraved upon the Tablets, so should the message of God be engraved on the human heart. It should be woven into the fabric of human expression and integrated into the self. This is the ultimate towards which an individual should aspire.

Freedom is not seen as the liberty to do what one feels like doing, but rather, it means to become what one really is, namely the individual who has etched Godliness within the self. Thus, *Read not engraved* [charuth] *but freedom* [cheruth], *for there is none who is free save one who is occupied with Torah study.* Only one who is occupied with Torah study perceives freedom in its true context, as a freedom towards realizing Torah values, rather than a freedom from this restraint or that obligation. Freedom itself is in a context, and oriented around a specific target.

Anyone who is occupied with Torah study will become exalted. Not everyone will become exalted in the sense enunciated in the previous *baraitha*, because that is a fulfillment which is realized only through studying Torah for its own sake, with diligence and serious application, on a steady basis. The *baraitha* here says that even less serious application to Torah, whilst it will not bring the ultimate benefits, will uplift the individual. The *baraitha* plays on the names of three sites in the Israelites' travels in the wilderness: Mattana, Nachaliel, and Bamoth. *Mattana* refers to God's gift, *Nachaliel* to God's heritage, and *Bamoth* to high places. There is a progression starting from God's gift to the people, the Torah.

If properly integrated into the self, this gift becomes God's heritage for the individual. When it becomes God's heritage, it will lead to high places, to the exaltation of the human being and to the thrusting of the individual onto a higher sphere of life.

These three places were journeys of the people of Israel in the wilderness, but they speak also of the journey of each individual in life. That journey should go on a progression upwards, starting with accepting the code of Torah, then integrating that code into the self, and finally letting the Torah carry the individual to the natural destination, exalted places.

ג הַלּוֹמֵד מֵחֲבֵרוֹ פֶּרֶק אֶחָד אוֹ הֲלָכָה
אַחַת אוֹ פָּסוּק אֶחָד אוֹ דִּבּוּר אֶחָד אוֹ
אֲפִילוּ אוֹת אֶחָת צָרִיךְ לִנְהַג בּוֹ כָּבוֹד, שֶׁכֵּן מָצִינוּ
בְּדָוִד מֶלֶךְ יִשְׂרָאֵל שֶׁלֹּא לָמַד מֵאֲחִיתֹפֶל אֶלָּא שְׁנֵי
דְבָרִים בִּלְבָד קְרָאוֹ רַבּוֹ אַלּוּפוֹ וּמְיֻדָּעוֹ, שֶׁנֶּאֱמַר
וְאַתָּה אֱנוֹשׁ כְּעֶרְכִּי אַלּוּפִי וּמְיוּדָּעִי. וַהֲלֹא דְבָרִים
קַל וָחֹמֶר, וּמַה דָּוִד מֶלֶךְ יִשְׂרָאֵל שֶׁלֹּא לָמַד
מֵאֲחִיתֹפֶל אֶלָּא שְׁנֵי דְבָרִים בִּלְבָד קְרָאוֹ רַבּוֹ
אַלּוּפוֹ וּמְיֻדָּעוֹ, הַלּוֹמֵד מֵחֲבֵרוֹ פֶּרֶק אֶחָד אוֹ הֲלָכָה
אַחַת אוֹ פָּסוּק אֶחָד אוֹ דִּבּוּר אֶחָד אוֹ אֲפִילוּ אוֹת
אַחַת, עַל־אַחַת כַּמָּה וְכַמָּה שֶׁצָּרִיךְ לִנְהַג בּוֹ כָּבוֹד.
וְאֵין כָּבוֹד אֶלָּא תוֹרָה, שֶׁנֶּאֱמַר כָּבוֹד חֲכָמִים יִנְחָלוּ
וּתְמִימִים יִנְחֲלוּ טוֹב. וְאֵין טוֹב אֶלָּא תוֹרָה, שֶׁנֶּאֱמַר
כִּי לֶקַח טוֹב נָתַתִּי לָכֶם תּוֹרָתִי אַל־תַּעֲזֹבוּ:

3 One who learns from a fellow a chapter, a law, a verse, an expression, or even a single letter, must behave toward that fellow with honor, for this we find concerning David, King of Israel, who learned only two things from Achithophel, yet he called him his master, his guide, and his beloved, as it is said — "But it was you, a man my equal, my guide and my beloved" (Tehillim 55:14). Can we not derive from this — If David, King of Israel, who learned only two things from Achithophel, yet called him his master, his guide, and his beloved, then one who learns from a fellow a chapter, a law, a verse, an expression, or even a single letter, ought all the more to behave toward that fellow with honor. And honor inheres in naught except the Torah, as it is said — "The wise shall inherit honor" (Mishley 3:35) "and the wholehearted shall inherit good" (Mishley 28:10). And the good is naught but the Torah, as it is said — "For I have given you a good teaching, do not forsake My Torah" (Mishley 4:2).

So important is the Torah in making it possible for the individual to realize one's purpose in life that one must be grateful to anyone who has helped in the Torah endeavor. There is no better example than *David, King of Israel, who learned only two things from Achithophel, yet called him his master, his guide, and his beloved,* as it is so explicitly written in the verse cited — "But it was you, a man my equal, my guide and my beloved." This is followed by the statement of David that together they would study the profundities of the law, which is the reason why Achithophel would be called David's master, guide and beloved.

Kings are accustomed to receiving honor rather than bestowing it. Yet the greatly honored King David acknowledged the wisdom he acquired from another person. How much more, then, should this apply to commoners who do not have to switch honor-roles as David did. They would have to acknowledge even the slightest bit of wisdom and Torah inspiration that has been given to them by others. It is a gratitude which should be natural, if one appreciates the value of Torah for one's life. What honor can one bestow on others? Surely not materialistic honor, or anything which is of a passing nature. Honor in this context must be seen in its profound expression — again, a Torah-oriented honor.

The wise shall inherit honor: those who have wisdom and who teach others shall be honored. *And the wholehearted shall inherit good*: the wholehearted, who are sincere in their appointed task of teaching and sharing of their wisdom, will inherit the good. In a word, the wholehearted wise will inherit honor and good. What is that which is good? Nothing but the Torah itself, "For I have given you a good teaching, do not forsake my Torah." That which is good is here equated with Torah. The Torah is good; the good is that which will be given to the wholehearted wise, as their honor.

The greatest honor one can give to an individual who has taught Torah is to revere that individual; to desire, yearn, and thirst to learn even more from the individual, thus acknowledging that individual as a great teacher.

כָּךְ הִיא דַרְכָּהּ שֶׁל־תּוֹרָה, פַּת בְּמֶלַח
תֹּאכֵל וּמַיִם בִּמְשׂוּרָה תִּשְׁתֶּה וְעַל
הָאָרֶץ תִּישָׁן וְחַיֵּי צַעַר תִּחְיֶה וּבַתּוֹרָה אַתָּה עָמֵל.
אִם־אַתָּה עֹשֶׂה כֵּן אַשְׁרֶיךָ וְטוֹב לָךְ, אַשְׁרֶיךָ בָּעוֹלָם
הַזֶּה וְטוֹב לָךְ לָעוֹלָם הַבָּא:

4 This is the way of the Torah: To eat bread with salt, to drink water by ration, to sleep upon the ground, to live a life of hardship, and to toil in the Torah. If you do this, you will be happy and it will be well with you; you will be happy — in this world; and it will be well with you — in the world to come.

The Torah is so vital to the human endeavor that one must be able to endure hardships and trials in order to achieve its perceived goals. An individual must be able to live on *bread with salt, water by ration,* and with *sleep upon the ground,* and thus live *a life of hardship* — and still *toil in the Torah.* The individual must be so dedicated to the Torah that it is possible to negate the material and to transcend circumstance. Once one places Torah into prominence as the essence of life, all else becomes secondary; it becomes much easier to surmount unfavorable conditions. If one is able to do this, that individual will be happy. There is a spiritual happiness in this world, which momentary pleasures cannot bring. And, "it will be well with you — in the world to come."

The *baraitha* is not recommending that one actually seek to deprive oneself in order to study Torah; rather, it indicates that being occupied with Torah is not consistent

ה אַל־תְּבַקֵּשׁ גְּדֻלָּה לְעַצְמְךָ וְאַל־תַּחְמוֹד
כָּבוֹד. יוֹתֵר מִלִּמּוּדֶךָ עֲשֵׂה, וְאַל־תִּתְאַוֶּה
לְשֻׁלְחָנָם שֶׁל־מְלָכִים שֶׁשֻּׁלְחָנְךָ גָּדוֹל מִשֻּׁלְחָנָם
וְכִתְרְךָ גָּדוֹל מִכִּתְרָם וְנֶאֱמָן הוּא בַּעַל מְלַאכְתְּךָ
שֶׁיְּשַׁלֶּם לְךָ שְׂכַר פְּעֻלָּתֶךָ:

5 Do not seek greatness for yourself and do not covet honor. Let your deeds exceed your learning and do not crave for the table of kings, for your table is greater than their table, and your crown greater than their crown, and your Employer is faithful to pay you the reward of your work.

---

with rampant sensual expression. In a situation where the individual is faced with the painful dilemma of only being able to study Torah in adverse circumstances, then the conviction of Torah's importance should make living in adverse circumstances manageable.

MISHNA 5

The Torah is indeed a great doctrine, one which legitimizes making great sacrifices. Nevertheless, in the pursuit of Torah, one should not seek greatness for the self and one should not covet the honor that other people have gained by being recognized as Torah-true personalities. The individual must embark on Torah for its own sake. *Do not seek greatness for yourself;* rather, *let your deeds exceed your learning.* Instead of seeking greatness, live a life of greatness.

Do not covet honor. Do not even *crave for the table of*

kings, because whatever glory one may envisage they have, one's glory is greater than theirs, one's table is greater than their table. What one digests has lasting value. Theirs is a gaudy but superficial show with no substance to it. The crown of an individual with integrity is greater than their crown, because it is qualitatively more solid, and proves to be everlasting.

One might question why the king is wearing the crown and not the individual. Your *Employer is faithful to pay you the reward of your work*. The real crown, the crowning achievement of one's life, will have its time for proper expression; not immediately, but eventually, and in an everlasting time-frame.

וֹ גְדוֹלָה תוֹרָה יוֹתֵר מִן־הַכְּהֻנָּה וּמִן־
הַמַּלְכוּת, שֶׁהַמַּלְכוּת נִקְנֵית בִּשְׁלשִׁים
מַעֲלוֹת וְהַכְּהֻנָּה בְּעֶשְׂרִים וְאַרְבַּע, וְהַתּוֹרָה נִקְנֵית
בְּאַרְבָּעִים וּשְׁמוֹנָה דְבָרִים. וְאֵלּוּ הֵן, בְּתַלְמוּד,
בִּשְׁמִיעַת הָאֹזֶן, בַּעֲרִיכַת שְׂפָתַיִם, בְּבִינַת הַלֵּב,
בְּשִׂכּוּל הַלֵּב, בְּאֵימָה, בְּיִרְאָה, בַּעֲנָוָה, בְּשִׂמְחָה,
(בְּטָהֳרָה), בְּשִׁמּוּשׁ חֲכָמִים, בְּדִבּוּק חֲבֵרִים,
בְּפִלְפּוּל הַתַּלְמִידִים, בְּיִשּׁוּב, בְּמִקְרָא וּבְמִשְׁנָה,
בְּמִעוּט סְחוֹרָה, בְּמִעוּט דֶּרֶךְ אֶרֶץ, בְּמִעוּט תַּעֲנוּג,
בְּמִעוּט שֵׁנָה, בְּמִעוּט שִׂיחָה, בְּמִעוּט שְׂחוֹק, בְּאֶרֶךְ
אַפַּיִם, בְּלֵב־טוֹב, בֶּאֱמוּנַת חֲכָמִים, בְּקַבָּלַת
הַיִּסּוּרִין, הַמַּכִּיר אֶת־מְקוֹמוֹ, וְהַשָּׂמֵחַ בְּחֶלְקוֹ,
וְהָעוֹשֶׂה סְיָג לִדְבָרָיו, וְאֵינוֹ מַחֲזִיק טוֹבָה לְעַצְמוֹ,
אָהוּב, אוֹהֵב אֶת־הַמָּקוֹם, אוֹהֵב אֶת־הַבְּרִיּוֹת,
אוֹהֵב אֶת־הַצְּדָקוֹת, אוֹהֵב אֶת־הַמֵּישָׁרִים, אוֹהֵב
אֶת־הַתּוֹכָחוֹת, וּמִתְרַחֵק מִן־הַכָּבוֹד, וְלֹא־מֵגִיס
לִבּוֹ בְּתַלְמוּדוֹ, וְאֵינוֹ שָׂמֵחַ בְּהוֹרָאָה, נוֹשֵׂא בְעוֹל
עִם־חֲבֵרוֹ, וּמַכְרִיעוֹ לְכַף זְכוּת, וּמַעֲמִידוֹ עַל־
הָאֱמֶת, וּמַעֲמִידוֹ עַל־הַשָּׁלוֹם וּמִתְיַשֵּׁב לִבּוֹ
בְּתַלְמוּדוֹ, שׁוֹאֵל וּמֵשִׁיב, שׁוֹמֵעַ וּמוֹסִיף, הַלּוֹמֵד
עַל מְנָת לְלַמֵּד, וְהַלּוֹמֵד עַל־מְנָת לַעֲשׂוֹת, הַמַּחְכִּים
אֶת־רַבּוֹ, וְהַמְכַוֵּן אֶת־שְׁמוּעָתוֹ, וְהָאוֹמֵר דָּבָר בְּשֵׁם
אוֹמְרוֹ. הָא לָמַדְתָּ כָּל־הָאוֹמֵר דָּבָר בְּשֵׁם אוֹמְרוֹ
מֵבִיא גְאֻלָּה לָעוֹלָם, שֶׁנֶּאֱמַר וַתֹּאמֶר אֶסְתֵּר לַמֶּלֶךְ
בְּשֵׁם מָרְדֳּכָי:

6 Greater is Torah than priesthood and kingship, for kingship is achieved through thirty advantages and the priesthood through twenty-four, but the Torah is acquired through forty-eight qualifications. They are: 1) by study; 2) by attentive listening; 3) by proper enunciation; 4) by an understanding and perceptive heart; 5) by reverence; 6) by awe; 7) by humility; 8) by joy; 9) by ministering to sages; 10) by attaching oneself to colleagues; 11) by keen discussion among students; 12) by calm deliberation; 13) by study of Scripture; 14) by study of Mishna; 15) by moderating business activity; 16) by moderating involvement in worldly matters; 17) by moderating pleasure; 18) by moderating sleep; 19) by moderating idle chatter; 20) by moderating jest; 21) by being slow to anger; 22) by having a good heart; 23) by trusting in the sages; 24) by acceptance of affliction; 25) by recognizing one's place; 26) by rejoicing in one's portion; 27) by putting a guard to one's words; 28) by not claiming merit for one's self; 29) by being beloved; 30) by loving God; 31) by loving humankind; 32) by loving acts of charity; 33) by loving rectitude; 34) by loving reproof; 35) by keeping distant from honor; 36) by not boasting of one's learning; 37) by not enjoying handing down decisions;

38) by sharing burdens with one's fellow; 39) by judging one's fellow charitably; 40) by leading one's fellow to the truth; 41) by leading one's fellow to peace; 42) by being studious in learning; 43) by asking and answering, listening and adding to knowledge; 44) by learning in order to teach; 45) by learning in order to practice; 46) by enhancing the wisdom of one's teacher; 47) by being exact in what one has learned; and 48) by reporting a statement in the name of its author, for thus you have learned — whoever reports a statement in the name of its author brings deliverance to the world, as it is said — "And Esther told it to the King in Mordechai's name" (Esther 2:22).

Baraitha six continues along the theme of the crown of glory. It indicates that there are crowns of glory in life, most notably priesthood and kingship, but that, in comparison with the Torah, they rank second. Kingship is acquired through thirty advantages and the priesthood through twenty-four. Even then, it is not human achievement which makes priesthood and kingship possible; rather, they are attributes of priesthood and kingship which come simultaneous with the position. Torah, however, is acquired through forty-eight human attributes, forty-eight qualifications which are the prerequisites for having the Torah crown bestowed on the individual's personality.

The Torah is acquired through *study*. It should be obvious that one can only become imbued with Torah if one studies Torah. *Attentive listening* is the quality of being receptive, or wanting to learn and wanting to understand. Understanding is enhanced by *proper enunciation*, by verbalizing what has been studied, such that one hears it, speaks it, and is thus more likely to remember what has been experienced through the senses.

The *understanding and perceptive heart* is vital for absorbing Torah. One can perform all the recommendations mechanistically, but one must really have the heart in it for the Torah to be integrated into the person. This integration is best achieved through *reverence* for the teacher who is transmitting the Torah and by the *awe* of the Torah itself, recognizing the Torah's greatness and revering those who have made it their obligation to teach it. This attitude will enhance the attentiveness towards Torah study.

The awareness of the majesty of the Torah brings with it a natural *humility*, which is a result of appreciating the magnitude of the Torah. This should lead to the *joy* of having been so blessed with the opportunity to live the greatness of a Torah-oriented life. The desire to live a Torah-oriented life is realized by *ministering to sages*, by seeing how they live a Torah-oriented life and have translated the Torah into their lifestyles. Moreover, it is important to *attach oneself to colleagues*, to place oneself in a Torah atmosphere and, in that atmosphere, to have *keen discussion among students*, to continually occupy one's conversation with Torah themes. In the eagerness to sharpen one's knowledge, one must always be careful to have *calm deliberation*, not to rush to conclusions, but to be patient and work things through to their proper end result.

Having achieved this general attitude and atmosphere, and having developed a pattern of learning, it is then important to become expert in the foundations of all Torah wisdom. The *study of Scripture* is necessary to become firmly anchored in the roots of all Torah expression. This is followed by the *study of Mishna*, by mastering the Mishna, the Oral Law which emanates from the Written Law.

Mastering wisdom is a never ending process. The more one learns, the more one perceives, the more one appreciates. It is important for the individual to *moderate business activity*, such that more time is available for Torah study. In the same sense, one should also *moderate involvement in worldly matters*, affairs which might be important but certainly do not rank on par with learning of Torah. It stands to reason that one should not indulge in too much sensual expression. One should not eliminate it entirely, but in order to properly appreciate Torah in its spiritual dimension, one should *moderate pleasure*.

There are other ways in which one may make Torah more available. *Moderating sleep* creates more time for Torah study. An individual who is excited about Torah opportunities will want to stretch the day. One way of doing it is by sleeping less. Another way is by *moderating idle chatter*, so that less time is wasted in trivia and in needless talk. Also, by *moderating jest*, one does not compromise on the seriousness of life, but rather keeps perspective on the imperative to constantly focus on that which is important.

Others may want to enjoy a good joke now and then, and this might be frustrating to the individual who desires to learn. Nevertheless, one of the ways in which Torah is acquired is by *being slow to anger,* by being patient with others. By getting excited, one can not only alienate others, but also make it more difficult to properly concentrate. A balanced approach is in order here.

In terms of relationship to others, it is also important to have a *good heart*, to rejoice when someone else makes a noteworthy achievement in Torah study and advances understanding, because everyone is the beneficiary of such insight.

Others may have uncovered or interpreted things which an individual does not yet fully understand. In the same way as the individual should be happy and have a good heart towards this, one should also be *trusting in the Sages*. If they offer an interpretation which does not yet fully register with an individual, one should nevertheless trust that their conclusions are valid, and should remain confident that in the future it will all fall into place. What is not completely understood intellectually should be accepted out of trust.

In a similar manner, what is difficult to comprehend in life should also be accepted out of trust. This refers to the *acceptance of affliction,* which the individual does not comprehend. If one accepts it and does not wrestle with it then one can better continue on the course of life. One's acceptance of affliction is made possible by *recognizing one's place.* In the acceptance of affliction, one recognizes that God has separate calculations, that one cannot assume God's place in charting the ups and downs of life.

Whatever bounty and good one is given in life should be greatly appreciated. Unlike affliction, which one lives with by almost ignoring it and transcending it, that which one has been granted which seems to be beneficial should be accepted in joy. *Rejoicing in one's portion* is an important aspect of maintaining the proper attitude towards a Torah lifestyle. The balanced perspective one has towards one's immediate condition should also pertain to how one expresses oneself. By *putting a guard to one's words* one makes sure to verbalize in moderation; not to indulge in extremes, but rather to walk the straight and middle path.

This meticulous care about life should mean simply living a responsible lifestyle; it is nothing special. By *not claiming merit for one's self* one acknowledges that this is the way one must be, it is nothing extraordinary. This type of balanced and modest approach will lead to an individual's *being beloved* by others, who see the unassuming greatness of such a personality. When the individual perceives the love of others for the self, such an individual will be grateful to God for giving the instrumentality for eliciting this love.

Being beloved leads to *loving God*. Loving God brings the recognition that God's major concern is for the enhancement of humankind. This leads to *loving humankind*, strongly desiring to help them in their approach to life. Loving humankind is an abstract. It has its concrete expression in *loving acts of charity* which, whether they be of material or emotional nature, help the individual become involved in ultimate destiny.

Even in helping one should be aware of the sensitivities of others. One should *love rectitude*, and make sure that anything done for others maintains the dignity of the other individual. The dignity of the other individual is important, but not so the dignity of the self, at least not in the sense of being above criticism. By *loving reproof*, the individual shows the proper orientation to self-betterment, the non-acceptance of the status quo as the end product. Reproof can raise the individual out of stagnation towards greater heights of achievement. By *keeping distant from honor*, one again affirms the idea that present achievements, however laudable they may be, and even above reproof, are, nevertheless, no excuse for resting on one's laurels.

One loves reproof in order to improve in the future, one keeps distant from honor in order not to become stultified in the present. The individual who keeps distant from honor is likely, as a next step, not even to see any reason for having honor bestowed. There will be *no boasting of one's learning*, no projection of one's achievements. The time that would be spent in boasting of one's learning is spent in increasing that very learning.

Even though one may be aware of having absorbed much learning, by *not enjoying handing down decisions*, one avoids imposing the gained wisdom, even the self, onto others. The Torah is there for others to gain, but is not to be forced onto others. Nevertheless, absence of enjoyment in handing down decisions does not imply becoming detached from the problems of others. Rather, the true Torah-integrated individual should *share burdens with one's fellow*.

If there is any judging to be done, it should be done by *judging one's fellow charitably*. This is judgment in a non-legal setting. If one sees another individual not so fortunate, not so well learned, one should judge that there are circumstances which explain this apparent deficiency. The awareness of such deficiency and the taking of such an affirmative attitude will likely result in *leading one's fellow to the truth*.

Recognizing that the individual was not fortunate in the past, and being concerned about the individual, one perceives the vacuum and tries to fill it by leading the individual to the true life orientation. In the process the beneficiary of wisdom is likely to be troubled by doubts, having been previously exposed to different thought patterns. Therefore, in leading another person to truth, one also should be mindful of *leading* him *to peace*. One must ensure that the values which have been imparted become harmoniously integrated in a peaceful, serene manner with the individual's personality, and are not something the individual is forced to wrestle with and fight.

One may be involved with the destiny of others, but it is still important to concentrate on Torah by being *studious in learning*, by recognizing that even though one has reached the point of being able to teach others, nevertheless, it is still important to continue being a student oneself. By *asking and answering, listening and adding to knowl-*

edge, one continues to probe, one continues to explore, one continues to expand the horizons of knowledge. By *learning in order to teach*, one further upgrades the desired end goal of the learning, and therefore lifts the learning into a higher dimension, the dimension of learning in order to teach, in which instance the learning is of a higher quality and yields greater results. Even more so, by *learning in order to practice*, one induces a higher form of comprehension, a comprehension of all the detail of observances which must be applied in the practice of Torah itself.

On a higher level, one can, in the probing for deeper knowledge, not only enhance the self but even enhance the very teachers who have brought Torah to one's attention. By *enhancing the wisdom of one's teacher*, one graduates to becoming an inspiration, in confidence, to the teacher, and becomes intricately involved in probing the depths of learning. Despite the fact that one now feels a greater sense of sharing with the teacher, in that one has given to the teacher, although not nearly as much as the teacher has given to the individual, nevertheless it is important to remember that the teacher is the teacher. By *being exact in what one has learned*, one maintains this balance. One understands that the teacher, however much the teacher may gain from the student, is, nevertheless, the revered individual whose words must be measured very carefully and digested in precise detail.

The individual, by engaging dialogically with the teacher, has become part of the higher learning process, part of the pool of Torah truth. Still, the individual must recognize at all times the achievements of others, their inferences, derivations, and ingenious interpretations. By *reporting the statements in the name of the author*, the individual shows that it is not embarrassing to admit that others have uncovered insights which may have eluded the self. One is so happy the insights have been made and that everyone is a beneficiary that one is naturally and spontaneously grateful to the one who has uncovered the insight.

The individual who *reports statements in the name of their author brings deliverance to the world,* deliverance from destructive selfishness. The proof is in the situation of "And Esther told it to the King in Mordechai's name." Esther found out from Mordechai that two men were plotting to kill the king. She could have alerted the king to this without saying who was the source of the information. The end result would have been the same; the king would have saved himself and would have killed the plotters. However, by telling this to the king in Mordechai's name, Esther placed the king in Mordechai's eternal debt. Later on, the king felt obliged to acknowledge that which Mordechai had done for him. This was the harbinger of a changed destiny which reversed the edict of destruction for the Jews. It is therefore important not only to make the observations, but to indicate by whom they are made. This establishes proper credibility and proper credit.

This *baraitha* projects very clearly a broadbased and enlightened notion of what is meant by the crown of Torah. It is not merely becoming wise; it includes having the proper attitude towards knowledge, towards oneself, towards others, and towards one's condition in life. It involves what may be called the integrated Torah person, who, in both the personal and social dimensions, brings out the best in the self and in others. An individual wearing the crown of Torah has incorporated within himself the attributes enumerated in this *baraitha*; he is a total human being.

ז גְדוֹלָה תוֹרָה שֶׁהִיא נוֹתֶנֶת חַיִּים
לְעוֹשֶׂיהָ בָּעוֹלָם הַזֶּה וּבָעוֹלָם הַבָּא,
שֶׁנֶּאֱמַר כִּי־חַיִּים הֵם לְמֹצְאֵיהֶם וּלְכָל־בְּשָׂרוֹ
מַרְפֵּא, וְאוֹמֵר רְפְאוּת תְּהִי לְשָׁרֶּיךָ וְשִׁקּוּי
לְעַצְמוֹתֶיךָ, וְאוֹמֵר עֵץ־חַיִּים הִיא לַמַּחֲזִיקִים בָּהּ
וְתֹמְכֶיהָ מְאֻשָּׁר, וְאוֹמֵר כִּי לִוְיַת־חֵן הֵם לְרֹאשֶׁךָ
וַעֲנָקִים לְגַרְגְּרֹתֶיךָ, וְאוֹמֵר תִּתֵּן לְרֹאשְׁךָ לִוְיַת־חֵן
עֲטֶרֶת תִּפְאֶרֶת תְּמַגְּנֶךָ, וְאוֹמֵר כִּי בִי יִרְבּוּ יָמֶיךָ
וְיוֹסִיפוּ לְךָ שְׁנוֹת חַיִּים, וְאוֹמֵר אֹרֶךְ יָמִים בִּימִינָהּ
בִּשְׂמֹאולָהּ עֹשֶׁר וְכָבוֹד, וְאוֹמֵר כִּי אֹרֶךְ יָמִים
וּשְׁנוֹת חַיִּים וְשָׁלוֹם יוֹסִיפוּ לָךְ:

7 Great is the Torah, for it brings life to those who practice it, in this world and in the world to come, as it is said — "For they are life to those who find them and health to all their flesh" (Mishley 4:22); and it says — "It shall be health to your body and marrow to your bones" (Mishley 3:8); and it says — "It is a tree of life to those who maintain it and those who uphold it are happy" (Mishley 3:18); and it says — "They shall be a garland of grace for your head, and necklaces around your neck" (Mishley 1:9); and it says — "It gives to your head a garland of grace, and will bestow upon you a crown of glory" (Mishley 4:9); and it says — "For through Me the number of your days will grow, and the years of your life will be increased" (Mishley 9:11); and it says — "Length of days is in its right hand, in its left hand are riches and honor" (Mishley 3:16); and it says — "For length of days and years of life and peace will they add to you" (Mishley 3:2).

The individual who has become a Torah-imbued personality, and who has acquired the crown of Torah, is doubly blessed. The Torah *brings life to those who practice it, in this world and in the world to come*. It brings life in the various dimensions of the term. It brings an extra dimension of quality, it brings a dimension of health, it brings a dimension of vitality. This very statement would seem to indicate that when the *baraitha* previously recommended bread with salt and water in measure, it was not to recommend starvation, but rather to recommend a life of moderation, of balance, which is conducive to health.

The *baraitha* now proceeds to a discourse of linking verses, all of which deal with the theme of life and health. "For they are life to those who find them and health to all their flesh." The Torah is *life* to the soul of individuals who find meaning in it and is *health* to the body of those individuals who live in Torah.

"It shall be health to your body and marrow to your bones." The Torah enhances one's physical well-being (health to your body) and also one's general vitality and vibrancy (marrow to your bones).

"It is a tree of life to those who maintain it and those who uphold it are happy." The Torah gives life in quantity and in quality. Those who uphold it are happy, have a much more positive and affirmative attitude to life.

"They shall be a garland of grace for your head, and necklaces around your neck." They shall ennoble the individual spiritually (garland of grace for your head) and also enhance the individual physically (necklaces around your neck).

"It gives to your head a garland of grace, and will bestow upon you a crown of glory." The Torah gives the individual an aura of importance such that others will accept the Torah-imbued personality with admiration and adulation (garland of grace). Others will acknowledge his contribution to life, his own majesty (crown of glory). Needless to say, the individual who feels this response from others is encouraged to progress in life and is thus given further impetus towards life's purpose.

"For through Me the number of your days will grow, and the years of your life will be increased." Through listening to God's Torah one will have extra days of life and the years of life which make up these days will be enhanced qualitatively as well as quantitatively.

"Length of days is in its right hand, in its left hand are riches and honor." The main ingredient is the dimension of life which is added through Torah (right hand), but there are side benefits (left hand), such as riches and honor, which make it easier to live and which inspire towards life.

"For length of days and years of life and peace will they add to you." This inspiration gives one a completeness, a sense of harmony with the world, which enables one to approach one's destiny. The combination of these ingredients brings to the individual, aside from extra days and qualitative years, the dimension of harmony and *peace*, of completeness and contentedness.

ח רַבִּי שִׁמְעוֹן בֶּן־יְהוּדָה מִשּׁוּם רַבִּי שִׁמְעוֹן
בֶּן־יוֹחַאי אוֹמֵר, הַנּוֹי וְהַכֹּחַ וְהָעֹשֶׁר
וְהַכָּבוֹד וְהַחָכְמָה וְהַזִּקְנָה וְהַשֵּׂיבָה וְהַבָּנִים נָאֶה
לַצַּדִּיקִים וְנָאֶה לָעוֹלָם, שֶׁנֶּאֱמַר עֲטֶרֶת תִּפְאֶרֶת
שֵׂיבָה בְּדֶרֶךְ צְדָקָה תִּמָּצֵא, וְאוֹמֵר תִּפְאֶרֶת
בַּחוּרִים כֹּחָם וַהֲדַר זְקֵנִים שֵׂיבָה, וְאוֹמֵר עֲטֶרֶת
חֲכָמִים עָשְׁרָם, וְאוֹמֵר עֲטֶרֶת זְקֵנִים בְּנֵי בָנִים
וְתִפְאֶרֶת בָּנִים אֲבוֹתָם, וְאוֹמֵר וְחָפְרָה הַלְּבָנָה
וּבוֹשָׁה הַחַמָּה כִּי־מָלַךְ יְיָ צְבָאוֹת בְּהַר צִיּוֹן
וּבִירוּשָׁלַיִם וְנֶגֶד זְקֵנָיו כָּבוֹד. רַבִּי שִׁמְעוֹן בֶּן־מְנַסְיָא
אוֹמֵר, אֵלּוּ שֶׁבַע מִדוֹת שֶׁמָּנוּ חֲכָמִים לַצַּדִּיקִים,
כֻּלָּם נִתְקַיְּמוּ בְּרַבִּי וּבְבָנָיו:

8 Rabbi Shimon the son of Yehuda says in the name of Rabbi Shimon the son of Yochai: Beauty, strength, riches, honor, wisdom, old-age and fullness of years, and children are becoming to the righteous and becoming to the world, as it is said — "Fullness of years is a crown of glory, it is found in the path of righteousness" (Mishley 16:31); and it says — "The glory of the young is in their strength and the beauty of the old is in the fullness of their years" (Mishley 20:29); and it says — "The crown of the wise is their riches" (Mishley 14:24); and it says — "The crown of the old is children's children, and the glory of children are their parents" (Mishley 17:6);

and it says — "The moon will be confounded and the sun ashamed, for the Lord of Hosts will reign in Mount Zion and in Jerusalem, and God's elders shall meet honor" (Yeshayahu 24:23). Rabbi Shimon, the son of Menasia says: These seven attributes enumerated by the sages for the righteous, all were realized in Rabbi Yehuda haNasi and his sons.

The quality of life which is bestowed upon those who live consistent with Torah dictates is one which involves different attributes. They include, according to this *baraitha*, *beauty, strength, riches, honor, wisdom, old-age and fullness of years,* and *children.*

All of these are realities which can be distorted if abused. One can use beauty to entice, but the righteous use beauty to attract and to inspire. Strength can be used to do wrong, but the righteous use strength to perform good deeds. Riches can be used for personal pleasure, but the righteous use riches for charitable purposes. Honor can be used to satisfy the ego; but it can also be used as a vehicle to teach. For example, an individual who is given a testimonial dinner can use that occasion to boast about achievements. But, since many have come to listen, the situation can be employed, and indeed the righteous would employ such a situation, to teach those who have come.

Wisdom can be used to distort, wisdom can be used to rationalize deviance. The righteous use wisdom by sharing of that wisdom with others. Old-age and fullness of years can signify the extension of something miserable over a long period of time. For the righteous, who use their years to the maximum, extra years, old-age and fullness of years are well utilized. Finally, those who are deviant only extend their deviance by having children who follow in their footsteps. The righteous have children who emulate their way.

Thus, because the righteous use all these ingredients properly, they are *becoming to the righteous and becoming to the world*, which gains so much from the commitment of the righteous.

The verses cited here serve to corroborate the statement of the Mishna. "Fullness of years is a crown of glory, it is found in the path of righteousness." A long life is a crown of glory only when it is lived in righteous expression, such that more years mean more goodness.

"The glory of the young is in their strength and the beauty of the old is in the fullness of their years." The young are exemplars by their deeds, by their actions, by what they do for others. As for those who have advanced in years and do not have those energies, their beauty is in the fullness of their years, in the experiences which they have had and which they share with others, thus helping them towards their value fulfillment.

"The crown of the wise is their riches." The majesty of the wise is best perceived in how they translate theoretical wisdom into real practice. The wise would logically recommend sharing, but it is only the really wise who will actually share if they are blessed with riches.

"The crown of the old is children's children, and the glory of children are their parents." The crown of the old is in having perpetuated the values which they ennobled in life through their children and through their children's children; the strength of their commitment is so all-embracing and awe-inspiring that their children adopt this commitment and are able to transmit it to the grandchildren. Parents themselves are the glory of children — the model which is admired, the model which is emulated.

Eventually, "The moon will be confounded and the sun ashamed, for the Lord of Hosts will reign in Mount Zion and in Jerusalem, and God's elders shall meet honor." In the future, it will become obvious that the moon's light and the sun's brilliance are directly dependent upon the brilliance of God. In the future, God will show that the ultimate source of light and of brilliance is the elders, who will meet honor, who will shine like the brilliance of the sun. It is fitting for them to have this honor, and indicative of how much of the world's master plan they have integrated into their existence.

The *baraitha* ends with an interesting statement, that these seven attributes *were realized in Rabbi Yehuda haNasi and his sons*. Rabbi Yehuda haNasi is none other than the editor of the Chapters of the Sages, who systematized chapters developing the notion of one's ethical, moral, and spiritual responsibility towards the self and towards others.

This statement indicates that Rabbi Yehuda haNasi's commitment and lifestyle were consistent with the recommendations contained in the Chapters of the Sages, and were so awe-inspiring that they were readily adopted by his children. In other words, the Chapters of the Sages does not limit itself to abstract ideas, but recommends something which can be, and in fact has already been, put into practice.

מ אָמַר רַבִּי יוֹסֵי בֶּן־קִסְמָא, פַּעַם אַחַת
הָיִיתִי מְהַלֵּךְ בַּדֶּרֶךְ וּפָגַע בִּי אָדָם אֶחָד
וְנָתַן־לִי שָׁלוֹם וְהֶחֱזַרְתִּי לוֹ שָׁלוֹם. אָמַר לִי, רַבִּי
מֵאֵיזֶה מָקוֹם אָתָּה, אָמַרְתִּי לוֹ מֵעִיר גְּדוֹלָה שֶׁל
חֲכָמִים וְשֶׁל־סוֹפְרִים אָנִי. אָמַר לִי, רַבִּי רְצוֹנְךָ
שֶׁתָּדוּר עִמָּנוּ בִּמְקוֹמֵנוּ וַאֲנִי אֶתֵּן לְךָ אֶלֶף אֲלָפִים
דִּינְרֵי זָהָב וַאֲבָנִים טוֹבוֹת וּמַרְגָּלִיּוֹת, אָמַרְתִּי לוֹ
אִם אַתָּה נוֹתֵן לִי כָּל־כֶּסֶף וְזָהָב וַאֲבָנִים טוֹבוֹת
וּמַרְגָּלִיּוֹת שֶׁבָּעוֹלָם אֵינִי דָר אֶלָּא בִּמְקוֹם תּוֹרָה,
וְכֵן כָּתוּב בְּסֵפֶר תְּהִלִּים עַל יְדֵי־דָוִד מֶלֶךְ יִשְׂרָאֵל
טוֹב לִי תוֹרַת פִּיךָ מֵאַלְפֵי זָהָב וָכָסֶף. וְלֹא עוֹד,אֶלָּא
שֶׁבִּשְׁעַת פְּטִירָתוֹ שֶׁל אָדָם אֵין מְלַוִּין לוֹ לְאָדָם לֹא
כֶסֶף וְלֹא זָהָב וְלֹא אֲבָנִים טוֹבוֹת וּמַרְגָּלִיּוֹת אֶלָּא
תוֹרָה וּמַעֲשִׂים טוֹבִים בִּלְבָד, שֶׁנֶּאֱמַר בְּהִתְהַלֶּכְךָ
תַּנְחֶה אֹתָךְ בְּשָׁכְבְּךָ תִּשְׁמֹר עָלֶיךָ וַהֲקִיצוֹתָ הִיא
תְשִׂיחֶךָ. בְּהִתְהַלֶּכְךָ תַּנְחֶה אֹתָךְ בָּעוֹלָם הַזֶּה,
בְּשָׁכְבְּךָ תִּשְׁמֹר עָלֶיךָ בַּקֶּבֶר, וַהֲקִיצוֹתָ הִיא
תְשִׂיחֶךָ לָעוֹלָם הַבָּא. וְאוֹמֵר לִי הַכֶּסֶף וְלִי הַזָּהָב
נְאֻם יְיָ צְבָאוֹת:

9 Rabbi Yose the son of Kisma said: Once I was walking on the road, and was met by a certain person who greeted me, and I returned the greeting. He said to me — "Rabbi, from what place are you?" I said to him — "I am from a great city of sages and scribes." He said to

me — "Rabbi, if you are willing to live with us I
will give you a million golden dinar and precious
stones and pearls." I said to him — "Even if you
were to give me all the silver and gold and
precious stones and pearls in the world, I would
not live anywhere except in a place imbued with
Torah." And thus it is written in the Book of
Psalms by David, King of Israel — "The teaching
of Your mouth is better for me than thousands of
gold and silver" (Tehillim 119:72); moreover, when
a person dies, neither silver nor gold nor precious
stones and pearls accompany that person, only
Torah and good deeds, as it is said — "When you
walk it shall lead you, when you lie down it shall
watch over you, when you awaken it shall talk
with you" (Mishley 6:22). "When you walk it shall
lead you" — in this world; "when you lie down it
shall watch over you" — in the grave; "when you
awaken it shall talk with you" — in the world to
come. And it says, "Mine is the silver and Mine is
the gold, says the Lord of Hosts" (Haggai 2:8).

The previous *baraitha* indicated that wealth is appropriate
for the righteous, that one of the side benefits of Torah may
be the bestowal of wealth. This *baraitha* nevertheless puts
a delicate balance on the relationship between Torah and
wealth. It tells a story, self-explanatory, of Rabbi Yose, who
had an offer others may think could not be refused, but
which he turned down. It was an offer for a million golden
dinar and precious stones and pearls if he would move from

where he lived, which was a place of sages and scribes, to another city. What is interesting is the response given by Rabbi Yose to the question — will you move for a million golden dinar? Rabbi Yose, instead of answering simply — No, because, as King David exclaimed, "The teaching of Your mouth is better for me than thousands of gold and silver [pieces]," injects a new ingredient. He says *Even if you were to give me all the silver, gold, precious stones and pearls in the world, I would not live anywhere except in a place imbued with Torah.* But he was not offered all the world's wealth!

Perhaps Rabbi Yose is adding a dimension in terms of the relationship of wealth to Torah. If Rabbi Yose were given all the silver, gold, precious stones and pearls in the world, he would obviously be able to build a city or even a country with that money. He would be able to attract individuals whom he would want to that city, offer them handsome salaries, and firmly establish them materially so that they have no more worries. He would be able to build beautiful edifices, houses of learning, which would attract the best teachers and the best scholars. Rabbi Yose, with all that wealth, could have made of any place, even the wilderness, a place of Torah.

But, he says, even with all that, he would not take the money and build, not because of laziness, but because, by so doing, Rabbi Yose would create an artificial area of Torah established not because of Torah orientation, but because of the wealth which enticed the scholars.

When asked where he came from, Rabbi Yose said *from a great city of sages and scribes.* By this, Rabbi Yose meant that the city became great because of the sages and the scribes, who invested unconditionally and without looking for reward, in the city. This was a city which purely and spontaneously evolved as a Torah community. So, says Rabbi Yose, I prefer a city which is poor, but where the vi: The Acquisition of Torah   271

Torah evolved purely, spontaneously, sincerely, and authentically, to the option of having all the material wealth at my disposal and thereby creating a Torah community. Such a community will not be as pure, as sincere, or as authentic, because it will evolve from ulterior motives.

Moreover, adds Rabbi Yose, the possession of silver, gold, precious stones and pearls is, under normal circumstances, useless, because these do nothing, they achieve no purpose, they remain as ornaments in an individual's home, but they do not translate into deeds. An individual, in this world, can only claim credit for what one has given to the world in terms of Torah study and good deeds. The acquisition of wealth is irrelevant towards this purpose because "Mine is the silver and Mine is the gold, says the Lord of Hosts." The silver and the gold have already been placed into the world by God. By acquiring wealth, one has merely switched owners. However, by increasing Torah and good deeds, one has given to the world what was previously non-existent, something real, which leads the individual in life, protects him in death, and crowns him in the world-to-come.

It is only in an authentic place of Torah that one should endeavor to live, for there one has the environment, the spirit and the inspiration to live according to God's plan.

חֲמִשָּׁה קִנְיָנִים קָנָה (לוֹ) הַקָּדוֹשׁ בָּרוּךְ
הוּא בְּעוֹלָמוֹ וְאֵלוּ הֵן. תּוֹרָה קִנְיָן אֶחָד,
שָׁמַיִם וָאָרֶץ קִנְיָן אֶחָד, אַבְרָהָם קִנְיָן אֶחָד, יִשְׂרָאֵל
קִנְיָן אֶחָד, בֵּית הַמִּקְדָּשׁ קִנְיָן אֶחָד. תּוֹרָה מִנַּיִן,
דִּכְתִיב יְיָ קָנָנִי רֵאשִׁית דַּרְכּוֹ קֶדֶם מִפְעָלָיו מֵאָז.
שָׁמַיִם וָאָרֶץ מִנַּיִן, דִּכְתִיב כֹּה אָמַר יְיָ הַשָּׁמַיִם כִּסְאִי
וְהָאָרֶץ הֲדוֹם רַגְלָי אֵי־זֶה בַיִת אֲשֶׁר תִּבְנוּ־לִי וְאֵי־
זֶה מָקוֹם מְנוּחָתִי. וְאוֹמֵר מָה רַבּוּ מַעֲשֶׂיךָ יְיָ כֻּלָּם
בְּחָכְמָה עָשִׂיתָ מָלְאָה הָאָרֶץ קִנְיָנֶךָ. אַבְרָהָם מִנַּיִן,
דִּכְתִיב וַיְבָרְכֵהוּ וַיֹּאמַר בָּרוּךְ אַבְרָם לְאֵל עֶלְיוֹן
קֹנֵה שָׁמַיִם וָאָרֶץ. יִשְׂרָאֵל מִנַּיִן, דִּכְתִיב עַד־יַעֲבֹר
עַמְּךָ יְיָ עַד יַעֲבֹר עַם־זוּ קָנִיתָ. וְאוֹמֵר לִקְדוֹשִׁים
אֲשֶׁר בָּאָרֶץ הֵמָּה וְאַדִּירֵי כָּל־חֶפְצִי בָם. בֵּית
הַמִּקְדָּשׁ מִנַּיִן, דִּכְתִיב מָכוֹן לְשִׁבְתְּךָ פָּעַלְתָּ יְיָ
מִקְדָּשׁ אֲדֹנָי כּוֹנֲנוּ יָדֶיךָ. וְאוֹמֵר וַיְבִיאֵם אֶל־גְּבוּל
קָדְשׁוֹ הַר זֶה קָנְתָה יְמִינוֹ:

10 Five acquisitions did the Holy One, blessed be He, acquire for Himself in His world. They are: the Torah — one acquisition, heaven and earth — one acquisition, Avraham — one acquisition, Israel — one acquisition, the Temple — one acquisition. How is this derived concerning the Torah? Because it is written — "God acquired me as the beginning of His way, before all His work, from of old"

272

(Mishley 8:22). How is this derived concerning heaven and earth? Because it is written — "Thus says God: The heaven is My throne and the earth is My footstool, what type of house will you build for Me and what type of place for My rest?" (Yeshayahu 66:1); and it says — "How manifold are Your works, O God, all of them You made in wisdom, the earth is full of Your acquisitions" (Tehillim 104:24). How is this derived concerning Avraham? Because it is written — "And He blessed him, saying Blessed be Avram to the Most High God, Acquirer of heaven and earth" (Bereshith 14:19). How is this derived concerning Israel? Because it is written — "Until Your people pass over, O God, until this nation You have acquired passes over" (Shemoth 15:16); and it says — "As for the holy who are in the earth, they are the noble through whom is all My will done" (Tehillim 16:3). How is this derived concerning the Temple? Because it is written — "The place, O God, You have prepared for You to dwell in, the sanctuary, O God, which Your hands have established" (Shemoth 15:17); and it is said — "And He brought them to the area of His sanctuary, to this mountain, which His right hand had acquired" (Tehillim 78:54).

This *baraitha* deals with the basic ingredients which are necessary for God's plan to be effective. The importance of the ingredients enumerated in this *baraitha* inheres in that God acquired these ingredients. God showed that they were so important they were acquired. It is an anthropomorphic expression. Human beings buy things which are valuable to them. The expression used here, consistent with verses which corroborate the statements, is one which employs human terminology to describe what God considered to be vital for the world.

There is the *Torah*, which is the basic blueprint of creation, that which justifies the world's having been created. "God acquired me as the beginning of His way, before all His work from of old." The Torah existed before all God's works, prior to creation. Creation could not have even been contemplated if there had been no Torah to be implemented subsequent to creation.

The second basic ingredient in the Divine masterplan is *heaven and earth*, a heaven towards which to aspire and an earth upon which to live. Heaven and earth are linked by God's presence — "The heaven is My throne and the earth is My footstool, what type of house will you build for Me and what type of place for My rest?" God stretches the expanse between heaven and earth. God permeates the universe; there is no house that can contain God and there is no place that is without God. Any place on this earth is eligible for potential fulfillment. "How manifold are Your works, O God, all of them You made in wisdom, the earth is full of Your acquisitions." All that was placed into this world — nature, trees, water, fish, "the fullness of the earth" — are both acquisitions of God in that He considers them important, on the one hand, and elements which help to sustain the individual while realizing his goal, on the other.

Avraham is the original expounder of God's message on earth. Avraham is the individual who raised the Torah ideal from an abstract into an applied reality. "And He blessed him, saying Blessed be Avram to the Most High God, Acquirer of heaven and earth." Malkizedek blessed Avram after Avram had involved himself in a bitter battle against the forces of evil and emerged victorious. Avraham was considered blessed to God, Who acquired heaven and earth and by so doing, bestowed blessing on heaven and earth. Avraham is identified with heaven and earth. Avraham's campaign to bring Torah righteousness to the world is the fulfillment of the basic creation blueprint and justification for the world.

Israel, in the communal dimension, carried forth the message first projected by Avraham, and established itself as a model community which implements the Torah, personally and societally. "Until Your people pass over, O God, until this nation You have acquired passes over." The people are Your people because they have accepted Your doctrine.

You have shown how important they are by acquiring the people unto Yourself. "As for the holy who are in the earth, they are the noble through whom all My will is done." These are the individuals within the community of Israel who, in their lifetime, were committed to Torah ideals and were the agents for bringing God's message into the world.

Finally, there is the *Temple*, which is the spiritual center of the Jewish people, the place in which the people are able to serve God in an ideal fashion. "The place, O God, You have prepared for You to dwell in, the sanctuary, O God, which Your hands have established." The goal of the Exodus was to bring the people towards service of God. It is a freedom towards religious obligation which Moshe here celebrates with the people. "And He brought them to the area of His sanctuary, to this mountain, which His right hand had acquired." Eventually, this original purpose was fulfilled in history, when the people arrived at and worshipped in the Temple. The Temple is the ultimate model where living and focusing around God's word finds its most profound this-worldly expression.

The five ingredients are the Torah, which is the blueprint; heaven and earth, where the blueprint is to be implemented; Avraham, who initiated the implementation of the blueprint; Israel, who expanded the blueprint onto a societal plane, and the Temple, which focused cogently and with precision on how the blueprint was to be expressed. All of these are acquisitions of God; all of these are considered as the vital conditions for living according to the Divine plan.

יא כֹּל מַה־שֶּׁבָּרָא הַקָּדוֹשׁ בָּרוּךְ הוּא
בְּעוֹלָמוֹ לֹא בְרָאוֹ אֶלָּא לִכְבוֹדוֹ, שֶׁנֶּאֱמַר
כֹּל הַנִּקְרָא בִשְׁמִי וְלִכְבוֹדִי בְּרָאתִיו יְצַרְתִּיו אַף
עֲשִׂיתִיו. וְאוֹמֵר, יְיָ יִמְלֹךְ לְעֹלָם וָעֶד:

11 Whatever the Holy One, blessed be He,
created in His world, He created solely
for His own glory, as it is said — "All that is
called by My Name and that I have created for
My glory, I have formed, even made" (Yeshayahu
43:7); And it says — "God shall reign for ever and
ever" (Shemoth 15:18).

All the ingredients enumerated previously, whose importance is illustrated by the fact that they are God's acquisitions, plus everything else in the world, was created by God
solely for His own glory. The forces, ideas, values and
events which coalesce to form human history, all have been
made and all are directed towards the culminating event,
the establishment of God's kingdom, when humankind will
acknowledge God's majesty and orient around Godliness.
"All that is called by My Name and that I have created for
My glory, I have formed, even made." This verse indicates
that all of creation plus that which was formed subsequent
to creation and implemented in the world, are directed
towards God's glory, as will be manifested by the glorious
deliverance and uplifting of the people of Israel. Through
this will be established God's kingdom; "God shall reign for
ever and ever."

At first glance, this *baraitha* may seem problematic.
Throughout the entire span of the Chapters of the Sages,

one of the key elements in the human endeavor is the concern for others and the rejection of the pursuit of honor. Here, we are told that everything God created in the world was made for God's honor. Ostensibly, this runs counter to the self-transcendence which is asked of human beings.

Upon closer reflection, orientation around God, by God, for God's sake, is really a Divine necessity — a denial of the human dynamic in the Divine dimension — in order that the human dynamic can be possible. The idea that everything is oriented around God is not directed at God; God does not need this reinforcement. However, this is considered the ideal blueprint for human-beings — to orient around God, and is consistent with the Divine plan. It gives ultimate justification and meaning to creation. To the extent that we transcend ourselves, and orient ourselves around God's word and around Torah values, to that extent do we become part of God's masterplan, and become able to experience the everlasting majesty of God. The living of an ethically pure and religiously sensitive life perpetuates itself and generates its own eternality. But it can only be achieved by orienting around Transcendence.

Indeed, God created everything solely for His own glory. This is made known to humanity to forcefully project the message of self-transcendence toward the Divine as the essential dynamic for a meaningful life and a meaningful world.

רַבִּי חֲנַנְיָא בֶּן־עֲקַשְׁיָא אוֹמֵר, רָצָה הַקָּדוֹשׁ בָּרוּךְ
הוּא לְזַכּוֹת אֶת־יִשְׂרָאֵל לְפִיכָךְ הִרְבָּה לָהֶם תּוֹרָה
וּמִצְווֹת. שֶׁנֶּאֱמַר, יְיָ חָפֵץ לְמַעַן צִדְקוֹ יַגְדִּיל תּוֹרָה
וְיַאְדִּיר:

Rabbi Chananya the son of Akashya says: The
Holy One, blessed be He, desired to make Israel
worthy, therefore He gave them Torah and commandments in abundance, as it is said: "God
was pleased for the sake of His righteousness to
magnify and glorify the Torah" (Yeshayahu 42:21).

About the Author

Reuven P. Bulka, rabbi of Congregation Machzikei Hadas in Ottawa, Canada, is a highly regarded author and editor. He was ordained at the Rabbi Jacob Joseph Rabbinical Seminary in 1965 and received his Ph.D. in Logotherapy from the University of Ottawa in 1971. Founder of the Center for the Study of Psychology and Judaism and editor of the *Journal of Psychology and Judaism*, Rabbi Dr. Bulka is the author of twenty-five books, including *What You Thought You Knew about Judaism*, *More of What You Thought You Knew about Judaism*, and scores of articles.